The Lost History of the
LADY
Aeronauts

For Ursula Taylor

The Lost History of the
LADY
Aeronauts

Sharon Wright

PEN & SWORD
HISTORY
AN IMPRINT OF PEN & SWORD BOOKS LTD.
YORKSHIRE - PHILADELPHIA

First published in Great Britain in 2018 and
reprinted in paperback format in 2021 by
PEN AND SWORD HISTORY
An imprint of
Pen & Sword Books Ltd
Yorkshire – Philadelphia

Copyright © Sharon Wright, 2018, 2021

ISBN 978 1 39900 538 8

The right of Sharon Wright to be identified
as the author of this work has been asserted by her in accordance
with the Copyright, Designs and Patents Act 1988.

A CIP record for this book is available from the British Library
All rights reserved. No part of this book may be reproduced or
transmitted in any form or by any means, electronic or
mechanical including photocopying, recording or
by any information storage and retrieval system, without
permission from the Publisher in writing.

Typeset in Times New Roman by
SJmagic DESIGN SERVICES, India.

Printed and bound by CPI Group (UK) Ltd, Croydon, CR0 4YY

Pen & Sword Books Ltd incorporates the imprints of Pen & Sword
Archaeology, Atlas, Aviation, Battleground, Discovery,
Family History, History, Maritime, Military, Naval, Politics, Railways,
Select, Social History, Transport, True Crime, Claymore Press,
Frontline Books, Leo Cooper, Praetorian Press, Remember When,
Seaforth Publishing and Wharncliffe.

For a complete list of Pen and Sword titles please contact
Pen and Sword Books Limited
47 Church Street, Barnsley, South Yorkshire, S70 2AS, England
E-mail: enquiries@pen-and-sword.co.uk
Website: www.pen-and-sword.co.uk

Or

PEN AND SWORD BOOKS
1950 Lawrence Rd, Havertown, PA 19083, USA
E-mail: Uspen-and-sword@casematepublishers.com
Website: www.penandswordbooks.com

Contents

Foreword vii

Chapter 1   Wonder Women 1
Chapter 2   Maiden Flights 12
Chapter 3   Sex, Scandal and Mrs Sage 29
Chapter 4   The Fabulous Birdwoman of France 56
Chapter 5   Mistresses of Misadventure 65
Chapter 6   The White-Knuckle World of Margaret Graham ... 78
Chapter 7   Queens of the American Clouds 101
Chapter 8   Champers and Hampers ... How the Other Half Flew 115
Chapter 9   Of Pluck and Parachutes 142
Chapter 10   The Lily Cove Mystery 154
Chapter 11   Balloonomania Sunset 170

Bibliography 178
Index 180

Foreword

If a work of art is never finished but merely abandoned, then exploring lost women's history can always be resumed. When *Balloonomania Belles: Daredevil Divas Who First Took To The Sky* appeared in hardback, there was a gratifying reception from readers who shared my astonishment that these courageous female pioneers had lain forgotten for so long. I couldn't shake the conviction, though, that there were still one or two mysteries to solve, some curious clues and overlooked events that could reveal yet more about these marvelous women.

So began the evolution of this updated paperback. Fresh detective work led to a discovery that finally explodes a sexist 236-year-old myth about Letitia Sage, first English woman to fly. I first encountered Lily Cove as a young reporter in West Yorkshire and it's a story I cannot leave alone. So when I took another look at her inquest, I was forced to see the Haworth horror story in a whole new light. Then there was Margaret Graham, whose incredible life story I laboured over and whose pauper's grave I visited. To my great delight I was able to talk with Mrs Graham's great, great granddaughter Ursula Taylor. Ursula was generous in discussing her family history, particularly in filling in the gaps around Margaret's death and sharing portraits of the daring diva. She began investigating her ancestor with her late husband Hugh and their son, Matthew Taylor, kindly helped us to compare notes. Mrs Graham lies in an unmarked grave but her glorious story lies in this book.

More light on how balloonomania swept through the lives and minds of Georgian women was shed by Chawton House, which holds a collection of works by early women writers. The twin joys of happenstance and collaboration led to Mrs Sage appearing in their excellent *Man Up!* exhibition, while I was invited to explore rare and beautiful books by female contemporaries of the aeronauts. I am indebted to chief executive Katie Childs for drawing my attention to a work by Harriette Wilson, to Emma Yandle, curator and collections manager, for her guidance and insight, and to communications and public engagement manager Clio O'Sullivan and Louisa Carpenter, former visitor experience manager, for embracing balloonomania.

I could not have written this book without the unfailing help and support of Brian Riddle, chief librarian of the National Aerospace Library in Farnborough, and John Baker, archivist at the British Balloon Museum and Library, the official museum of the British Balloon and Airship Club. I am indebted to the trustees of the Dolly Shepherd Pioneer Parachutist Archive, Julie Carlsen of the Berg Collection at the New York Public Library, Haworth historian Steven Wood and Dan Sudron, archivist at the West Yorkshire Archive Service, Calderdale, for his transcription of the entry in Anne Lister's diary (reference SH:7/ML/E). Also to Lucinda Dharmasena, Ann Dinsdale, Abigail Halley, Julie Akhurst, Diane Park and Tim Harrison, and Laura Hirst at Pen & Sword for their encouragement and US balloon legend Bob Sparks for our unforgettable day in Philadelphia. Thanks too to Jennifer Jones, retired chartered librarian, translator of Enlightenment French and public records expert. If there are any errors in this book, they are mine alone.

Welcome to the revised and updated and yet more uplifting story of early female flight. The lady aeronauts are not lost any more.

Sharon Wright, Spring 2021

Chapter 1

Wonder Women

In 1783 the balloon went up in more ways than one. Radical thinking swept across Europe and America, the spirit of change churning the air of politics, philosophy, fashion and art. The months were so stuffed with marvels they became known as an annus mirabilis, year of wonders. A giant comet cut a fiery path across the heavens and epic volcanic eruptions in Iceland sent sulphur pouring into the jet stream to cause weather chaos. Events in the sky above Enlightenment Europe were as dramatic as those on the earth when most wonderful of all, humans learned how to fly. A beautiful balloon hung in the French sky at Versailles above an astounded crowd of Parisians. As brothers Joseph-Michel and Jacques-Étienne Montgolfier unlocked the secret of soaring above the earth, the watching women, from Queen Marie Antoinette down, shared a single thought: the eighteenth century equivalent of 'what's not to love?'

Balloonomania was unleashed, spreading like wildfire through France, then all Europe and quickly on to America. Commentators also called it balloon mania and when it proved so infectious, balloon influenza. It was a 'craze', a 'rage' and all so maddeningly thrilling it held European and American society in thrall. From the earliest days, women were in on the act. The first female aeronauts were flamboyant, fashionable or just plain fearless as they embraced ballooning and all it promised. The craze swept the world and its pioneering women in the late eighteenth and early nineteenth centuries, evolving into a fabulous story of female flight that stretched across 120 years before the first aeroplane left the ground.

Balloon legend puts women at the very dawn of ballooning. One theory is that Joseph Montgolfier saw a washerwoman place a petticoat on a wicker frame to dry over a stove and it began to rise. Another has the unmentionables of Madame Montgolfier drying as her inventive husband became fascinated by how smoke drifted upwards to lift a chemise. As he and Étienne puzzled over how to prevent a smoke-filled paper bag from leaking, did the widow next door poke her head through the window to suggest they tie the bottom? The story was good enough for Victorian balloonist Gertrude Bacon but whatever their real role at the birth of ballooning, women were at the heart of everything that followed. Down on the ground they were trapped in subordinate roles imposed by the law and rules of society. Up in the sky they were free.

The mania for balloons happened very quickly. A string of historic breakthroughs came thick and fast over just six months in the year of wonders. The Montgolfiers fired the starting pistol in the south of France where they lived. Scientists by inclination, they were paper manufacturers by profession. The family had made paper for generations and in 1783 they were suppliers to the king, Louis XVI. Two brothers among sixteen siblings, unkempt Joseph was a drifter and a dreamer who once ran away from the family trade, while Étienne trained as an architect and had a good head for business. They had nothing in common until they invented the balloon.

They unveiled the floating linen bag, fastened by buttons and lined with paper, in Annonay on 5 June 1783, three months before they risked it in front of royalty. Eight sweating men hung on for dear life as the red and yellow balloon measuring 110ft around was filled in front of invited VIPs. At the signal to let go astonishment spread among the dignitaries in the town square, and terror among the peasants where it landed. The balloon rose to 6,000ft, flew for ten minutes and bobbed to earth a mile and a half away. There it caught fire and was left to burn by field hands convinced the moon had fallen from the sky and the day of judgement was upon them. It caused a sensation. News flew by letter and word of mouth to Paris. The sensation earned a name – aerostation – and the Montgolfiers became its first megastars. The inflatable invention, immediately dubbed a montgolfier, was the talk of the town. The race was on to replicate the experiment. For French scientists, philosophers and leaders of fashion, nothing really counted until it had happened in Paris.

On 27 August, a young physics professor called Jacques Charles launched the *Globe* over the enthralled capital. He had not actually repeated the experiment, though. He was misled by an inaccurate account that said the June balloon was filled with hydrogen, the 'inflammable air' discovered by British recluse Henry Cavendish a few years earlier. It was a serendipitous mistake, leading to an intense but friendly rivalry between the Montgolfiers who filled their balloons with smoke (not realizing it was hot air doing the work) and Charles who championed hydrogen. Less friendly was the reception the *Globe* received when it fell to earth fifteen miles from Paris. No-one had alerted people living in the countryside. For unsuspecting spectators a deflating balloon looked horribly like a writhing visitor from hell. Men and women panicked when the terrifying object fell to earth, billowing like a monster in its death throes. The daggers, pitchforks, muskets and rocks used to 'kill' the world's first hydrogen balloon are captured in a contemporary drawing, *General Alarm of the Inhabitants of Gonesse occasioned by the fall of the air balloon of M.Montgolfier.*

Soon Étienne Montgolfier was in Paris too, answering the summons to demonstrate a balloon before King Louis XVI, Queen Marie Antoinette and a vast crowd at Versailles. The city buzzed with excitement and traders cashed in by selling miniature balloons. In *The History and Practice of Aerostation* written the following year, Tiberius Cavallo describes how mini montgolfiers popped up in Paris amid burgeoning balloon mania:

> 'As the price of these balloons did not exceed a few shillings, almost every family satisfied its curiosity relative to the new experiment, and in a few days time balloons were seen very frequently flying about Paris, and soon after were sent abroad. Thus this curious experiment was spread in the world with an unparalleled rapidity.'

The showcase event on 19 September 1783 was awash with all the pomp the French court so enjoyed. The balloon was 57ft tall and dubbed *Aérostat Réveillon* by Étienne, after the wallpaper designer who helped create the blue, gold and red taffeta beauty. Cannons fired to mark liftoff but the ascent also had a practical purpose; to discover whether living creatures could deal with great height. Hence the first aeronauts were a sheep, a cock and a duck, perhaps underwhelming for the duck, if not its flightless companions. When they landed neither dizzy nor dead, the implications were enormous. If a sheep could fly without its head exploding (an actual worry at the time), could a human being?

The Cuthbert-Hodgson Collection and Major B.F.S. Baden-Powell Collection of Aeronautical Cuttings in the National Aerospace Library at Farnborough record several attempts to fly like the birds long before the first aeronauts finally pulled it off. From the legend of the British king Bladud of Bath who strapped wings to his arms in 850BC and unintentionally jumped to his death from the temple of Apollo in ancient London, to a Paris convict in 1777 being 'surrounded with whirls of feathers' and dropped 70ft, descending slowly if not actually flying, the idea wasn't new. A Brazilian priest called Bartolomeu Lourenco de Gusmão demonstrated an unmanned one to the king of Portugal in 1709. The father then designed a balloon car resembling a hollow pigeon to carry passengers but gave up when people decided it all smacked of witchcraft and reported him to the Portuguese Inquisition. A Russian called Kria Kutnoi also annoyed the clergy by flying a balloon into a church tower in 1731 and was excommunicated. Both were deemed to have invented unholy floating fire hazards.

Sustained and repeatable human flight only truly arrived with frères Montgolfier but the cautious duo left hair-raising trials of their contraptions to other people. Celebrated for their contribution to the age of enlightenment in paint, poetry and prose, they were usually watching proceedings with feet planted firmly on the ground. Étienne never flew and Joseph only once. That flight ended terrifyingly quickly with a rip in the balloon that sent it crashing back to earth. He never tried again. Hydrogen hero Jacques Charles also gave up on ballooning when it gave him earache. The test pilots for the very first flight were daring young volunteers. On 21 November 1783 the science teacher Jean-François Pilâtre de Rozier and soldier François Laurent, Marquis d'Arlandes, became the first men to fly.

Once again it was Paris that witnessed the epoch-making event. At first the huge audience fell into stunned silence as it watched the first humans head for the clouds. When it sank in that the ascent was a success, the crowd went suitably wild. By December 1783 balloon events were drawing phenomenal numbers. The largest recorded gathering of people the world had ever seen turned up to watch the first manned flight of a hydrogen balloon. More than 400,000 men and women saw Jacques Charles and Ainé Robert take off from Paris, enough people to fill modern day Wembley Stadium four and a half times over. By now balloons were big news everywhere and when this one came down twenty miles away the pitchforks stayed in the barns. The king sent out a proclamation to warn people they would be seeing more monsters and not to panic as they were harmless and might even prove useful.

Witnessing the initial trips to the clouds, Cavallo suggested that 'a few years hence, the most timid woman will perhaps not hesitate to trust herself to the same experience.' In fact women were raring to go, very far from timid and certainly not prepared to wait years for a balloon ride. Within a few months the first female aeronauts claimed their place in the history books. On 20 May 1784 the Marchioness and Countess of Montalembert, the Countess of Podenas and their companion Miss de Lagarde became the first women in the world to fly, boarding a tethered balloon in, of course, Paris. A fortnight later on 4 June the charismatic Elisabeth Thible ascended from Lyon to become the first woman in the world to fly entirely free of the earth.

WONDER WOMEN

The age of flight had begun and ballooning gripped the public imagination. The invention flooded fashion and philosophy from the street to the salon. The rage for all things aerostation was entirely in keeping with the overwrought mood of the times. Scientific discovery, revolutionary philosophy and political tumult were as much in vogue in late eighteenth century society as a Montgolfier medallion. The ink was barely dry on the Treaty of Paris, which ended the American War of Independence, when the hot air balloon made its royal debut a few miles away. Louis XVI and Marie Antoinette enjoyed the spectacular show at Versailles never guessing their days were numbered. Before the decade was out some in that crowd would storm the Bastille and trigger the French revolution.

Ballooning arrived when the natural world seemed upside down, too. The wonders of 1783 were often terrifying or deadly. Enormous volcanic eruptions from the Laki fissure in Iceland wrought havoc with the climate. They began just four days after the Montgolfier demonstration at Annonay in June and continued for eight months, killing a fifth of Icelanders and sending sulphur spewing across Europe as acid rain. The hottest summer on record was followed by a bitterly cold winter. The sky turned white with ash, crops failed and tens of thousands more died from breathing the killer smog that settled over Norway, Germany, France and Britain.

Nine days before Pilâtre de Rozier and Laurent became the first balloonists, a giant comet known as a flying dragon scorched across the August sky above Scotland, England and France. In the midst of such portents, political crises and climatic confusion people seized on the delightful distraction of the balloon craze. Marie Antoinette stands accused of telling the restless poor of the 1780s to eat cake. She may just as easily have advised blotting out their worries by watching balloons.

Thus balloon-inspired art, fashion and entertainment blossomed in the late eighteenth and early nineteenth centuries. Balloons themselves were made to look gorgeous. Aeronauts competed to impress princes and public alike, ascending in montgolfiers made of hand-made paper, kid leather, linen or silk, striped or painted with ornate designs. Much as modern balloons display the logos of their sponsors, the Montgolfiers decorated their early aerostats (another name for balloons) to flatter the king. Royal emblems were picked out in gold on sky blue backgrounds. The Royal Aeronautical Society's Cuthbert-Hodgson Collection holds a fragment of the balloon that lifted Pilâtre de Rozier and the Marquis d'Arlandes aloft. A rare piece of printed chintz from the 1780s depicting a balloon flight demonstrates how quickly the craze caught on in fashionable homes. By Christmas 1783 there was no shortage of balloon-themed gifts in the shops. The montgolfier motif appeared on everything from silk fans to exquisite furniture, cufflinks to handkerchiefs. French craftsmen turned their talents to producing rococo delights such as crystal chandeliers, delicate jewellery and elaborate clocks. Potteries produced plates, tiles, teapots and tureens. Artists sold paintings and prints of famous ballooning scenes. People rode in montgolfier-shaped coaches and balloon ascents were the hottest tickets in town.

Women were in the vanguard of the vogue, piling their hair high to echo the shape of a balloon or sporting hats and skirts that did the same. To be a fashionista was to be a balloonista. There were few places a dedicated female follower of fashion did not put a balloon, according to an account from 1784:

> 'The *balloon influenza* rages with more violence than ever– added to balloon hats, balloon bonnets, balloon caps, balloon ribbons, and balloon pins, the ladies have *double balloon earrings* and *balloon side-curls;* so that there are no less than seven balloon articles appertaining to the decoration of the most *beautiful balloon* in nature–the head of a pretty woman!'

Satirical writers and artists had a field day. Skits on the crazy clamour to be in a balloon, wear a balloon or talk about a balloon were everywhere. The Major B.F.S. Baden-Powell Collection of Aeronautical Cuttings shows English pens were first off the mark, miffed as they were by the French stealing a march on the clouds. One 1783 cartoon shows a Montgolfier brother perched on a balloon, steering with the aid of an ass, a fool and a monkey. Balloon madness did not catch immediate hold among the English, possibly because the French had beaten them to it and feigned disdain seemed more dignified than a scramble to catch up. The first Brit in a balloon was Scotsman James Tytler in August 1784 but it was an Italian, Vincent Lunardi, who made the first ascent from English soil in September of the same year. At that point Blighty did catch balloon influenza and wags enjoyed sending up the fad that had invaded from France.

Horace Walpole, the arch wit and chronicler of his age, was irritated by the widespread frenzy, calling balloons 'as childish as the flying kites of school-boys' and complaining, 'Balloons occupy senators, philosophers, ladies, everybody.' Cartoonists had not tired of the topic by 1825 when renowned caricaturist George Cruikshank lampooned the pastime. His illustration *A Scene In The Farce of "Lofty Projects" as performed with great success for the Benefit & amusement of John Bull* shows balloons lined up like taxis beneath a crowded sky.

Theatres threw themselves into the fun too, with a pantomime at Covent Garden in London called *A Flight from Lapland in an Air Balloon* enjoyed by 'an overflowing audience' with 'the loudest laughter and applause'. As the first women took to the skies in 1784, the English playwright Elizabeth Inchbald premiered her hit farce *The Mogul Tale; or The Descent of the Balloon* set in a foreign land and employing colonial language. She also appeared in the comedy that revolved around three English people in a balloon blown off course in India and forced to run around pretending to be, variously, concubines and the Pope in order to escape again. Inchbald wasn't the only one to mine the zeitgeist for comedy. Funny verse and songs sprang up everywhere. Her contemporary George Keate penned a prologue with a topical twist that begins:

> 'When half the world are soaring to the moon, Buoy'd up by fashion's trumpery *balloon*; When cats, dogs, women, cleave the yielding air, to make the gaping croud look up and stare, And madly, in philosophy's defiance, their folly sanction with the name of science; Tho' when they thro' the atmosphere have roll'd, All they can tell us is, '*twas very cold.*'

For filling newspapers, balloons were unbeatable. Every tragedy, triumph, near miss or outbreak of fisticuffs was splashed across the press. The cuttings collections at the National Aerospace Library show the thousands of column inches devoted to the fashions, feuds, fires, falls, fatalities and letters of outrage that followed from rampant balloonomania. Sometimes it was the fate of the fans, as in this report from Rome in June 1786:

> 'The balloon-mania was productive of a most melancholy disaster here last Sunday, when a number of persons having assembled to see one of these aerial machines let off, in a gallery erected for that purpose, one of the rows suddenly gave way; in consequence of which accident upwards of twenty of the spectators were either killed or desperately wounded.'

Sometimes it was the rage of the crowds who lost the plot when a balloon failed to go up. Balloon riots broke out quite regularly when ascents went awry. Chevalier de Moret was one of the contenders jockeying with Lunardi to be England's first aeronaut, but his attempt near the Star and Garter in Chelsea on 11 August 1784 ended badly. A vast crowd turned up and stood for three hours as he burned straw in a bid to fill the balloon with smoke. The disgruntled punters decided they had been conned out of their sixpences and mobbed the balloon, tearing it to shreds. Moret only escaped thanks to the dense smoke and a few good Samaritans in the mob.

A reliable source of sensational news was the unfortunate flip side to balloonomania – pyromania. Using the Montgolfier method of burning rubbish to create hot smoke was a particularly combustible pastime. When people sent up little balloons for fun it only took a small combination of mishaps to end in chaos. Known as the fire balloon, it lived up to its name according to a newspaper in October 1784:

> 'A letter from Paris gives an instance of the danger there is in sending up lighted balloons, One of this description fell some days ago on a building at the fair of St. Laurent, where wild beasts are kept for show, such as lions, tigers, &c. providentially, however, the exertions of the firemen, and the place being tiled over, prevented the dreadful consequences which otherwise must unavoidably have taken place.'

There were numerous reports of disaster being visited on hapless victims. When 'an illuminated air balloon' fell on a Kensington barn, it was prevented from incinerating the grain stored there only by frantic owners flinging ditch water and loose earth over the flaming invader. It really was most tiresome, cautioned another:

> 'The following narrow escape ought to be a warning to those gentry who divert themselves every evening with sending up fire balloons; one of the above description descending on Thursday night upon the stables of the Golden Cross Inn, Charing-cross, not a yard from the place where it fell, was a tile broke; had it fell on that place, the whole premises would have been consumed.'

The use of hydrogen was hardly a health and safety improvement. An infamous inferno claimed the life of the most celebrated aeronaut of all time, thanks to the unwise proximity of inflammable air and fireworks. Sophie Blanchard became balloonomania's first female fatality when she plunged to her death in a burning balloon over Paris.

Yet ballooning seemed here to stay according to one weary letter to *Town and Country Magazine*:

> 'It was generally believed that the rage for air-balloons had subsided as the winter advanced; but we find that the aerial Quixotes are not to be deterred by frost or snow, rain or hail ... in all likelihood the rage of air-ballooning will be as violent in 1785, as it was in the two preceding years.'

Indeed, the rage would last for many years to come. Pages were devoted to landmark flights along with science and engineering developments. And there was always room for more salacious stories with an irresistible combination of sex and ballooning. Letitia Sage became the first Englishwoman to fly in 1785, but was forever dogged by speculation over exactly why she briefly bobbed out of sight alongside the gentleman with her. In 1808 two Frenchmen held a duel in the sky in a fight over the favours of a ballet dancer with the opera called Mademoiselle Tirevit. One fired his blunderbuss at the other's balloon and sent his rival to be 'dashed to pieces on a housetop'. Whether they were right to assume Mlle Tirevit would wed the winner goes unrecorded.

Historians often confine balloonomania to the final decades of the eighteenth century and the beginning of the nineteenth. But though the frenzy for all things balloon themed eventually faded among fashionistas, balloon mania as an ecstatic devotion to aerostation never went away. In Britain the Georgian era gave way to the Victorian age with ballooning in full swing. When Queen Victoria took her throne in 1837 and made herself comfy for the rest of the century, dozens of female aeronauts were making their mark. In 1838, the year of her coronation, the balloonist and musician Thomas Monck Mason produced a brief history of flying, listing forty-nine women among the 471 most important aeronauts in the world. Of these twenty-eight were English, seventeen French, three German and one Italian.

Once the initial thrill of watching people fly wore off, aeronauts had to finance their calling through ever more inventive ways to attract the crowds. Science and spectacle were an unbreakable bond among early aeronauts. Only the very wealthy could afford to take off without a paying audience. During the nineteenth century balloonists needed to constantly reinvent their acts to keep interest alive and women often used their novelty value to gain their place in the sky. When respectable dress for a woman was still floor-length skirts, restrictive corsets and gloves, the sight of an actual female leg climbing into a balloon basket induced palpitations. Knickerbockers, bloomers or tights counted as scantily clad. Among the most scandalously attired was Fanny Godard, part of the French troupe of aeronauts that toured Europe and America from the mid-nineteenth century. Her trademark skimpy sailor suit caused a sensation.

The early female aeronauts were supremely skilled, mastering the demands of early flight and showing no fear in the face of considerable danger. This alone was often enough to draw the crowds. Women were seldom allowed – and therefore seen – to put their talents to work in the public sphere. From the ladies of the Age of Enlightenment to the emancipated Edwardians, the life of an aeronaut became a ticket to independence and adventure open to very few other women.

Across the world the aeronauts ignored convention to find fulfilment in the skies. They did this by making ballooning pay. They wore wonderful outfits and ramped up the razzmatazz. We find an admiring appraisal of a female aeronaut by another woman in the work of English author and courtesan Harriette Wilson in 1825. First she wrote her best-selling memoirs of life as a mistress among the nobility, blackmailing lovers into paying to keep their names out of it. Then she published a satire on the English in France called *Paris Lions and London Tigers* that includes an evening at 'Tivoly':

'For my part, I could not help pitying the poor lady, who went up in the balloon, dressed in a plume of white ostrich feathers; you would charge a guinea a piece, for such feathers, the very lowest. Yes, poor soul! she left a gay scene to dangle, and twinkle, in the air, till, at last, we could not distinguish the balloon, which had about fifty large lanterns fastened to it, from a star. However, she went up, in high spirits, seemingly, for she bowed, and bent, and curtsied ...'

Along with the adrenaline and the applause, though, came perpetual danger. The constant whiff of peril helped to sell tickets but the risks women ran for a living often ended with them dying instead. Aerostation was never for the faint hearted. For every Margaret Graham who died in bed in her sixties, there was a Sophie Blanchard who was smashed to death on a rooftop. While Dolly Shepherd lived to fly with the Red Devils in her nineties, her contemporary Lily Cove died at 20 when her parachute failed to open.

These feisty airborne entertainers usually used balloons to escape a lack of prospects on the ground. They turned natural courage, market savvy and pure skill in the air into successful careers. Meanwhile aeronauts such as Wilhelmine Reichard in Germany, Mary Myers in America and Gertrude Bacon in England were fascinated by the scientific opportunities of ballooning. Others were serious about sport. Vera Butler co-founded the

Aero Club of Great Britain (now the Royal Aero Club) in 1901, ensuring it was open 'equally to ladies and gentleman'. Alongside the showgirls, sportswomen and scientists a proto jet set of aristocratic aeronauts flourished. High society balloonists such as Vittoria Colonna, the Princess of Teano and May Assheton Harbord cultivated ballooning's cachet in the golden age before the First World War.

The one thing these women all shared was the exhilaration they felt when floating thousands of feet above the earth in a balloon. The extraordinary stories of the female aeronauts reveal a feisty breed of performers, scientists and pioneers with nerves of pure steel. From the 1780s to the advent of the First World War, long before they won fundamental freedoms such as the vote, the liberation women achieved among the clouds was unparalleled. The life of a lady aeronaut – even when it was cut short – was a glorious, soaraway adventure.

Chapter 2

Maiden Flights

Paris in the spring of 1784 thrummed with a new passion. The city of love had lost its heart, its reason almost, to aerostation. The Montgolfier brothers had unlocked the airy realm just as the previous summer had turned to autumn. The age of flight had arrived and for the philosophers and fashion conscious of France, absolutely nothing was sexier than a balloon.

Naturally it was in Paris that women enjoyed their first exquisite taste of leaving the earth. The capital was the epicentre of the new science and Faubourg St Antoine was where beautiful balloons were conjured into being. The district was home to Jean-Baptiste Réveillon, the man who made montgolfiers look gorgeous. He worked with the Montgolfier brothers, also in the paper trade, to create the outer shell of the balloon that so astonished the court at Versailles in September 1783. The breathtaking balloon was named *Le Réveillon,* decorated in the wallpaper factory beneath his apartments and tested in the grounds. The mansion was the natural venue for women with the nerve and status to be the very first to take flight. On 20 May 1784 four elegant ladies stepped aboard a balloon in Faubourg St Antoine and were released into the sky. It was a small step for the women and an almighty leap for womankind.

At the front of the queue for a ride above the earth were the Marchioness of Montalembert, the Countess of Montalembert, the Countess of Podenas and a companion, Miss de Lagarde. Joseph Montgolfier himself was in charge of the private, experimental flight assisted by the Marquis of Montalembert, who may also have been in the basket. The balloon almost certainly rose from the beautiful grounds of Réveillon's mansion, Titonville, on Rue de Montreuil, where Réveillon and Montgolfier usually tested their creations. Though few details survive of this landmark moment, their courage is recalled by supreme balloonomaniac Jules Verne in one of his adventure stories. *A Winter Amid the Ice and Other Thrilling Stories* imagines an aeronaut being hijacked by a deranged inventor and the pair wrestling for control of the balloon. The hijacker urges the petrified pilot to rise ever higher by citing the courage of the women:

> 'What is nobler than to overlook the clouds which oppress the earth? Is it not an honour thus to navigate on aerial billows? The greatest men have travelled as we are doing. The Marchioness and Countess de Montalembert, the Countess of Podenas, Mademoiselle la Garde, the Marquis de Montalembert, rose from the Faubourg Saint-Antoine for these unknown regions, ... all left the traces of their glory in the air. To equal these great personages, we must penetrate still higher than they into the celestial depths! To approach the infinite is to comprehend it!'

The four women gazed down upon a Paris, at least, that they comprehended from the comfort of the ruling class. Réveillon's property radiated prosperity from its wallpaper factory on the ground floor, sumptuous apartments above, wine cellar below, immaculate gardens in front. In 1784, it was where the wealthy and well-connected indulged their love of balloons. In 1789, it was where the French revolution began to break out. Réveillon once again found fame, only this time the wallpaper baron gave his name to a riot rather than a balloon. Wage cut rumours led a mob to smash up the factory and Réveillon, who lent his art and his name to the flying machine that astonished the world, was reduced to climbing over the garden wall and running for his life.

The first women aloft left the traces of their glory in the air but they too faced an inglorious future. The marchioness fled to England, where she was abandoned and divorced by the marquis. Tragedy came first, though, to Charlotte, the young Countess of Podenas. On a beautiful day in May she was among the first of her sex to fly and by December she lay in her grave. Charlotte died in childbirth aged just 22. An exciting world was opening to women in the sky but they faced the same mortal dangers on the ground. Miss de Lagarde presumably lived to be glad she was not a titled lady but simply an aerostatic pioneer and citizen of the new France.

We can only guess at whether the Paris pioneers were invited to fly or had insisted on the trip, but the first untethered female flight was the very opposite of a private experiment. The ascent of an opera singer two weeks later in Lyon was marked by drumrolls, royal pomp and impromptu arias. Balloon mania swept Lyon as thoroughly as Paris, not least because its chief industry was silk weaving. Lyon also had a royal visitor to impress,

THE LOST HISTORY OF THE LADY AERONAUTS

Gustav III of Sweden. Half of the population worked in silk so what better way to represent the style-conscious city than with the en vogue invention. Add a smart venue, a diva with an impressive bearing and voice that could carry miles and the stage was set.

The demonstration was planned for 4 June 1784 in the chic district of Brotteux and the diva in question was the opera singer Elisabeth Thible. According to Gaston Tissandier in the Victorian ballooning bible *Histoire des Ballons*, Elisabeth was pretty, she was born in Lyon and she had been abandoned by her husband shortly after their wedding. What bearing this had on her role in making aerostatic history is unclear, though it was probably to explain why there was no M Thible around to object. On the day, she rose as magnificently to the occasion as the montgolfier that carried her. Elisabeth was awarded the role in the royal performance by Count Jean-Baptiste de Laurencin. He yielded his seat so that she could ascend with a painter and balloonist called Monsieur Fleurant. One reason may have been that the nobleman was still recovering his nerve after a traumatic experience earlier that year. He was among the passengers who ascended from Lyon in *Le Flesselles* in January with Joseph Montgolfier. The gigantic balloon ripped at 3000ft and it was a miracle that the seven men on board survived the landing.

Elisabeth would have been only too aware of the spectacular accident. She almost certainly witnessed it. Though there had been no fatalities so far, lots of balloons caught fire or crashed and usually both. The balloon buzz was everywhere but most people preferred to watch from a safe distance. Being an aeronaut came with very real danger. Yet Elisabeth did far more than simply cling to the car and paint on a smile. If she was going to ascend in a balloon for the king of Sweden, she was going to do it in style. Impressing Gustav was important. France and Sweden became allies under a treaty signed in July 1784 and he was on a diplomatic visit to seal the deal. As thousands gathered for the glamorous balloon ascent, Elisabeth dressed to impress. She emerged at 4pm in the costume of Minerva, the Roman goddess of wisdom, art and war. The balloon was the blue and yellow of Sweden and called *La Gustave* in tribute to the royal guest. The king did not arrive until 6pm but made a beeline for the balloon enclosure. He was fascinated by the machine and was shown around the interior workings.

The king took his seat. It was time for the spectacle to commence. Elisabeth gathered her goddess skirts, adjusted her feathered headdress and took her place in the gondola. At ten past six a drumroll was the signal to light the fire beneath the aperture and the balloon began to inflate. At a second drumroll, the external ropes were attached to the gondola and at the third, the planks holding the balloon down were removed. When the fourth drumroll sounded, the balloon began moving towards the gallery where the king was seated, spooking some of the ladies. They were preparing to flee when they realised the balloon had stopped its forward movement, according to Tissandier. The fifth and final drumroll sounded and this was the big moment for Elisabeth. The ropes fell away and she became the first woman to fly free into the sky. *La Gustave* rose, wrote the historian:

> 'straight up into the air, with no rocking, with the regal assurance of a body disdainfully leaving the earth in order to establish its empire in the heavenly regions.'

As they floated majestically into the air, Elisabeth and her companion waved a flag at the cheering Swedish king and his fellow balloon maniacs. Fleurant reported rising to such a great height that the houses of Lyon looked like a shapeless heap of pebbles. Seven minutes into the flight they were waving a second flag for the benefit of the distant spectators when they were hit by the altitude. Elisabeth and the pilot suffered a sudden chill and a loud buzzing filled their ears. To their intense relief, the unpleasant sensations passed off and were replaced with a sweet sense of wellbeing. Seizing this perfect moment, the goddess burst into song. Her powerful voice rang out from the sky as she sang *I triumph, I am Queen*, an aria from a popular opera called *La Belle Arsène*. Fleurant did his best to respond with *What, journeying in the clouds* from the comic opera *Zemire and Azor*. 'After having so poetically expressed their aerial impressions,' reports Tissandier:

> 'the travellers perceived that their supply of combustible material had almost all been used up; they descended above a wood which Fleurant avoided by feeding the flame, and landed fortunately in the middle of a wheatfield, about two leagues from their departure point.'

The descent was going smoothly until it touched down, when they heard part of the rig break and the balloon shell fell onto them both. Fleurant pulled out his knife and cut a window in the cloth, searching frantically for his companion. Elisabeth had managed to move clear of danger, though she had twisted her left ankle in the crash. People ran towards the wreckage from every direction. In the melee the cry went up that there was a casualty but Fleurant and Thible insisted they were fine. The mystery was solved when Fleurant realized someone was trying to lift the balloon to help them emerge. A well-dressed man explained how he had seen them about to land, raced to meet them and almost set himself alight when the balloon grazed past. The flames of the burner had charred some of his clothing but not his skin and he was able to joke with the aeronauts about their lucky escapes.

Then, as so often at early ballooning events, things descended into pandemonium. The crowd grew around the deflating balloon and amid the melee it fell onto the burner and went up in flames. What scraps survived were quickly pilfered as souvenirs. *La Gustave* was gone, but King Gustav did not care. He was delighted by the demonstration and eager to meet Madame Thible and her companion. They were carried in triumph to his royal highness, who Tissandier records, 'congratulated them on their beautiful experience, one of the most remarkable to have been made up till then by balloons with fire'.

Elisabeth was panache personified. She had serenaded her home town and his highness from the clouds and emerged with dignity from a crash landing and friendly mobbing. She had handled the performance with perfect aplomb and Fleurant gave her great credit for her practical role too – the young Minerva fed the fire box and proved a fearless companion.

Count de Laurencin was also beside himself with admiration for the limping diva. He wrote to Joseph Montgolfier praising her courage and aplomb:

> 'A thousand persons of her sex, have shown us that courage is not solely a male attribute; but I assert that no woman has furnished better proof of this than Mme Tible; that no woman has shown more sang-froid or genuine determination; that no woman, proud of an unknown danger, has been more happy to face it.'

Across the English Channel aeronauts began frantic attempts to ascend with a woman. By early 1785 the battle had become almost comic. Male aeronauts wanted the kudos of being the first to squire a lady into the air and ladies were only too happy to volunteer. A letter to the editor of *Lady's Magazine* from the Cuthbert-Hodgson Collection reveals how avid women were for the latest news. 'Your readers may wish, in the present rage for balloons, to have a short and accurate account of the different aerostatic voyages which have been made since Mr. Montgolfier's discovery,' the correspondent writes, giving a brief account of Elisabeth Thible's success as 'the first lady who ascended'.

While Madame Thible's ascent had been a triumphant affair, every attempt to have a similar success in England seemed doomed. The contenders were the foreign aeronauts who brought the balloon craze to Britain. Count Francesco Zambeccari launched the first hydrogen balloon here in November 1783; his fellow Italian Vincent Lunardi made the first manned flight in September 1784 and Frenchman Jean-Pierre Blanchard made the first balloon crossing of the English Channel in January 1785. Balloons did not come cheap and all three were locked in a constant battle to woo high society purses with their aerostatic displays. The scientific establishment was still very dismissive of balloons but they were hugely popular as entertainment. Among the first aeronauts, status and funding relied on an exhausting quest to provide something new. For this, women were brought in on the act.

If women themselves had been allowed any say in the matter, the first British woman to go ballooning would have been Georgiana, the Duchess of Devonshire. In November 1784 she asked the American doctor John Jeffries if she could replace him on an ascent with Pierre Blanchard in London. He refused, even when the Prince of Wales pressed her case. The only way Jeffries was willing to include women was by lobbing little billet-doux from aloft, addressed to his many lady friends.

Just before Christmas 1784 Count Zambeccari began making it known he wanted to find a woman willing to make an ascent. He put his *British Balloon* on display at the exhibition rooms of the Lyceum in the Strand, where people could pay a shilling for a look, and 'wishes to be accompanied by a British Lady and Gentleman' on its next aerial outing. By the new year of 1785 he had secured a wealthy gentleman passenger in rear admiral Sir Edward Vernon and was desperate for a lady:

> 'A gentleman of the first distinction has engaged to attend Count Zambeccari in his approaching Aerial Excursion, and it is his ambition to be favored with the company of a British Lady, but this happiness he must forego, and content himself with a second Gentleman, unless some Lady, whose rank, &c. in life would obviate every objection, is speedily proposed.'

As the hunt continued, he took swipes at his rivals, claiming his balloon was superior because of its construction not 'from any arts calculated to exaggerate its merits, for mercenary purposes.' He wants to attract the shillings while distancing himself, without naming names, from the likes of Lunardi and Blanchard. Zambeccari is all about lofty goals, he says in the Lyceum advertisement, not swindling the public.

> 'He wishes to address himself to the good sense of the respectable public, and to build his pretentions to their favor, upon the solid basis of truth and sincerity, not plausibility and deception, as practiced by those whose views extend no farther, than to the gratification of their interested pursuits; who are insensible to the dignity of genuine honor; and who, under the specious pretence of respect and gratitude, insult the generous unsuspecting credulity of the public, by pretending to advance the noble cause of philosophy, without the ability to give a rational answer to the simplest question upon a scientific subject.'

It was this endless self-aggrandizement that so often went before a fall in the unpredictable world of the early aeronauts. They made very big promises and if they did not keep them, all hell broke loose. Zambeccari would discover that the respectable public made little distinction between philosophers and pretenders when it came to not getting their money's worth. By 23 March 1785 he had found a lady willing to board the *British Balloon*, though he never deigns to use her name when giving his version of what happened next. She was Miss Grice, about whom we know nothing except she had the courage and drive to be the first woman to take flight in Britain. She was there so the count could fulfil his much-trumpeted 'ambition to be favored with the company of a British lady.' Then he ditched her in the most humiliating and public fashion. The count and the admiral treated her like so much ballast. In the Italian's self-penned words:

> 'At 35 minutes after three o'clock, Admiral Sir Edward Vernon, Count Zambeccari, and a Lady, entered the Boat, and immediately the balloon was left to itself; but after two or three attempts, its power being found inadequate to raise the annexed weight, the lady, who was only an accidental passenger, was obliged to leave the boat, which she did with evident reluctance.'

Who can blame her? Miss Grice did not feel like 'only an accidental passenger' until that moment. She was furious and had to be virtually ordered out of the car. A captioned engraving of *Count Zambeccari's Balloon* records the moment when 'Miss Grice was obliged to get out.'

Another report gives a fuller account of her foiled attempt to be the first British woman to fly (though here she is called Grist along with other typos). It may give a clue to how she found her way into the balloon car, if not the sky. It seems likely that she was there thanks to her own initiative. The exact time and venue for the ascent had been kept a secret. The only way to find out was by buying a ticket (five shillings for the cheap seats, half a guinea for first class). As the count was still missing his British lady with only a day to go, Miss Grice simply took her chance. She may have known the gentlemen, but it seems possible she won her seat by simply presenting herself as British lady aeronaut material:

> 'Just on the eve of their departure, a Miss Grist, of Holborn, offered to accompany of [sic] the Aeronauts, which offer was accepted, and she entered the car; but notwithstanding they threw out a great quantity of ballast, after making three or four attempts, the heroine was obliged to give up the pleasure of ascending, the balloon being incapable of taking more than the two gentlemen; on the Lady's quitting her seat, it ascended with amazing velocity.'

Zambeccari did not spend another moment on the fate of his poor lady passenger, describing instead the rest of the flight as more male derring-do. She had won her place at the eleventh hour and at the fifty-ninth minute, saw it snatched away. Hopefully the enterprising Miss Grice decided she must laugh or else she would cry as she trudged home to Holborn. Everyone else seemed to find it quite funny, as a bawdy new song *The Air Balloon Fun* from a newspaper in the Cuthbert-Hodgson Collection attests.

> 'You frollicksome lads and lasses draw near,
> And an air balloon ditty you quickly shall hear,
> An amiable lady, as people report,
> Would go a ballooning being fond [of] the sport. Fall lara.
>
> 'Fam'd Count Zambeccari form'd a balloon,
> And some people say 'twas as big as the moon;

THE LOST HISTORY OF THE LADY AERONAUTS

Where Cupid before his arch tricks never play'd,
By which a young lady was to be convey'd,
We cannot but speak now in praise of the fair,
The balloon was got ready, some thousand were there,
When the lady was in that his thing would not rise,
The people did gaze on the Count with surprize.

'But as disappointments crowd on us a-pace,
The lady was forc'd to alight from her place,
Some praising her courage, whilst others they cry'd,
I am sorry, dear madam, you're depriv'd of your ride.

'The Count and brave Vernon ascended, we hear,
A beautiful prospect the sky being clear,
I'll bet five to one, had the charmer been there,
She'd have felt the effects of inflammable air.

'Near Horsham in Sussex the air balloon fell,
The wind being brisk yet they manag'd it well,
Some cordage gave way from the tube or the cawl,
Which had lik'd to have caus'd them a terrible fall.

'Full thirty five miles in one hour it run,
And just like a whirlwind the air balloon spun,
They heard such a terrible noise in the air,
They thought that Old Belzebub follow'd them there.

'But since that the Ladies all hazards will run,
This summer will bring forth some air balloon fun,
The charming young creatures so artful are grown,
They now go in search of philosophers stones.

'You lads and you lasses I'd have you prepare,
You may couple together like birds in the air,
And if you shou'd get a young daughter or son,
You sure will remember the air balloon fun.'

Jokes about erections and conceptions reflect the real conversations in the balloon-mad crowds that turned up to watch aeronauts in their supposedly scientific endeavours. To an eighteenth century reader a philosopher's stone was associated with the alchemy of mercury, a treatment for venereal disease. Such sniggers made the women who braved the ever-present innuendo in that summer of 1785 all the more impressive.

While the Italians slugged it out to the amusement of the British press, the indefatigable Frenchman Jean-Pierre Blanchard stole a march on them both. In January of that year he found fame with the first balloon crossing of the Channel. Of all the early aeronauts, none was better at giving the punters what they wanted, especially when they wanted flying women. He went on to marry one of his protégées, the great Sophie Blanchard, but in the spring of 1785 he was hauling his balloon around Britain. At the beginning of May he announced his latest attraction in the press.

> 'Mr. Blanchard having finished a Balloon and Gallery, on a new construction, has the honor to inform the public, that at the particular solicitations of several persons of distinction, he will To-morrow, the 3^d of May, accompanied by a Lady, make an aerostatic experiment, at the extensive and commodious situation, known by name of Langhorne's Repository, in Barbican.'

Langhorne's was a yard for buying and selling horses. At midday Blanchard promised to perform some fresh moves with his new machinery and tickets were five shillings a head.

The lady was actually a 14-year-old girl who had grown up on the stage. Rosine Simonet came from a family of French dancers and had been performing since she was at least seven. Daughter of Louis and Adelaide, Rosine worked in London theatres with her younger sisters Leonora and Theresa. Her first appearance was at Covent Garden Theatre in 1777, shortly after the family arrived from France. By the time she met Blanchard, she was a respected performer with a long list of credits from the Covent Garden, Drury Lane and King's theatres.

On 3 May 1785 Londoners were spoilt for choice. The beautiful day dawned with two aeronauts promising to take the first woman into the English skies. In Tottenham Court Road, Zambeccari was now proposing to take a Miss Hall up in his *British Balloon*. Over at the Barbican, Blanchard vowed to make Miss Simonet fly. As Zambeccari had already failed on the female aeronaut front, Blanchard drew the bigger crowd.

Rosine had tremendous nerve but she was still only 14. For a moment, she showed her age:

> 'The Lady was much frightened when the balloon first rose, but soon after appeared to have recovered herself; and M. Blanchard, in sight of a great number of people, saluted her.'

Louis Simonet's heart lurched as he watched his young daughter master her fear. He could not relax until she had landed safely. He jumped on a horse and galloped along for an hour, beneath the balloon where she could see him. Tissandier reports:

> 'Among the riders who followed the balloon, Mlle Simonet could make out her father, who took her into his arms after they had landed and took her back to London, to general acclamation.'

Rosine had travelled six miles by air, becoming the French girl who made English history. She was the first female to take to the air from British soil. The balloon and its occupants were escorted back to the city by the relieved Louis and two other men on horseback. 'When the Procession arrived at Barbican, the Lady alighted,' reports *The Oxford Journal*:

> 'A Correspondent observes, that tho' Miss Simonet, who ascended with Mr. Blanchard on Tuesday last from Barbican, may not be allowed to be the *greatest* Woman in England, she is certainly a Lady of *higher* Rank than any in the Kingdom.'

As the papers went to press declaring that 'the ingenious M. Blanchard made his fourth aerial experiment in England, accompanied by a lady', they also relayed the news of the disastrous end to the rival display by Zambeccari. Blanchard's success stood in stark contrast to the flop across town when they were reported side by side. 'Same Day,' notes one paper:

> 'the Proprietors of that Balloon with which Count Zambeccari and Sir Edward Vernon ascended, drew together a considerable Body of the People [to] witness a second Experiment, in which they advertised that a British Lady was to make a Adventure in the upper Regions of the Atmosphere; they took a vast Deal

of Pains to accomplish their Purpose, but there was evidently a Want of Intelligence. The Assembly was very patient, until about Four, the Machine burst, when John Bull became outrageous, and considerable Injury was done to the premises.'

John Bull (aka the English public) never missed an opportunity for a spot of hooliganism when aeronauts let them down. Once again, a game woman was persuaded to accompany Zambeccari in his balloon and once again, she lived to regret it. Another report describes a floppy balloon and a terrifying scene:

'Count Zambeccari, and afterwards a young Lady of fortitude, whose name we understand to be Hall, took their stations in the boat, but in vain. Indeed, the spectators were at a loss to determine whether the boat was suspended by the balloon as it should have been, or the balloon from the boat. This failure must truly be attributed to an unforeseen accident; a small opening had burst at the top of the balloon. The company seeing this was the case, were satisfied with Count Zambeccari's endeavours to please them, and only regretted that his hopes were frustrated. Not so the populace. They tore down the scaffolding, reduced part of the wall into ruins, and had committed more mischief, but for the appearance of the guards. Fourteen of the rioters were taken into custody.'

Who Miss Hall was or how she escaped the Count's latest fiasco, we do not know. She had arrived that day hoping for a shot at immortality as the first British aeronaut of her sex. She fled with the cries of rioters ringing in her ears to fade back into obscurity. Just like Miss Grice, no-one even remembered her first name. Zambeccari was known in some quarters as the Mad Count of Bologna. Certainly would-be female aeronauts learned to give him a wide berth.

Meanwhile Lunardi was attempting his own launch of 'an English lady', with a much-heralded ascent announced for 13 May from the Artillery Ground. As we will see later, this too was a disaster. By mid-May, the failed attempts of Lunardi and Zambeccari to ascend with their ladies left them laughing stocks. Blanchard, on the other hand, was a hero:

'The peculiar circumstance of being the first Aerial Voyager who has crossed the sea, and the first who has carried up a

> LADY in his boat, are additional causes of satisfaction to Mr. Blanchard, as they have been of pleasure and gratification to the great Metropolis.'

After her ascent in the first week of May, Rosine returned to dancing in the theatre while Blanchard planned the next novelty. Notices appeared in the press announcing a display of falconry from the balloon he used to cross the Channel. Unfortunately, Colonel Thornton the falconer was too portly to lift. 'The balloon proved to be insufficiently inflated, and the colonel, who was a sizeable and weighty man, was forced to remain on the ground,' explains Tissandier. A balloonist was only as good as his last ascent and Blanchard was not happy:

> 'I was particularly annoyed, in as much as Colonel Thornton, being the greatest falconer in England, had promised to set his raptors to hunt from the balloon, which would undoubtedly have been very entertaining; but, as he could not go up, he ordered his servants to set flight to the pigeons and falcons, and this pursuit was of great interest to the large crowd.'

An aeronaut who disappointed a large crowd was never far from a riot and Blanchard had to think quickly before the bird show finished. As he pondered what to do he was surrounded by women begging to take the colonel's place. Male aeronauts were often mobbed in this way. If the fashionistas were balloonistas, then the groupies were balloonies. 'Being determined to ascend by myself at precisely two o'clock, I got in to the gondola; all the ladies around me seemed set on coming with me,' he reports. It took a fellow famous aeronaut to tell him that actually, a woman could save the day:

> 'M Pilatre de Rozier, who had recently arrived from London, made his way through the crowd and came to tell me (on behalf of M Simonet) that the younger Mlle Simonet desired the same favour as her elder sister.'

Leonora was only 13 years old and also a child dancer. Blanchard may have moved on but the Simonet sisters had discovered a passion for flight. Leonora was desperate to do what her sister had done. She begged her father and he asked de Rozier what he could do. Like so many of the female pioneers, little Leonora was in the right place at the right time. Blanchard needed a new companion before the crowd turned ugly. He got straight to the point and asked how much the girl weighed. Weight, as the colonel was forced to reflect, could make or break a balloon display. Blanchard was only 114lbs so when he heard Leonora weighed a mere 83, he agreed at once:

> 'M de Rozier, taking her into his arms, placed her in my gondola, removed my ballast, and drew us into the wind so as to avoid the danger of hitting the tall trees. Thus we escaped from his restraining hands to the unanimous acclamation of the entire crowd.'

Leonora found her balloon legs faster than her sister. Several reports of Rosine's ascent stated, 'The young lady not being used to such excursions was air sick, and fainted several times.' Leonora felt fine and simply gazed out across London, enchanted, as they floated low along the skyline at the height of St Paul's. Blanchard had to draw her back 'from the ecstasy which she retained at the sight of London town and its neighbourhood,' says Tissandier, to warn her they were about to descend. Leonora begged him to carry on flying but he had promised not to cover more than four or five miles. He pointed to the riders below who were following their progress and said 'a longer journey would exhaust a great number of these fine horses'. The girl gave in with a sigh.

> 'Blanchard and his little companion were at once surrounded by thousands of people. Mlle Signoret, a fluent speaker of English, acted as interpreter for the aeronaut. The balloon was not deflated; kept attached to the gondola by means of ropes, it was triumphantly drawn back towards London in a captive state, Blanchard and the young traveller remaining in the gondola.'

Leonora enjoyed a heroine's welcome from her sister Rosine and a jubilant crowd. Tissandier reports Blanchard saying:

> 'If my return from my flight with the elder Mlle Simonet was a grand occasion, this return was no less so. We passed through the most beautiful areas around London. The town was deserted; all the roads leading towards it were completely crowded. M Pilatre de Rozier came to meet us; he told us how

pleased he was, and made every effort to encircle us so that the crowd did not inconvenience us – it was only with the utmost difficulty and effort that he succeeded. And so, with his help, we arrived at the place from which we had set off ... The two Mlles Simonet were shown to the public, who had been shouting loudly for a sight of them.'

The irrepressible pair became the darlings of England. As at home in the circus as a serious ballet, Blanchard's balloon became just another venue. The child stars played fairies and Cupid on the stage and now delighted audiences with real life antics in the air. They were troupers, used to the demands of regular performances and dancing for their supper. As the *Kentish Gazette* observed 'that the rage for balloons is no while abated' they made the most of being the only female aeronauts in Britain. For the rest of May they were on a roll. Rosine put airsickness behind her and was happy to perform on demand. One report says:

'by particular desire of several persons of distinction, Miss Simonet ... was elevated alone several times, amidst the acclamations and huzzas of the beholders, for the space of a quarter of an hour, after which time she descended.'

Everyone loved the sisters, even if they were not always sure which one they were watching:

'Mr. Blanchard and one of the Miss Simonets ascended in the balloon from South Lambeth, and took an aerial tour for about twenty minutes, descended in a field behind the Green Man, near the turnpike on the Greenwich road, from whence the boat was carried on men's shoulders with the two voyagers in it, and the balloon held down by cords, in procession to the place [of] their ascent, when Miss Simonet alighted.'

The teenagers shared ballooning as happily as they shared the stage. They were very close, often dancing or singing together, and a joint aerial adventure was what they had hoped for. Ballooning was not their permanent calling, though. Once they had danced through the clouds and taken all their bows, they returned to the theatre. Rosine and Leonora had been performing together since they were small children and their careers intertwined. They danced and sang together at the Royal Circus, the Haymarket and the Royalty. It was probably Rosine who became Mrs Wilde when she married an actor called William. They toured the country but she often used Simonet as her professional name. In 1791 the sisters were part of a group of leading European dancers assembled for a new opera at the Pantheon, so often the venue for aeronauts drumming up money with their balloons. Fittingly, it was here that Leonora made her final performance in 1792 before disappearing from showbusiness at the age of 19.

Stars of the stage were peculiarly suited to being the first women aloft. They were professionals, with the ability to master their nerves and perform under pressure. They were also glamorous and enjoyed the attention. When Elisabeth Thible achieved her ascent with such *savoir faire* she proved that performers made perfect aerial pioneers. Aside from their professional skills, they had a measure of social approval for such a public role (though then, as now, people loved to speculate on celebrity sex lives). It was the era when the great tragic actress Sarah Siddons brought new respectability to the profession. Hence whenever a London aeronaut announced he planned to take 'a Lady' aloft in 1785, she usually came from the theatre. Miss Grice and Miss Hall may have had different stories, but a theatrical background was a definite advantage if you had aerostatic ambitions. Many actresses of the late 1700s were connected both through their work and their families. Adelaide Simonet, the mother of Rosine and Leonora, was the aunt of Maria Theresa de Camp who married Charles Kemble, the brother of Sarah Siddons. These theatrical dynasties had many daughters and no playhouse could accommodate the size of crowd attracted to an early balloon ascent. Whatever its scientific pretensions, aerostation was always nine-tenths showbusiness.

The late eighteenth century provided precious few opportunities for women to enjoy the same adventures as men; little wonder balloons received an ecstatic greeting by ladies of every age and station. Flying was so fashionable and exciting that no-one thought to ban women from the party. Lighter-than-air travel was an unexpected frontier in the fight for an exciting role outside of the home. The battle for a balloon ride, though, was a free for all. Few women were hand picked to take an aerial voyage, so most had to resort to simply throwing themselves in the way of their heroes. Like a modern girl might yearn to be pulled on stage by her idol at a pop concert, young ladies of the Georgian era vied for the eye of an aeronaut.

Women took to the sky as Enlightenment thinkers fought for rights on the ground. The Age of Reason allowed some chink of light to fall on the role of women, though it was usually to discuss what kind of mother and homemaker they should be. For a taste of liberty, balloons had it all. They were the perfect metaphor for freedom. In a balloon a woman could leave the confines of society and rely on her own ability and resilience in the limitless sky. Women knew their route to the clouds lay in their novelty value. If that was the price of flying, so be it.

It was a time when female voices rarely managed to wrestle their way to any kind of a hearing. The law made women the property of their fathers and then of their husbands. They had no rights within marriage, their bodies and children were owned by the man.

A few independently wealthy women gained the freedom that came with holding their own purse strings, through widowhood or not marrying in the first place, and others gained some voice through the status of male relatives. Intellectual upper class women enjoyed genteel tea and thinking in gatherings of the bluestockings in the London homes of hostesses such as Elisabeth Montague. It was artists who fought to be heard as themselves by making a place in the world outside of the home. The women of the Enlightenment included Mary Wollstonecraft, who was struggling to keep her radical school for girls open in 1785 and would go on to write *A Vindication of the Rights of Women* – her daughter Mary Shelley would write *The Last Man*, a story of the future where balloons were the new buses. Elisabeth Inchbald was an actress and playwright making her name in the thick of the Georgian theatre where lady aeronauts were so often recruited. Fanny Burney carved a place as a novelist. Real equality, however, was almost two hundred years away.

The brutal fact was that men had all the power in 1780s Europe and balloons offered unexpected liberation for a select vanguard of women possessed of courage and flair.

Rosine and Leonora Simonet delighted the crowds with their youth and daring and opened the English skies to women. They were, however, French. The summer of 1785 arrived and for British women, there was still all to play for. The early aeronauts jostled for cash, prestige and public acclaim in a London seething with balloon frenzy. Everyone wanted to see an English woman ascend and it was another actress who showed outstanding grace under fire. She was the first to give voice to her own story and no-one would ever forget her first name. She was Letitia Ann Sage.

Chapter 3

Sex, Scandal and Mrs Sage

Early ballooning was all about showbusiness and no-one was more at home in the limelight than Letitia Sage, the first Englishwoman to fly. She was a West End actress whose steely determination and plunging neckline brought va-va-voom to the balloon. Letitia did not suffer stage fright, even when her performance was delivered thousands of feet above ground. However, exactly what that performance consisted of was the source of ribald rumour the poor woman never quite managed to outrun. Her landmark voyage into the London sky had all the comedy, drama and suspense an actress could expect. With more unexpected twists than a hit farce, a Georgian playwright could not have given the Mrs Sage balloon show of 29 June 1785 a better plot.

The suitably theatrical debut came two years after the Montgolfier brothers unveiled their invention and the year after the first Frenchwomen took to the sky. The lag was largely due to the English trying and failing to blank ballooning when it was invented by their age-old rivals. During 1783 their stock response was ridicule. Press and public figures united in scorning the Gallic gas bags. What possible use could there be for such things? King George III was interested enough to call for an inquiry, but this elicited a sniffy response from the Royal Society stating that no good whatsoever would come from ballooning. One newspaper instructed its readers to mock this great waste of French time and to laugh balloons out of existence. Another starts a verse 'In Ridicule of the Prevailing Rage for Air Balloons':

> 'Men have long built castles in the air: how to reach them
> Montgolfier has now first the honour to teach them.
> How odd this whim to mount on air-stuft pillions!
> 'Twill ruin all our coachmen and postillions…'

Balloons were pretty hard to dismiss, however. Aerostation had all Europe a-flutter and newly-independent Americans were equally enthralled.

THE LOST HISTORY OF THE LADY AERONAUTS

Scotland had its first aeronaut in the impoverished but ingenious inventor James Tytler. He managed to leap, as he put it, over an Edinburgh garden wall and land in a dung heap in August 1784. It was only a matter of time before England succumbed to the craze. That time came with Vincenzo (Vincent) Lunardi, the Italian who brought balloonomania to Britain.

Lunardi arrived as a junior diplomat but felt destined for higher things and nothing came higher than being England's first aeronaut. He made the first ascent from English soil on 15 September 1784, rising from the Artillery Ground in front of 150,000 people, including the Prince of Wales. The vast audience in London reacted exactly like the one for the Montgolfiers in Versailles one year earlier. Witnesses went bananas. Even the prince threw his hat in the air. Lunardi knew how to make an impression. The flamboyant 31-year-old floated past George III's window, wine in hand, place in history secured, balloonomania taking hold among the crowd below.

The coup gave Lunardi immediate celebrity status and his reputation was only enhanced when an unscheduled stop in Hertfordshire allowed him to hand over the cat he had with him. The puss began to shiver and shake with the cold and he felt sorry for it. The feline aeronaut also became a celebrity. A report from the time notes that Lunardi left his traumatised pet with an old lady who lived in Southgate. The pensioner found herself besieged by people wanting to see 'Balloon Puss' who wore a silver collar engraved with the date she declined a career among the clouds. Charming, handsome and kind to kittens, Vincent was surrounded by female fans wherever he went. The world of high fashion embraced him as a trendsetter. Lunardi hats with a wide brim and floppy, balloon-like crown became all the rage. Lunardi medallions made of silver, copper and bronze were everywhere. The balloonistas adored Vincent and Vincent adored them right back. One snippet in the Major B.F.S. Baden-Powell Collection of Aeronautical Cuttings at the National Aerospace Library in Farnborough reports an encounter, with helpful italics, between Vincent and what was probably a witty sex worker. He was at an entertainment palace in London, the Pantheon near Oxford Street, where his balloon was exhibited, when:

> 'Lydia Lovely again manoeuvres about in the circles of fashion; she sported the Pantheon on Saturday morning, attended by her *mature* Duenna. On her first entrance, with a loud laugh, and Cyprian smile, she fixed hold of Lunardi, expressed her astonishment at the enormous *swell* of his *balloon*, and declared her greatest satisfaction would be to see *it rise!*'

Balloons were so ripe for double entendre that few people bothered to resist.

While Lunardi cultivated his image as 'the daredevil aeronaut' about town, Letitia Sage was described as 'an incomparable beauty'. Mr Lunardi loved the playboy lifestyle that came with his fame and wanted to remain the darling of London. Mrs Sage was a glamorous actress who turned her talents to publicity events when the stage roles dried up. They were a perfect fame-hungry match. Lunardi needed to boost his waning popularity with another success. Letitia also needed a profile-raising role. Eight months after his historic flight from the Artillery Ground, he was turning into yesterday's news. Unlike her more successful sisters, Letitia's acting career had fizzled. Like Vincent, she desperately needed to star in a hit show. Her moment arrived with his invitation to ascend in a stylish silk balloon in front of anyone who was anyone in fashionable London. Lunardi needed to prove he was still the nation's number one aeronaut – and nothing was going to stop Letitia Sage from becoming the first English woman to fly.

Letitia was an actress, aeronaut and wardrobe keeper, according to her impressive CV in *Biographical Dictionary of Actors, Actresses, Musicians, Dancers, Managers &Other Stage Personnel in London, 1660-1800*. Born Letitia Ann Hoare she arrived into the theatrical branch of an ambitious family. The dictionary says her relatives included Henry Hoare, a wealthy Fleet Street banker who co-founded the Church Missionary Society and possibly the artists William and Prince. Letitia's parents were probably actors outside of London and they put all three of their daughters on the stage. Letitia and her sisters Sarah and Katharine became actresses in the capital. Katharine married fellow thespian Sparks Powell and Sarah wed actor-manager Thomas Achurch Ward. Letitia, however, fell for a haberdasher in the City of London and called herself Mrs Sage, though she does not appear to have actually been married.

The Hoare sisters were well known in theatrical circles but Letitia did not land as much acting work as her siblings. She made her stage debut in a Restoration comedy at Covent Garden Theatre in April 1773, playing Lady Townly in *The Provok'd Husband*. It was another seven years before she appeared on stage again, this time as Lady Macbeth. While her sisters Mrs Powell and Mrs Ward went on to enjoy successful acting careers, the resilient Mrs Sage had to find other ways of earning a living. She may have joined casts in theatres outside of London or worked behind the scenes in the costume mistress role she settled on in later life. According to Leslie Gardiner in *Lunardi* she was understudy to the undisputed queen of Drury Lane, Sarah Siddons. Whatever the twists and turns of her career, she remained a well-connected member of London's thriving theatrical world. This may even have been where she first met George Biggin, who went on to become a trustee of the theatre. Or possibly she was part of Vincent's fan club.

Letitia's ballooning fame began in Spring of 1785 when Lunardi began a series of announcements about his return to glory. On 13 May the Italian would ascend once again from the Artillery Ground, this time in his new balloon and accompanied by 'an English Lady and Gentleman'. The lady was Letitia Sage and the gentleman was George Biggin. George was a wealthy young scholar who 'takes a peculiar delight in scientific experiments' according to *The New London Magazine* and was besotted by ballooning. With Lunardi constantly chasing subscriptions (funding), a rich English gentleman was a very useful friend to have. The balloonomaniacs became friends before the Italian's historic flight the previous September. Indeed, George should have been standing next to Vincent as he took off from the Artillery Ground, sharing the glory of England's first manned ascent. Lunardi had left him behind, ostensibly breaking his promise because the balloon would not rise with two people. Whatever the cause, Lunardi had sole claim on the fame.

The thirteenth dawned and it was unlucky from the start. Letitia and George were ready to fly but the balloon was not. Though an elegant red and white striped beauty, the looks of Lunardi's balloon were not enough to impress the immense gathering of London's fashionable people when inflating it became a problem: 'The expence of filling that Balloon, I understand, amounted to nearly four hundred pounds, and yet it was unequal to its task. It involved poor Lunardi in a great number of very unpleasant matters…' writes Letitia in her memoir, *A Letter Addressed to a Female Friend*.

Unfortunately, a picture designed to celebrate the ascent contributed to the general public relations disaster. An engraving by Francesco Bartolozzi (another Italian based in London) from a painting by John-Francis Rigaud – called *V. Lunardi Esq., Mrs Sage, G. Biggin Esq* – was published on the day showing the trio taking off. In reality Lunardi had to admit defeat and ascend alone for little more than a feeble hop because the balloon refused to budge with all three on board. The image merely underlined Lunardi's failure and was taken for hubris. The press did not hold back, as this piece in the *Kentish Gazette* shows:

> 'The friends of Mr. Lunardi had been industrious in whispering the names, and in giving a favourable impression of the talents of Mrs. Sage and Mr. Biggin, who were to return from an

aerial tour to the Continent, fraught with sentimental and philosophical observations.

'The event, however, was something similar to that of the conjuror's promise to get into a bottle; for when the company, to the amount of four or five thousand in the ground, and eighty or a hundred thousand in its neighbourhood, were assembled; rumours of ill usage and dissention were propagated; it was seen by the preparations, that the power of the balloon had been falsely estimated; and Lunardi, getting into his car a little after one, in order to be led over the ground as the advertisement had taught the company to expect; the rope was cut; and he ascended partly to fulfill his promise, partly to escape embarrassing interrogations. ... The business appears to have been conducted without sufficient knowledge of the *very little* science which has been hitherto introduced into aerostation ... Mr Lunardi must have very good reasons to justify the disappointment, or his future pretensions will be consigned to contempt.'

It was all very embarrassing, according to Letitia:

'Various have been the opinions respecting the failure of this experiment. I think it could have arisen from no other cause than some unforeseen accident in the process of filling it. Let the cause be what it may, it has been the occasion of those great expences which Mr. Lunardi has been at, to remove the reflections of ignorance, and of the mortification we all experienced, at being obliged to disappoint the most brilliant assemblage of fashionable people that ever were collected on a similar occasion.'

Scathing reports did not paint Vincent or Letitia in a good light. Some suggested that he never intended to take her along, others that she lost her nerve at the last minute. Such insinuations left her furious. For one, she knew Lunardi had spent a lot of time and, more important, money on staging her flight and it was very unfair to accuse him of secretly planning to leave her behind:

'I had, besides, a stronger obligation to perform my engagement, than even my own inclination for the voyage. Mr. Lunardi had put himself to great expence, in order to gratify my wish to be of the party with him and Mr. Biggin ... I, who knew the natural honesty of Lunardi's sentiments, was perfectly convinced that this reflection upon his character was unjust and cruel in the highest degree.'

She was even more indignant that 'others attributed my *not* going at that time to cowardice in me.' How dare people say she had lost her bottle? 'I was piqued also that I should be suspected of a weakness, which is not in any degree a trait in my character, if I am to judge of myself.' She says there were 'a thousand opinions' flying around about why Lunardi had to leave herself and Biggin behind, from the coating of the balloon to the process of filling it with enough hydrogen to do the job. The simple upshot of the not-as-advertised ascent was that Lunardi had to work fast to fix his reputation and faster still if he was to keep his promise of putting the first Englishwoman into the air. Letitia sums up the May disaster with:

'I never thought myself competent to judge *how* the matter *did* happen; he failed: and the only way to extricate him from the imputation of ignorance, was to make an attempt gratis, to prove that he was right in his estimate, and that the Balloon, *properly* filled, was equal to carry up the proposed weight.'

She does not specify whose weight was the heart of the matter. The voluptuous star weighed 200lbs and it was an issue Lunardi could not ignore forever.

The Italian embarked on a hasty tour of the country to scare up enough iron to use in the manufacture of hydrogen for the second attempt to fly with Letitia and George. It was a scarce commodity. Lunardi's many rivals also had balloons to fill. On his travels, he was entertained by Letitia's sister in Liverpool, which she mentions in her memoir:

'I thank you for your attention to him when at Liverpool. He speaks of *you* and *yours* with great friendship, and I find it will not be long before he pays you a second visit.'

There he would show 'the goodness of his heart' by only recouping his expenses for proposed ascents and giving the rest of the proceeds to charity. This may have been goodness, or it may have been a vain attempt to deflect the critics who pounced on his every mishap. Vincent wrote to George from Liverpool later that summer. Far be it for the aeronaut to go on about his charity work... except to say:

> 'If the prayers of one grateful Heart are offered up for me I shall be supremely happy! Perhaps a Ray of Joy may beam on the disconsolate Widow's, or helpless Orphan's Bosom; – Perhaps the Father of a numerous Family, rescued from the Miseries of immediate Want, may bless me as his Benefactor, and, seated by his happy Fire-side, teach a lisping Infant to pronounce LUNARDI'S Name!'

He throws in an ode written, he claims, by an admirer that opens with:

> 'To thee, true Hero, who, without a fear, First soar'd aloft in England's Atmosphere, The Muses haste, to dedicate their Lays, And crown thee with unfading Wreaths of Bays!'

It continues in such vein about Lunardi 'the GOD-LIKE HERO'.

Such habitual self-promotion was perhaps understandable if a little over the top. Lunardi and Letitia were professional performers and both understood that funding for aeronauts depended on putting on a good show. The June ascent had to be a success. So Lunardi ordered his iron, pinned down the venue and publicized the flight. Six weeks after the embarrassing false start, Mrs Sage was ready to board the balloon car. This time nothing would force her to step out again until she had made her name as England's first female aeronaut. With only four days to go and in the triumph of hope over experience, E. Wyatt published a new version of Bartolozzi's print. Now called *The Three Favorite Aerial Travellers,* George has acquired a hat and Vincent a sword and Letitia looks even more beautiful centre stage. Again, it proved a pretty picture rather than a true record of events.

As the ascent drew closer Letitia refused to listen to doom-merchants, including anxious friends who thought the escapade far too dangerous. It was taking place just two weeks after ballooning's first fatalities. Jean-François Pilâtre de Rozier and Jules Romain died on 15 June attempting to cross the English Channel from France. Though sobering, it did not deter Lunardi and crowds always relished a bit of danger. As Horace Walpole remarked, 'The balloonomania is, I think, a little chilled, not extinguished, by Rozier's catastrophe.'

THE LOST HISTORY OF THE LADY AERONAUTS

The people Letitia visited on the eve of her ascent were spooked by the recent tragedy and did their best to talk her out of it. Her sister, she writes, will not be surprised that they failed to sway her. If anything, she was even more determined to succeed if only to draw a veil over the May fiasco:

> 'I passed the day with some of our friends, whose entreaties were all exhausted, to prevail on me to relinquish my scheme; you, who saw the cool determination of my conduct, when it was intended I should accompany Mr. Lunardi and Mr. Biggin, on a former occasion, will not be surprised I could withstand their persuasions.'

Secretly scared or not, this was Letitia's best shot at immortality. The race was on to get an English woman in the air and Miss Grice had almost beaten her to it when Count Francesco Zambeccari invited her on board, then cruelly ordered her off again.

Lunardi was more agitated by the logistics of getting the balloon to rise than passenger safety. Delays were never good in the volatile world of early aeronautics. Disappointing a big crowd could provoke a riot, as Chevalier de Moret had proved the previous summer in his failed attempt to beat Lunardi to the first manned flight in England. The mob was furious and Moret had to run for his life. 'The result was entirely disastrous, and must have acted for months to come as a warning to would-be adventurers in the air,' notes J.E. Hodgson in *The History of Aeronautics in Great Britain*.

It surely did and Lunardi was never free of the fear of failure and its impact on his reputation. He was in a constant state of anxiety about every ascent until the moment of liftoff. The iron he ordered from Birmingham did not arrive until the eleventh hour, thanks to 'some mistake' according to Letitia. He knew the amount of hydrogen needed to raise his passengers was considerable and did suffer more than his fair share of calamity, as he admits in a later letter to Biggin. 'You must have remark'd the odd Fatality that attends me; at the Beginning of every Enterprize some unlucky Incident deranges my Plan of Operations…'. Letitia, however, held her nerve and planned the performance of a lifetime.

The day of the rescheduled ascent arrived with beautiful skies and no immediate signs of an unlucky incident. On 29 June 1785, Letitia Sage dressed to impress and awaited the gentlemen who would escort her to the show. She chose a low-cut plum dress with lace cuffs and a large hat adorned with every balloonomania belle's favourite, plumes of white feathers. Her cleavage barely veiled in flimsy gauze, Mrs Sage was ready for her close-up. 'The auspicious morning came,' she writes:

> 'I went, in company with Mr. Down and Mr. Bell, about ten o'clock, to the Rotunda, in St. George's Fields; a place built by Mr. Arnold, for the purpose of launching his Montgolfier called the Royal George.'

She was very happy to see the process of inflating the balloon showed no signs of ending in disaster like the previous month:

> 'On our getting to the Rotunda, we found the Balloon about one-fourth inflated, and the business going on in a very regular manner, under the joint direction of Mr. Lunardi and Mr. Biggin. And here, I must observe, how much it is to be regretted, that they did not take this part of the business under their own care on the 13th of May.'

Like the Montgolfiers at the French court, Lunardi knew how to pander to his audience. The balloon was a giant union jack and named the *Royal George* in honour of the king. Aware of making the crowd feel entertained in the build-up, Lunardi made sure everyone could watch the aerostat take shape:

> 'They began filling the Balloon about nine o'clock; and, in order to make the process an object of gratification to the whole neighbourhood of St. George's Fields, Mr. Lunardi had raised a stage, upon which the Balloon was suspended, so that every thing was distinctly seen by each anxious and curious individual.'

It was tense going for Lunardi, she observes, as problems played out in front of the swelling crowd:

> 'By eleven o'clock they had exhausted the whole of their iron, and found a difficulty in getting water, so that business was suspended for a full hour; they at length got a fresh supply, and went on at an astonishing rate. At this time the company began to assemble, and, before one, there were more than an hundred thousand persons within the circle of St. George's Fields.'

The stage was set, the audience was gathered, the marvellous Mrs Sage was ready to make her entrance. Rather than mill around as the men did the donkey work, she stayed hidden away:

> 'As I did not like to be seen, until the very moment of getting into the gallery, I sat in the coach, where I escaped those remarks which I knew would naturally be made, had the *multitude* once got an idea of the woman who was about to make so bold an attempt.'

Meanwhile, George Biggin had arrived early and was enjoying his hands-on role in preparing for the ascent. He had been sorely disappointed twice. This was more than a case of third time lucky for Lunardi's generous supporter. The young gentleman's ride in the Italian's balloon was embarrassingly overdue. If anyone had to miss out this time, it was not going to be him. George Biggin Esquire was every bit as determined to fly that day as Mrs Letitia Sage.

This determination turned flinty when it transpired Lunardi had invited two more people to join the ascent. After failing to get three people aloft in May he suddenly seemed ready to try it with five. Worst of all, from Letitia's point of view, the latecomers included another woman. As far as the actress was concerned, she alone was topping the bill that day and some flavour of the *froideur* that descended comes from Letitia, leaving her rival nameless:

> 'The Balloon being as much inflated as was thought necessary to carry up three, if not four persons, at ten minutes after one o'clock (the time specified by Mr. Lunardi for his ascension) I was conducted into the Rotunda, and placed myself in the gallery, in which were Mr. Lunardi, Mr. Biggin, Colonel Hastings (a gentleman to whom Mr. Lunardi had given a promise, that should the Balloon be capable of carrying up more than the *intended three*, he should have a place in it) and another lady whose name I do not know.'

The lady whose name she did not know proved no match for Letitia. The balloon would not lift. The heaviest person there showed no sign of moving. It was game over for the luckless rival. 'The other Lady was the first to quit the gallery,' reports Letitia, 'which was merely an act of justice, yielding to my *prior* claim.'

And then there were four. Letitia was not blind to her ample figure and the impact such *en-bon-point* ('in good condition', the polite term for plump) had on proceedings. At fourteen stone, she was a voluptuous lady and it took a lot of hydrogen to lift her. She still was not getting out, though. It was hardly her fault, she reasoned, that they had not filled up on enough gas:

> 'They then began to try the rising power of the Balloon, before they took in either the ballast or Mr. Biggin's apparatus for observation; and I really believe the Balloon, properly filled, would be fully sufficient to the taking up four, if not *five* persons; I will not tell you that they shall all be so much *en-bon-point* as your friend.'

Even without the fifth passenger the balloon refused to move. Things were not going well. The scene was becoming chaotic and it looked horribly likely that this too would end in ignominious failure. She writes:

> 'It then could not stir. The neck of the Balloon was tied with the string of the valve. When Mr. Biggin perceived it, he desired it might be set free. Some person officiously tied it to the cords of the net. Mr. Biggin was then under the necessity of desiring it to be cut. In short, so great was the crowd and hurry on the scaffolding, that while Mr. Lunardi and Mr. Biggin were arranging matters on one side, others were deranging them on the other. From these circumstances, we lost so great a quantity of inflammable air, that the Balloon could not take up three.'

Courtly but desperate, Lunardi did the decent thing and stepped down from the basket:

> 'Lunardi, with a polite liberality that did him credit, gave up his place to Colonel Hastings. Conceive what must have been my feeling at the moment, and judge how alarming my apprehensions! Uncertain, in the hurry and confusion of the instant, whether I should not a *second* time meet with a disappointment in my favourite pursuit. I however kept my resolution; and although some of the papers have said, I was agitated *almost* "to fainting," I never was more mistress of my reason.'

Then there were three. Colonel Hastings still clung to the hope that he was going on a balloon ride. He was desperate to stay in the gallery but left with little choice when neither George nor Letitia were willing to step down and things were now frantic:

> 'Mr. Lunardi said delays were dangerous, and immediately prepared for our departure. Colonel Hastings very reluctantly quitted the gallery, for he appeared to have set his whole soul upon the voyage…'

The colonel may not have given up without a fight but Lunardi accepted his fate, according to *The New London Magazine*:

> 'The day was clear, and the sun shone with uncommon splendor; but Lunardi did not ascend. That natural politeness which all foreigners possess, in acts of obliging their friends, induced him to give way to the pressing solicitations of Mrs. Sage and Mr. Biggin, when it was found that the balloon would not mount aloft with the three adventurers: the master of the ceremonies therefore mortified himself by staying behind, and to permit his friends to make their visit in a duet to the clouds.'

So then there were two. Two who had never flown in a balloon before. However, George had studied every detail of aerostation and Letitia worked in the hectic world of theatre where the show must always go on. In the scramble, they were forced to leave behind the oars that Biggin kept calling for (aeronauts yet to accept that oars were as much use in a balloon as a shivering cat). With enormous gumption, they took to the air, Letitia throwing kisses as the experienced balloon pilot Lunardi became merely a speck on the earth below.

The audience went wild and finally Letitia could enjoy her moment of triumph. She had held her nerve. She had faced down another contender. She was the first Englishwoman to fly:

> 'At five and twenty minutes after one, Mr. Biggin gave the signal for cutting the cords, and your happy friend found herself secure from disappointment, and floating in the boundless regions of the air. We arose in a slow and majestic manner, forming a most beautiful object, amidst the acclamations of thousands, whose hearts at that moment

appeared to feel but one sentiment, and that for the safety of two adventurers; who, notwithstanding the discouragement so recently given, by the bursting of that *identical* Balloon, and the more melancholy fate of poor Pilatre de Rozier, had fortitude enough to banish from their minds every idea of fear, or even doubt.'

Though seldom modest, Letitia was brave. So was George, only 25 and with no experience of ever ascending in a balloon let alone being the pilot. Suddenly he found himself flying for the first time with only another novice for company. There was no time to panic because no sooner had the cannons fired to mark their ascent than they almost crashed. 'At about fifteen or twenty yards from the earth, making it's [sic] direction towards Astley's Amphitheatre, against which it probably would have struck, if Mr. Biggin had not thrown out a considerable quantity of ballast,' *The New London Magazine* reports.

Without his cool head and quick thinking, the ascent could easily have ended in tragedy and Letitia gives him his full due:

'Mr. Biggin's character is too well known to stand in need of any compliment from *my* pen; but as he is the principal link of the great chain by which I now hang, and I am an enthusiastic admirer of the principles on which he appears to think and act, I cannot let this moment pass without giving you some faint idea of what I felt respecting his manly and becoming fortitude, and that at a moment which bears the strongest affinity to the last awful breathing of this transitory existence.'

Unfortunately, while Letitia contemplated higher things there were those in the crowd with earthier imaginations. When she dipped out of sight a naughty aeronautical legend was born:

'We were crossing the Thames above Westminster Bridge; it was then Mr. Biggin began to lace the apperture of the gallery which served to let us in, and which had been left open by mistake at our ascension. Some other matter at that moment requiring his attention, he desired I would stoop down and finish it; and thinking it better to go upon my knees to do so, gave rise to the report that I had fainted.'

Fainting was the least of the rumours but that was her story and she was sticking to it. Letitia's explanation seems reasonable and the speculation was pretty insulting. Balloons carried with them the whiff of scandal, with Georgian imaginations working overtime when they watched a man and a woman head off into unchaperoned cloud. They went down in history, so to speak, as an attractive pair. In his memoirs of the era Covent Garden actor Michael Kelly notes:

> 'Mr. Biggin, who was once called in London the handsome Biggin, and who ascended in a balloon from Sloane Street, with the pretty Mrs. Sage…'

When Mrs Sage took to her knees while Mr Biggin steadied her by the shoulder, they would forever be suspected of inventing the mile high club. The double standards of the day meant the gossip could only enhance Mr Biggin's reputation while threatening to ruin hers and the story has followed her down two centuries of aviation history.

Whether it was simply a case of straightening the curtains or impromptu passion, no-one can ever know but it seems more likely it was simply the kind of smutty story Georgian London so loved. In Letitia's account of their relationship Biggin is always the perfect gentleman. Even when Letitia knelt on his prized scientific equipment, preventing him from recording their height during the voyage, he took it on the chin. It was those pesky laces again.

> 'When I knelt down to lace the gallery, I unfortunately put my knees upon the barometer and broke it, so that we were entirely without a barometer, and of course Mr. Biggin could form no perfect opinion respecting our altitude.'

No matter, they were enjoying themselves hugely and picking out the places they knew. George wielded a flag and Letitia mused on whom he hoped to impress. Apparently, she felt her own nearest and dearest would not be watching:

> 'In crossing over Westminster, we distinctly viewed each part of it; we hung some time over St. James's Park, and particularized almost every house we knew in Piccadilly. The appearance of the two parks were beautiful to a great degree: we remarked a number of persons collected, but not individually; Mr. Biggin here waved his flag; perhaps in compliment to some fair inamorata, who might just at that crisis be sending up her prayers for his safe return. The

objects of my affection or esteem were at that time (and are still indeed) so very distant from me, and so perfectly unacquainted with my situation, that I seemed to exist but for myself.'

Resourceful Letitia had taken a notebook with her to jot down her impressions as they happened. George was keen to record their adventure too and shared his scientific knowledge as they drifted along. She did this on her knees too:

'I continued most of the time in this situation, having no table or seat; and being determined to pay attention to every minute circumstance that should occur; for which purpose I had taken a book with me; and Mr. Biggin, seeing my anxiety was very great, at the same time thinking it no degradation to communicate his observations to a woman, of whose understanding, I am proud to think, he had not a contemptible opinion, gave me the most pleasing and unaffected explanations you can conceive. It is from his conversation that I am enabled to entertain you with some remarks, which would have been, perhaps, beyond the compass of my own observations.'

The barometer was destroyed but Biggin had other instruments and Letitia helped him with his observations. The balloon was roughly following the Thames and they had been aloft for about half an hour when they came to a halt, hanging above the Ranelagh pleasure gardens in Chelsea. Letitia looked down on the Rotunda, a beautiful rococo building decorated in paint and enamel, 'which, I remarked, appeared to resemble a tea-caddy.' They floated on past London's last wooden bridge for more sight-seeing, more waving at spectators.

'Mr. Biggin made me observe the beautiful appearance of Battersea Bridge. At this time we could perceive a great number of people collected in different situations; each of these parties Mr. Biggin saluted with his flag.'

The balloon spun around before Letitia had taken her fill of the Chelsea views and Biggin made a gallant attempt to stop the spinning using all he had in the absence of his oars.

'I complained to Mr. Biggin that I had lost sight of some particular objects which I was contemplating with great pleasure: he told me that he would endeavour to stop, and with the speaking trumpet rowed against the motion; it stopped instantaneously, and then took a motion on its axis, in the same direction that he moved the trumpet, which he again changed, and we proceeded in a direct line.'

Whether the trumpet was actually having any effect, the sun was definitely heating the hydrogen. The balloon began to climb rapidly and the remarkably relaxed pair prepared to enjoy a late lunch in the clouds. They had no qualms about tossing an empty wine bottle over the side, interested only in how long it took to fall out of sight. Letitia writes, 'we now very comfortably sat down, ate some ham and chicken, and drank a glass of Florence wine; threw out the bottle, and Mr. Biggin saw it above twenty seconds in falling.' Forty minutes into the flight Letitia was perfectly at home in the sky and did not panic when the air pressure and cold began to bite.

> 'Vapours began to appear under us ... Mr. Biggin said we should soon pass some clouds, and that I was to expect some wet. I was very cold for above five minutes, and felt a difficulty in respiration; but it was not an unpleasant sensation. The cold had not the same effect upon Mr. Biggin; but his ears were affected with an unusual sensation; this he seemed to think proceeded from the rarefaction of the air contained in the cellular organs, which extended the tympanum, particularly, as on the descent he found himself a little deaf, which seemed to indicate that the condensation of the air, and consequently the relaxation of the tympanum, had taken place.'

They coped with the discomfort and by the time they reached their highest point Letitia was an enthusiastic laboratory assistant. Despite a sudden snowstorm she helped her curious companion to explore the clouds using wax, magnets and more litter:

> 'Paper flung out descended with nearly its usual force on earth; that is, gently. Mr. Biggin tried the magnet frequently, but it had no variation. We here passed through a good deal of small sleety snow, which did not appear to descend, but floated about us, and that pretty thick. We had some white clouds under us in lines, and we saw the objects on earth through them as if through gauze. We kept close to the direct line of the Thames,

and consequently crossed its meanders frequently. Apparently we were here stationary for three minutes. Mr. Biggin flung out a roll, and saw it falling about a minute; and a bottle empty about the same time, which his sight lost whilst falling.

'Mr. Biggin tried a small bell, with an intention of observing any local difference of sound; but the effect was as usual. He then prepared an electrical experiment, with an electrometer, armed, as he expressed it, at the bottom with silver wire, terminating in a great number of points, by which he meant to form a conductor. On applying a stick of sealing wax, which he had previously rubbed on his coat, the pith-balls in the electrometer visibly separated; and on exposing it as far as the arm could extend, to a cloud we were then passing, the separation increased, and the balls diverged to the side of the glass: he then dried a glass, and after some friction applied it to the ball, which, immediately on the application, united. From this observation he told me his conclusion; which was, that the electricity of that cloud was negative.'

After almost two hours in the air, scientific experiments and lofty philosophy gave way once again to high comedy. If the takeoff had been hair-raising, the descent promised to be no less dramatic. The balloon began to collapse and descend. Game first-timer George had to get them safely back to earth with only his wits, bits of paper and trusty trumpet for help. 'From this time, Mr. Biggin was employed in preparing for our descent, which the papers gave us notice we were doing rapidly,' reports Letitia. George threw out the anchor and line, closely followed by 'our eatables, and other useless things' in a bid to slow their descent. He held the anchor rope in one hand and the last remaining bag of ballast in the other as they fell to earth.

They had travelled around fourteen miles from Southwark and were now hurtling towards a farmer's field near Harrow. The labourers looked up, astonished, and it was clear what George had to do. 'He spoke with the trumpet to some hay-makers in a field,' calling for help as they attempted to land.

'When the grapple was within a hundred yards of the earth, he threw out the ballast; the grapple soon after reached the ground, and on the Balloon's touching the earth, he rolled off the check with the cord. The instant the grapple felt the force of the Balloon it slipt; and we continued skimming and grazing the earth. It was then I hurt one of the tendons of my foot, by its striking against a piece of broken iron, which was not to be avoided, from the astonishing power the wind had upon the Balloon at our descent.'

Strong gusts tugged at the deflating balloon as obliging locals tried to bring it to rest and she describes the farcical scene as one after another grabbed the rope:

'The first assistance that presented itself to us was a single man, who got hold of the gallery; but he was of no service, as he was laid flat on his face. The people soon collected to the number of six, but the wind was so high as to pull them all after the Balloon: by the addition of two or three more we were completely stopped. I got out.'

Injured and winded by her inelegant landing, she nonetheless alighted with as much dignity as she could muster. George, meanwhile, had a desperate plan to fly on for a while without her. This was not part of Mrs Sage's plan at all and she once again ruthlessly deployed a few diva tactics:

'After a delivery of *two hundred* pounds of *human weight*, Mr. Biggin intended furnishing himself with almost an equal weight of ballast, and after leaving me in the care of some of the hospitable people of the neighbourhood, he meant to ascend again, and continue his voyage as long as the Balloon would carry him. It was then that a little trait of female weakness, I confess to you, crept into my heart. I wished *him* not to proceed further than I could accompany him.'

George had more success standing up to Mrs Sage than the woman with no name and thwarted Colonel Hastings, but his victory was short lived. The damsel in distress let it be known to her rescuers how very upset she was to be left all alone. More pressingly, the farmer turned up in a towering rage.

'[A]s it appeared to be so much wished by Mr. Biggin to proceed, I bade him adieu with infinite pleasure; and only looked forward to his safe return. A number of concurrent circumstances willed it might not be so. The place where he descended is a large common field, near Harrow on the hill: the crop upon it was nearly got in, some beans only remaining. The master of the fields is one of those beings, who, though they bear the *external* marks of humanity, have very little of the real character in their soul. And so you'll say when I tell you, that upon seeing a *trifling* injury done to his property, he was abusive and savage to a great degree. The greater part of his companions were silent; and had it not been for some genteel persons who came up to us, I make not a doubt but the Balloon would have been sacrificed by these unfeeling people.'

They were saved from the wrath of the farmer by Joseph Drury, the headmaster of Harrow School, and his pupils appearing over the hill and racing to their aid. They soothed the farmer's ruffled feathers and promised to pay for the damage. It was a narrow escape. 'The attention they paid, to assist Mr. Biggin, is not easily to be described to you,' writes Letitia, 'and he tells me it was principally owing to them that the Balloon was saved from destruction.'

George, an old Etonian, made a last ditch attempt to return to the clouds but he had no spade to collect more ballast and found himself taken to one side by frowning Harrovians:

'To make the matter worse, some of the gentlemen who had surrounded me seeing that I could not walk, went to Mr. Biggin, and told him that I was greatly hurt. *Supposing* this to be the case, he immediately determined to give up the idea of going further ... I went to take my leave of Mr. Biggin, he had begun to let out the gas.'

Mrs Sage having her own way once again and the balloon packed off in a cart, the public schoolboys carried her to the pub. The evening was devoted to celebrations and the aeronauts accepted separate dinner invitations. George went off to be wined and dined by the Drury family while Letitia accepted an invitation from a Mr and Mrs Wilson a mile away in Henwell Green. There was no shortage of gentlemen to help the injured leading lady to her after show party and she revelled in an adoring crowd and indulging young fans with souvenirs:

'There was a large party there, and were I to tell you the many flattering attentions that were shewn me, you would think me vain indeed. It is enough to say, that I did then, and ever I hope shall, feel the strongest sense of their politeness. Here I left behind me a bottle of harts-horn [smelling salts], which I had taken with me for fear of fainting; but as I never had the least idea of doing so, it had not been opened. Several other trifling things I distributed amongst the young girls who came to pay me their rustic compliments.'

When Letitia and the rustics had had their fill, Biggin sent a carriage to collect her. She arrived in Harrow to find a group of friends who had spent the day in overland pursuit, enjoying the new game of balloon hunting. There were more extravagant leave takings from the students and masters who were entirely smitten by the gorgeous actress who fell from the sky. 'No words can describe the expressions of joy, and the acclamations of applause that we were saluted with at parting with these fine young men,' she says. 'Not satisfied with giving us repeated cheers at Mr. Drury's door, they followed us out of the village, and placing themselves at certain distances on the road, reiterated their good wishes for our safety, until we lost the sound.'

The cheers of teenage fans ringing in her ears, Letitia's extraordinary day concluded at her home at 10, Charles Street (now Wellington Street) in Covent Garden. She limped through the door at midnight to find another impromptu party awaiting its guest of honour. Still high on the adrenaline and adulation she arrived 'in perfect health and spirits, and I was received by a numerous party of friends with sincere marks of joy.' As the curtain came down, there was no doubt that the amazing Mrs Sage was a hit.

Letitia awoke on 30 June 1785 with a throbbing foot but a happy heart. Every detail of her eventful voyage was fresh in her mind and as she was forced to rest her foot she wrote her memoir there and then. Propped up in bed, she began her famous letter to her sister:

'At length, my dear Friend, I have accomplished my favorite experiment; our aerial flight took place on Wednesday. All is now over, and I feel myself more happy, and infinitely better pleased with my excursion than I ever was at any former event of my life.'

Whether she would have produced such a vivid and immediate account if she had not been laid up is doubtful, though she was keen to tell the tale to her sister now the trip was safely accomplished. She hints that her correspondent in Liverpool is pregnant and she wanted to save her from worry. 'I considered the delicacy of your situation, and felt it highly improper to distract your mind with any fears upon my account.'

It was only when she took up her pen to recount her adventure that she admits to a small panic in the air about entering the region of the almighty. Some clergymen were in two minds about whether flying in a balloon (sometimes called 'the devil's horse') was altogether a proper activity for Christian people and Letitia suffered a fleeting fit of the collywobbles:

> 'You'll say I begin to prose, and indeed the present turn of my mind, shut up by myself, and reflecting, every line I write, upon the idea that I was daring enough to push myself, as I may say, before my time, into the presence of the Deity, inclines me to a species of terror; but I will lay down my pen, till I can reason myself out of my melancholy, and then go on with my narrative.'

After a little break to pull herself together she ploughs on:

> 'I take up my employment again with great pleasure ... Though the retrospection gave me a little gloom just now, assure yourself that I never had, since I first took up the idea, the least apprehension of danger. My mind was so perfectly made up as to the event, that I really felt no other sensation than a most pure and perfect tranquillity of soul, during the whole time we had withdrawn ourselves from every earthly connection, where not a murmur was heard to break in upon our peace, but all was sweet tranquility.'

Letitia succeeded in writing her whole extraordinary story in one day and it remains the fullest and earliest account from a woman of the heady early days of ballooning. She produced her account quickly so she could turn to the clamour for her company, which she clearly enjoyed. 'The door is never quiet a single instant, and I suppose when I go out I shall be as much looked at as if a native of the aerial regions had come down to pay an earthly visit,' she writes. The letter written and her foot recovering, she signed off to her sister as an aeronaut. 'Remember me to all you value most; and believe me, whether in heaven or earth, I shall be always, Most affectionately yours.'

Then she was ready to receive her many visitors and venture out to enjoy her celebrity status, half hoping to be mistaken for an angel.

Letitia Sage was feted in the press for her achievement. Her courage won her kudos in the *New London Magazine*:

> 'It is perhaps a true observation, That there is no enterprise, however dangerous or difficult it may be, but the female mind can summons courage enough to undertake it. An instance of this we have in Mrs Sage, who unites to the tenderness peculiar to her sex, that manly fortitude that constitutes the heroine.'

There is also a reference to her looking 'a little agitated' at takeoff, which doubtless annoyed her. The account of her adventures is accompanied by 'A Portrait of Mrs Sage, the first Female Aerial traveller'. George Biggin's account gets second billing but his face appears next to hers.

Lunardi was happy and relieved that George and Letitia brought him reflected glory, at least, rather than more ignominy. The Italian came out of it rather well for surrendering his seat to the lady and paraded in triumph at the Pantheon. If Letitia was to cement her place as the nation's leading lady aeronaut she could not rest on her laurels... or her crutches. Six days after her painful crash landing, she too was holding court at balloon-business central, reports *The Morning Herald and Daily Advertiser*:

> 'Mrs. Sage, we understand, who is at this time very much indisposed from a contusion on her foot, which she received in quitting the balloon, has been prevailed upon to make her appearance this day at the Pantheon, contrary to the advice of her surgeon, rather than be a means of disappointing Mr. Lunardi's friends of any information they may wish to receive from her, regarding her late excursion.'

She would also be selling *A Letter* hot off the press for a shilling a copy. Her first-hand account promised to avoid 'as much perplexity as possible' and 'convey her ideas in the clearest manner'. Like the controversial curtains, Letitia wanted the record straight: 'She presumes that it may be considered as a full answer to every proper question that can be proposed to her on the subject.' The Mrs Sage show rolled on, not least because her elfin French rivals were still making the papers. *The Public Advertiser* of 7 July announced the publication of *A Letter* on the same page as a listing for 'the two Miss Simonets' (Rosine and Leonora) at the Theatre Royal in 'a new Dance, called THE FEMALE BALLOONISTS, or, The Ladies In The Air.' Lunardi the irrepressible impresario lurched on with his seat-of-the-pants career, heading straight to Liverpool for a series of ascents. There he received some new copies of the famous picture, now a souvenir of success rather than a reminder of failure. 'I have just received some Prints one of which, the three Aerial Travellers, now lies before me, and I contemplate it with unspeakable Delight!' he writes to George from Merseyside. Lunardi loved this celebrated picture of the balloonomania era. It was often mistaken for an accurate image of the takeoff, even by balloon historians. Gaston Tissandier described Lunardi's supposed flight with his friends in *Histoire des Ballons* in 1887.

Letitia enjoyed her moment in the sun. She was much in demand by admirers in July 1785. *The Morning Herald, and Daily Advertiser* noted that the beautiful balloon was 'in the exact condition in which it ascended with the agreeable Mrs. Sage, whose intrepidity has greatly excited the public curiosity, and her affability has equally received the commendation of the most respectable persons who have been at the Pantheon to converse with her.'

Unfortunately, she suffered the fate of celebrities of every era. Her achievement was overshadowed by scandalous gossip. What exactly *was* she doing on her knees as she and Mr Biggin flew over Piccadilly? Was she really just tidying up and taking notes and trashing barometers? Bawdy London preferred its own scurrilous scenario for an actress and young buck all alone in a balloon. The problem was that as soon as balloons reached Britain, men began taking bets on whether it was possible to have sex in them. Nowhere was gambling more rife than in the gentlemen's clubs of London, where princes and politicians were ready to bet on anything during drunken nights in gaming rooms. The members of Brooks's in St James's Street were particularly fond of outrageous wagers. A charming entry in the club betting book in 1785 shows the sky was not the limit:

> 'L[or]d. Cholmondeley has given two guineas to L[or]d Derby,
> to receive 500 G[uinea]s whenever his lordship fucks a woman
> in a Balloon one thousand yards from the Earth.'

There was a fortune to be had from founding the (half) mile high club if such bragging was to be believed. Sex in the sky was an actual goal among macho balloon maniacs. Edward Smith-Stanley, the Earl of Derby, was an inveterate gambler and no stranger to sexual scandal. His wife walked out on him and their children following her very public affair with the Duke of Dorset. They may both have been old Etonians but gallant, earnest young scientist Mr Biggin was not dissolute Lord Derby. The wager shows only that copulation among the clouds was a lively subject for debate when Letitia and George accidently took to the sky on their own. Imaginations were already working overtime so when Letitia got on all fours the innuendo was inevitable.

Added to this, the satirists of the day were merciless. James Gilray, George Cruikshank and others lampooned the balloonomania that engulfed late eighteenth century London. The shape of the balloon; the language of rising and swelling and hot air; the vanity and whimsy of devotees and the unpredictable behaviour of something so at the mercy of luck and prevailing winds. It was an irresistible package for cartoonists. When Letitia set sail for the clouds, sex and balloons were inextricably linked in the public imagination. In October 1784 a drawing entitled *Love in a Balloon* appeared in the satirical *Rambler's Magazine,* seemingly about Lunardi the ladies' man. A couple are in a clinch over London, he declaring, 'Ah Madame it rises majestically.' She replies, 'I feel it does Signor.' Underneath spectators sit on the roof tiles, one observing, 'Damn he's no Italian but a man every inch of him.'

At least this lady is wearing all her clothes and a smile on her face (the magazine claimed to be 'the annals of gallantry, glee, pleasure and the bon ton', or good manners). The same cannot be said for *Madame Blubber's Last Shift or The Aerostatic Dilly*, a coloured etching by James Gillray of an airborne woman in April of the same year. This image appeared more than a year before Letitia took to the sky and is not, as is often supposed, a rude reference to her 200lbs of en-bon-point. The subject is gambler and socialite Lady Albinia Hobart (later Countess of Buckinghamshire), her bottom on display as she is launched into the sky thanks to a 'little accident' inflating her skirt like a balloon. The real butt of the joke is her support for a relative at Covent Garden hustings for the Westminster Election. Gillray took a particular dislike to Albinia and often portrayed her in balloonish ways.

The enduring myth about Letitia's adventure, however, was not fuelled by crude wagers and cartoons alone. One overlooked culprit is the satirical poem that linked that summer's sensational divorce case to Letitia's ascent in the vivid but confused public imagination. *The Female Aeronaut* is 'addressed' to Mrs Sage but 'dedicated' to Mrs. Errington. All these two women had in common was becoming famous at exactly the same time.

Harriot Errington was the wife of rich London lawyer George Errington and either a libertine or a sex addict, depending on your outlook. While Letitia was making flight history, Harriot was on trial for adultery at the Bishop of London's court in the City. Graphic witness statements were published as *The Trial of Mrs. Harriot Errington* just a fortnight after Letitia's ascent and while she was at the Pantheon. *The Trial* was 'Embellished with three amorous scenes, elegantly engraved, from the following trial, viz 1. THE SQUIRTING SCENE. 2. THE BED-CHAMBER SCENE; and 3, THE BAGNIO [brothel] SCENE.' Harriot was accused of athletic liaisons with a series of lovers, including several army officers, a curate, a postmaster 'and many others'. Lurid details were supplied by servants before the divorce was granted.

Step forward *The Female Aeronaut* poet with promises of 'many ludicrous and well-known Characteristical Incidents. Dedicated to Mrs Harriot Errington.' The poem has not survived but withering reviews tell us much. Critics decided the poem was smut – and not even good smut. *The Monthly Review* did not mince words:

> 'We have heard of ass-races, in which he that came last was victorious. On the same principle, had a reward been proposed for the worst poem on the subject of Mrs Sage's ascension in Mr. Lunardi's balloon, we make no doubt that the indecent and illiterate performance before us would have gained the prize.'

The Critical Review expressed similar distaste:

> 'We have never read any attempt at poetry so utterly destitute of metre, common sense, and even grammar. It is even destitute of the quality of which it boasts; yes, such is the licentiousness of the age, that indecency is now boasted of, and each successive editor promises to exceed his predecessors. It is, however, stupidly dull from beginning to the end.'

The Female Aeronaut was published by William Smith in Charles Street, St James's, near Brooks's club. It seems likely one gentleman made it to the printers with some sexist jokes, disastrously conflating the reputations of Harriot and Letitia in the process. Thus the unjust myth of Mrs Sage was born, gaining purchase over time until in the 21st century it is held to be fact by TV researchers. Host Stephen Fry declared Mr Biggin and Mrs Sage went 'all the way' and 'were the first members of the mile high club, as it were' on an all-male episode of the BBC general knowledge panel game *QI* as recently as 2014.

THE LOST HISTORY OF THE LADY AERONAUTS

Soon after she penned her *own* invaluable account of her *actual* adventure, which she published herself, Letitia drops out of view. Exactly what she did in the 20 years after her extraordinary achievement is a mystery. Maybe she earned enough from her best-selling book to enjoy some leisure and dine out on her story. *A Letter* ran to at least three editions and was sold by John Bell in his bookshop called the British Library on The Strand. He was the perfect choice of publisher. Bell was an important figure in popular books and entertainment, producing the 21-volume *Bell's British Theatre* just before Letitia's memoir. He also launched a string of newspapers and periodicals, including a London daily called the *Morning Post,* so his authors were never short of publicity.

It is often suggested that she went to ground because of the innuendo over her controversial curtain moment, but it seems more likely that the pragmatic flying actress simply carried on with her adventures. Being the toast of London for whatever reason was better than obscurity. One theory is that she took up with a purser of an East Indiaman who was the son of a theatre manager in Edinburgh. The East India Company ships included the 'tea clippers' that sailed between Britain and the subcontinent and were frequent prey to pirates and shipwreck. Then again, Letitia may have been glimpsed seeing out the eighteenth century with a tour of America with another actor.

She only pops up properly in 1804, now going by the name of Mrs Robinson and with a successful career in costume. She worked as a dresser and wardrobe keeper at Sadler's Wells Theatre when it was enjoying a makeover to attract a classier clientele. Her boss was the writer, composer and manager Charles Dibdin the younger (to distinguish him from his father). He specialized in lavish productions and Letitia was there when he installed a giant water tank. Always in the fashionable vanguard, Letitia had moved on from the balloon craze to work on the aquadrama fad at the start of the nineteenth century. The stage was flooded in 1804 so Dibdin could recreate the siege of Gibraltar, crowding the eight thousand gallon lake with 177 ships for a spectacular sea battle between the English and Spanish.

After dressing the cast for such splashy escapades Letitia went to Dublin in 1805 to work for Dibdin's business partner, Frederick Jones at the Crow Street Theatre. Dibdin was there at the same time but returned to Sadler's Wells after losing a fortune in the failing Irish theatre. Letitia too headed back to London and the fourth Theatre Royal, also known as the Drury Lane Theatre. The sumptuously rebuilt theatre opened in 1812 (the last one burned down, despite having the world's first safety curtain) with Letitia as a woman's dresser. The theatre opened in October with *Hamlet* and she worked there for a year, returning for a second stint from 1816 to 1817. After her one unforgettable day as Lunardi's leading lady, immortalized in print and paint as England's first woman of the air, Letitia accepted her backstage role. She earned nine shillings a week among the elaborate theatrical costumes of the regency era, her fashion sense one of her many marketable gifts.

Mrs Sage's ascent is often told as a simple tale of one woman stepping into a basket to do the honours as England's first lady aeronaut. In reality, her path to claiming the record was far from smooth and relied on steely determination, courage and charisma. Décolletage, daredevils and being carried off to the pub by adoring young swains earned her a place in flying's hall of fame but they were never enough to pay the bills. The painting by Rignaud hangs in the Museo del Prado in Madrid and the print by Bartolozzi belongs to the British Museum. The ascent in the great Union Jack of a balloon was immortalized in oils by Julius Caesar Ibbetson. Her portrait is held in prestigious public and private collections. Letitia, however, lived on her nine shillings and the kudos that came with her achievement.

On that historic flight through the summer sky over London, V. Lunardi Esq was not waving his hat and G. Biggin Esq did not foresee his equipment being smashed in *some* kind of kneeling incident. But the marvellous Mrs Sage was definitely as advertised, calm and magnificent in her aerodynamic dress, taking her place as the first English Female Aerial Traveller.

Chapter 4

The Fabulous Birdwoman of France

The extraordinary French aeronaut Sophie Blanchard enjoyed the kind of celebrity usually reserved for saints and royalty. Her exploits as the queen of balloonists in early nineteenth century France earned her the adoration of both Napoleon Bonaparte and King Louis XVIII.

Madame Blanchard's skill as an aeronaut was impressive, but as important was a flair for keeping her star status steady while France itself was rocked by enormous political turbulence in the decades following the revolution of 1789. No-one stands as a more elegant, courageous or enduring emblem of French balloonomania in all its glory. Born a shy country girl, Sophie died an adored superstar of both the Napoleonic and Restoration eras.

Marie Madeleine-Sophie Armant was born on 25 March 1778 in the village of Les Trois-Canons near the port of La Rochelle in South West France and was an unlikely candidate for daring lady balloonist. Small and nervy, she was frightened by loud noises and hated crowds. Luckily, she was born just as history delivered a way to escape from the racket of everyday life for a girl brave enough to take it. Sophie was only about six when the Montgolfier brothers were 240 miles away, sending the first people into the air in Paris. The sensitive child could not know she would join the pioneers of flight with her own spectacular career… and sensational death.

Sophie's life changed forever when she married the world's first professional aeronaut, Jean-Pierre Blanchard. She may only have been 16 when she met the showman 24 years her senior but soon discovered she shared his devotion to ballooning. Had she not it is doubtful she would have remained Madame Blanchard for long. Jean-Pierre had already ditched a wife and four children in his ruthless quest to build his reputation across Europe. Sophie also shared his birdlike stature, though while Jean-Pierre was described as a little hero by admirers she was his small, ugly, nervous wife with sharp bird-like features. Only when she became the darling of state occasions was she promoted by the press to small and beautiful.

Her first ascent took place in Marseilles in the winter of 1804 when she was 25 years old. Standing beside Jean-Pierre in the basket, Sophie discovered a sense of liberation that remained with her for the rest of her life. Fearful and painfully shy on the ground, she was fearless and bold beneath the balloon and described flying as an incomparable sensation. There was a peace to be found in the air that vanished when she landed. Tiny, skittish and only at home in the sky, Sophie felt a true affinity with the birds.

If she was easily startled as a child in her sleepy hamlet by the sea, Sophie faced infinitely more shocks as the wife of a famous adventurer in the cities of Europe. Jean-Pierre made his name as the relentlessly ambitious aeronaut who scored a string of ballooning firsts. He was not from a wealthy or well-connected family so had to make ballooning pay. When Sophie plighted her troth she also promised that the Blanchard show must go on.

Jeanne-Pierre had already made the most celebrated journey of his life with the first balloon crossing of the English Channel in 1785. It was financed by the American doctor John Jeffries. Science was served by Jeffries' intention to collect air samples but for Blanchard, it was all about the glory. He had no intention of sharing the victory and fully intended to fly solo. His solution was ingenious, if a little unhinged. He paid a tailor to make a lead-lined jacket to wear at the pre-flight weighing in so he could claim his backer must stay behind. It might have worked, too, if the pesky tailor had not delivered the heavy garment to the scientist by mistake. Whatever awkwardness ensued, the doctor climbed pointedly in beside his fellow pioneer on 7 January 1785 and they ascended into the air. After a hair-raising ride Jean-Pierre successfully flew them to France, lead-lined suits tactfully consigned to history.

The achievement made Blanchard a by-word for balloonist across the world and it may have been during the triumphant tours of France that followed that he first met Sophie. By then he had also chalked up the first balloon flight in America – watched by the president, George Washington – and a guest appearance at the coronation of Leopold II as King of Bohemia.

Sophie quickly learned that while her husband toured Europe to great acclaim and was invited to headline the pomp and ceremony events of the day, he had absolutely no head for business. By 1804 Jean-Pierre was teetering on the brink of bankruptcy. For France it was the year Napoleon Bonaparte seized power to become emperor. At Chez Blanchard it was when Sophie climbed aboard the balloon to help dig them out of debt.

THE LOST HISTORY OF THE LADY AERONAUTS

She had found her element and in 1805, on only her third ascent, became the first female in the world to fly solo. The little woman scared of horses and loud noises, so shy she found conversation a strain, was the picture of courage as she rose from the garden of the Cloister of the Jacobins in Toulouse to take her place in the history books.

A lady aeronaut was a novelty that sold more tickets, just as the Blanchards had hoped. Sometimes Sophie flew alone, sometimes with her husband and always to a roar of approval from the growing crowds that gathered to watch. It was flying she embraced, however, not parachuting. She went up in a balloon and she went down in a balloon. Though her husband had actually introduced the parachute to balloonists, she never entertained the idea of using one, then or later. With her performances proving a hit, Sophie hoped the shadow of financial ruin was receding for good. It wasn't. Jean-Pierre had earned a fortune from his endless performances at fairs and fetes and the patronage of fashionable people, but it all slipped through his fingers. He had lost it all and now owed a fortune instead.

On Sophie's eleventh ascent, this time with Jean-Pierre in Rotterdam, the couple suffered a nasty accident. The crash in 1807 left Jean-Pierre with a serious head injury and Sophie mute with shock. The *Tyne Mercury* reports:

> 'In ascending, the balloon unfortunately caught by a tree, and, after much agitation, was rent, and M. and Madame Blanchard were precipitated to the ground. M. Blanchard received a violent contusion on the head, and particularly on one ear. We are happy to add, no fatal consequences were apprehended. Madame Blanchard was taken up without further injury than the effect the alarm had upon her mind.'

They recovered and soldiered on for another two years until a much worse disaster called on all the courage the birdwoman could muster. Despite Sophie's newly found celebrity, money worries loomed large. The stress was enormous and took its terrible toll when Jean-Pierre ascended over The Hague in 1808. Without warning he clutched at his chest, gripped by a heart attack. He tumbled forward out of the basket and plunged to earth. This time there was no coming back. His injuries were crippling and incurable. Sophie turned devoted nurse but Jean-Pierre knew his wife's future looked bleak. During his last days he was distraught, knowing that she faced destitution. As she sat by his deathbed he reportedly gave her a grim choice. When he was gone she could hang herself or she could drown herself. He could see no other option. Jean-Pierre finally succumbed to his injuries a year after the heart attack and fall, leaving his 30-year-old widow to battle the huge debts he left behind.

Though grief-stricken, Sophie was not about to accept the horrible fate Jean-Pierre had laid out for her. She was not going to commit suicide. She was going to make money and do it the only way she knew how – with a balloon. However timid she appeared as the impoverished little widow, she had her balloon to keep her strong. With no choice but to make it work, Sophie found she had a much better business brain than her quixotic husband. She made savings immediately. Small and slim, she could ride in a much lighter basket and swap hot air for hydrogen. A flimsy-looking gondola like a child's cradle reduced the gas bill and ended the need for tending a burner to heat the air. She also made a smaller balloon for going solo. Radical restyling of the kit whittled her costs down to bare essentials. That left Sophie free to pep up the performance side of her shows, rising to the occasion in every sense.

Sophie would not say boo to a goose on the ground and was terrified of riding in a carriage through Paris. Horses continued to spook her. She never stopped hating being in a crowd. She was still prone to bursting into tears at a loud noise and feared accidents in the street – but no such agitation followed her into the clouds. She seemed born for ballooning, far more happy and relaxed in the air than her huckster husband had ever been. Despite all the people chasing her for money, Madame Blanchard really loved her job.

She particularly enjoyed night flights when the wind is at its most quiet, sometimes riding in the restful air until morning. Her confidence grew and with it her fame across early nineteenth century France. No longer in the shadow of her egotistical husband, Sophie discovered her own ambition. The basket she once shared with Jean-Pierre now resembled nothing more than a tiny silver perch as her risk-taking grew alongside her cachet. To crank up the drama she began using fireworks on tethered night flights, gaily dropping them from the basket on little parachutes or firing them into the sky. She adored the spectacle of her pyrotechnics despite friends' warnings that silk, hydrogen, gunpowder and matches are not a good combination anywhere, let alone high in the sky.

Her untethered long distance journeys by balloon also became more audacious. On one flight across the Alps she went so high and the temperature dropped so low that she slipped into unconsciousness. It was not the only time she reached such an altitude that she passed out.

Coming down was no picnic either. During a flight over Naples she found herself descending too quickly, splash landing in marshland where she almost drowned. During another dangerous outing she was forced to stay aloft for more than 14 hours to escape a hailstorm. A newspaper report from 1811 says:

> 'Madame Blanchard, in one of her late ascents from Paris, was caught in a storm of hail and rain; but, notwithstanding, ascended so high, that she was lost in clouds and whirlwinds, and did not alight from her balloon near Vincennes til between six and seven in the morning of the day after she arose from Paris. In consequence of the prodigious height the balloon ascended, Madame Blanchard fainted, and continued insensible for some time. Her ascension occupied 14 hours and a half.'

Her poise in the air earned her a devoted and enduring following across France and Europe. Nothing better demonstrated Sophie's gift for adapting rapidly to her circumstances than her ability to survive the seesaw politics of her day. Her carefully cultivated image and great skill with a balloon allowed her to weave her career around the ever-shifting political realities of power and patronage. She saw the French revolution in 1789, the Terror that engulfed the country with countless beheadings at the guillotine, the rise and fall of Napoleon Bonaparte and the return to power of the Bourbon royal family. As political fortunes surged around her, Sophie offered a simple, unifying example of French élan from aloft.

Though the France of the early 1800s was frequently in uproar the universally admired Madame Blanchard was serene in the sky above, her beautiful balloon at the service of all. Balloonomania was in full swing and business as a lone lady aeronaut was booming. Careful cost-management and relentless hard work paid off. Sophie managed to clear the debt she inherited from Jean-Pierre. She had not thrown herself into a pauper's grave, as advised by her dying husband. Instead she created her own career as a ballooning superstar, only she was solvent.

Now definitely deemed 'small and beautiful' the indefatigable Sophie was an A-list performer and no prestigious public event was complete without her. Madame Blanchard and her balloon were simply de rigueur. Chief among her admirers was the emperor, Napoleon Bonaparte. He fell completely under her spell, adoring how she personified the glory of France. He made her the new aeronaut of official festivals, stripping the title from the disgraced Andre Garnerin who had botched the balloon display at Napoleon's coronation. Now Sophie had the responsibility for laying on balloon demonstrations at official events.

For Sophie, the brand of female freedom that came with a balloon was very real. Though female demands had been part of the French revolution, come the 1792 constitution women were banned from taking part in public life. Napoleon turned the screw in 1804 by denying women any legal or marital rights. Sophie appeared to be the exception to the 'little corporal's' rules. He wanted Sophie to fly over Paris like an angel to mark his wedding to Marie Louise of Austria in 1810 (he divorced Josephine earlier in the year, sans balloon fly-past). Napoleon stood with his bride, watching intently as Sophie ascended into the air from the Champ de Mars. When his son Napoleon II, king of Rome, arrived in 1811, it was Madame Blanchard who took to the Paris skies to scatter birth announcements. She was also in aerial attendance at the Château de Saint-Cloud for the baptism.

Sophie cultivated a trademark look for her prestigious bookings, immortalized in the 1811 engraving by Luigi Rados of her night ascent in Milan on Napoleon's birthday. The elegant pose on her silver gondola remains one of the iconic images of the balloonomania era. A white empire-line dress gathered under the bust drops in folds to her dainty slippers. On her head sits a white hat with plumes of feathers. The whole ensemble designed to be seen from a distance and reinforce her reputation as the most fashionable queen of the air. Her 'bird-like' features, tiny frame and snowy outfits all served to suggest a dove.

Napoleon's infatuation with Sophie's command of the sky knew no bounds and he became convinced he could use her aeronautical knowhow for military ends. One moment Sophie was working on her music and outfits, the next she was in hush-hush meetings with the emperor as he picked her brains on how to attack England by balloon. He may have got the idea from Joseph Montgolfier who once boasted he could fly soldiers over the heads of the English enemy into Gibraltar. So Napoleon made Sophie his chief air minister of ballooning and hatched an astonishing plan to have her spearhead an invasion of England by airborne troops. Alarmed and nonplussed, Sophie played along but was saved from being restyled as a flying general by the simple reality of how balloons work. The prevailing westerly winds in France would never waft battalions of balloons over Britain.

Fortunately, Sophie's popularity was more enduring than the emperor's and by 1815 she could relax about being in charge of a balloon army. Napoleon was in exile, a king was back on the French throne and Madame

THE LOST HISTORY OF THE LADY AERONAUTS

Blanchard seamlessly transferred her favours to the new Bourbon regime. Louis XVIII wasted no time in claiming Madame Blanchard for the new court, bestowing the title of official aeronaut of the Restoration. The responsibilities of this role were confined to ornamenting royal occasions rather than swooping on enemies from the sky.

Again her place at the heart of momentous national events was captured by artists of the day. Numerous drawings and paintings commemorating the entrance of Louis XVIII into Paris on 3 May 1814 feature Madame Blanchard hanging above the celebrations. She is shown variously hovering above the royal entourage, waving flags or releasing doves.

Sophie achieved a level of popularity that Jean-Pierre could only have dreamed of. Over the course of her ten years as a solo artiste she grew skilled and fearless, constantly upping the ante to push the boundaries of her profession. She took greater risks, almost recklessly seeking out new ways to test her own mettle. But however intrepid she was as a balloon pilot, she never resorted to using a parachute in her demonstrations like her great rival Elise Garnerin. It was flying that provided Sophie with the incomparable sensation, not skydiving.

In her quest for ever bigger and better spectacle with which to wow her crowds, Sophie became addicted to the drama of fireworks. She adored staging night flights illuminated by increasingly ambitious bursts of colour and shooting stars. In July 1819 her Bengal lights show at the Tivoli gardens in Paris promised to be spectacular. Madame Blanchard would rise in the moonlight like a stately meteor, her basket dotted with fireworks. It was a mesmerizing proposition. It was also unimaginably dangerous. She had to fly into the air beneath a huge ball of hydrogen gas, the balloon itself made of flammable silk, wielding a pole with a naked flame on the end and little packages of gunpowder hanging from her seat. It did not take much spelling out how risky this was but Sophie was deaf to the warnings of her worried friends. Her much-trumpeted entertainment must go ahead. She would not disappoint her public or put a hole in her takings.

On the night of the fete things grew riskier still when a violent summer wind whipped up. Sophie was brave but she wasn't stupid. She had planned everything to the final detail and was confident of her skills, but she did feel uneasy. One newspaper reported:

> 'Every account agrees in stating that Madame Blanchard, who had always displayed the most undaunted intrepidity, had been assailed previous to her ascension, by gloomy forebodings.

At the moment of rising, she said to one of the persons who surrounded her, "I know not why, but I am not at ease this evening."'

Another said:

'It is singular that previous to her ascension Madame Blanchard, usually so intrepid, testified a degree of disquietude resembling fear, it seemed as if she foresaw the approaching danger.'

Despite misgivings, Madame Blanchard dressed in her signature outfit of white dress, hat and feathers, then pinned on her smile and climbed into the doll-sized basket. At 10.30pm the cannon sounded, music filled the Paris night and the dauntless aeronaut began her slow sixty-seventh ascent. Almost as soon as she left the ground things began to go wrong, the gusting wind crashing her into trees and forcing her to throw ballast overboard to clear the branches. Recovering her composure – and unaware that the bump had dislodged the pyrotechnics hanging beneath the gondola – she began dropping fireworks by parachute. She watched the trail of silver stars before bending to ignite the Bengal lights hanging beneath the basket. Soon the balloon was bathed in blue light as Sophie waved her flag and the crowd roared in appreciation. She disappeared into a cloud but emerged to light another bundle of fireworks to drop by mini parachute over the side of the basket.

As she lit the match there was a blinding flash and a series of pops before flames suddenly shot out of the top of the balloon. She had failed to close the gas vent properly and the nightmare had finally happened – the hydrogen was on fire. At first the crowd went wild for what they assumed was all part of the show, calling out, 'Beautiful! Beautiful! Viva Madame Blanchard!' Then came the realization that the balloon was in flames and plummeting before their eyes. 'Immediately a dreadful blaze struck terror into the hearts of all the spectators, leaving them in but little doubt as to the deplorable fate of the unfortunate aeronaut,' reports *Bell's Weekly Messenger* of 18 July 1819. 'Cries of lamentation burst from all sides; numbers of females fell into convulsions; consternation was painted on every face! Some *gens-d'armes* rode off at full gallop towards the spot where it was supposed the fall might take place.'

Even in these desperate moments courageous Sophie kept her head and fought to bring the balloon down safely, throwing ballast from the basket in a frantic bid to slow the 400ft descent. It was hopeless. Out of control and hurtling towards houses in the street nearby, Sophie realised she could not save herself and cried out for help. The hydrogen burned off and the whole rig fell like a stone, crashing onto the roof of number 16 Rue de Provence and pitching Sophie out of the basket. The roof gave way, caving in to a depth of four or five feet and she sprawled forward, unable to catch hold. Screaming for help and tangled in the ropes, she plunged to the street below.

'The inhabitants of the house say they heard dreadful shrieks,' reports *The Messenger*:

> 'Madame Blanchard almost immediately fell from the roof into the street. At the moment she was taken up, she gave one or two deep sighs; her body was still enveloped by the ropes and the boat. She was immediately carried in an arm chair to Tivoli, and examined by several physicians, who tried, but in vain, to recal her to existence.'

Though terribly battered, Sophie was not disfigured by the fatal fall and seems to have escaped the flames at least. Her white dress had not a single singe mark. The crowd could only witness the carnival turn to carnage in stunned disbelief. The scene was too awful to take in. The daring Madame Blanchard lay broken and still. Back at the smashed roof in Rue de Provence her pretty bonnet hung from a piece of timber beside one forlorn and tiny slipper. The fete finished on the spot, music falling silent as people turned away to trudge home in terrible distress. The Tivoli management quickly arranged a collection at the gate as they left, intending the 3,000 francs raised to go to Sophie's children. They only discovered later that she did not have any. Unlike when Jean-Pierre died, no-one was left facing destitution with Sophie's passing. Her canny management of her one-woman business meant she left a fortune of 30,000 francs to the eight-year-old daughter of a friend.

The dramatic death of Madame Blanchard made headlines across the world and a vivid etching *Mort de Mme Blanchard* featured in a set of 1890 postcards, now in the Tissandier collection in the Library of Congress in America. Sophie was laid to rest at a Protestant funeral at the Père-Lachaise Cemetery in Paris. Seven mourning coaches plus others bearing her family formed a sad escort to the grave. The money raised during the hasty collection at Tivoli was spent on a stone memorial depicting Sophie's spectacular death. Beneath a carved balloon in flames lie the words, 'Victim of her art and intrepidity'. The astonishing life of Madame Sophie Blanchard, the barnstorming birdwoman of France, was over.

Chapter 5

Mistresses of Misadventure

The working class teenager fighting her way through the crowds thronging the City Road on 25 May 1824 was on a mission. Jane Stocks was determined to reach the Eagle Tavern, a hugely popular venue for entertainments of every kind. Today it was the turn of Thomas Harris and his great, big, gorgeous balloon the *Royal George*. Jane was a poor but dedicated balloonomaniac and her eyes were fixed not on the stars, but the clouds. When she floated into the sky one sunny afternoon at the tail end of the Georgian era, Jane was to endure a nightmare that she barely survived and could never forget. Within half an hour of soaring above a thousand cheering admirers she was in one of the most notorious balloon accidents of all time. It did not put her off, though.

The 18-year-old Jane was 'said to be rather of a romantic turn of mind' and she yearned for a ride in a balloon. She was bright and she was ambitious with 'a very intelligent countenance' according to the press. She was also 'petite, though well formed' and her appearance was deemed altogether 'extremely interesting'. One of seven children of a poor millwright in Shoreditch, Jane had been in service since she was old enough to work. She had just left her job over a boyfriend, according to the *Oxford Journal*:

> 'Her last situation was that of an attendant in the shop of a pastry cook in Barbican, which she quitted only Saturday last, in consequence of a love affair (not in the smallest degree discreditable to either party) with a young man.'

Jane had nothing to lose. As she made a beeline through the crowd her romantic mind was fixed not on her lovelife or work. It was fixed on the *Royal George*.

Thomas Harris was a respected aeronaut and had ascended from Soho the previous summer with his famous friend, George Graham. Gas balloons had not changed much in the 40 years since they were pioneered by Jacques

THE LOST HISTORY OF THE LADY AERONAUTS

Charles. Thomas believed a scientific advance was long overdue and was certain he could improve on the landing system. He designed a new kind of valve to release the gas quickly and stop the balloon dragging across the ground.

A flight to demonstrate the invention was arranged at the Eagle, in the heart of the silk-weaving district of Spitalfields. He began filling the balloon at 11am with the aid of his balloon committee of friends and supporters, including his uncle, a fellow aeronaut (whose day job was plumber and glazier) called Mr Rossiter. Thomas's wife and little girl also helped out as the crowd duly gathered. At least a thousand well-dressed people were waiting to watch the balloon ascend. Among them were wealthy gentlemen ready to pay to ride in the car. Jane was spent up once she had paid her two shillings and six pence admission but when she heard that Thomas was looking for a companion she said, 'I'll go, Sir, if you will let me.'

There were clearly those who had their doubts that Jane's adventure was down to pure luck and timing, as *Bell's Weekly Messenger* felt the need to point out that Jane:

> 'was a total stranger to Mr. Harris. But as many false reports of the circumstances attending the offer of Miss Stocks to accompany Mr. Harris have been circulated, it may be proper to supply the following particulars, which are said to be authentic.'

These were that Thomas had advertised for a paying companion, the price of joining him pegged at 50 guineas. Three men approached the aeronaut as he oversaw the inflation of the balloon, each offering 30 guineas 'but for some private reasons, these offers were declined by Mr. Harris.' Holding out for his fee, Thomas went to get ready and that was when Jane decided it was now or never:

> 'On his retiring from the Committee-room to dress for the ascent, Miss Stocks came to the window of the Committee-room, and intimated that she had seen the advertisement for a person to accompany Mr. Harris, and was herself willing to do so.'

A committee member told her it was a 50-guinea ride and the unemployed girl from the poor end of town 'appeared considerably disappointed'.

Her nerve impressed the organisers and they told the aeronaut about the girl at the window. 'Her application being mentioned to Mr. Harris, he went to her, and seeing her display much of the cool courage so necessary in a perilous enterprise, offered her a seat in his car.' Yes, he said. He would let her go with him.

Jane's moment had come, but she was still a teenager and she refused to wear a coat:

> 'Miss Stocks was then introduced to some female friends of the Committee ... but would not accept the offer of additional covering, which some thought necessary, as she was dressed in white, without a shawl.'

Jane was in a snowy muslin dress and straw hat with roses for the occasion and was not about to ruin her outfit with anything sensible. Instead she strolled around arm in arm with Mrs Harris until the balloon was ready. Word quickly spread and the crowd strained for a glimpse of the surprise star. 'About an hour before the ascent took place, a strong degree of interest was excited by an announcement that a young lady named Stocks, would ascend with Mr. Harris,' reports the *Examiner*. Thomas, short but impressive in a blue naval uniform embroidered with gold and a white hat, offered Jane his arm as the band struck up *See the Conquering Hero Comes*:

> 'The young adventuress soon after made her appearance. She appeared to be about 18 years of age, of rather delicate frame and complexion. The intrepid girl mounted the stage with but a slight appearance of fear in her manner, and was instantly greeted with the warmest cheers from the spectators.'

The enormous balloon strained at the ropes. Harris had paid more than £600 for the silk to be made by the Huguenot weavers of Spitalfields. It was a small fortune but the result was breath-taking. The balloon was 120ft in circumference and towered 52ft high. The wicker car was shaped like a canoe, decked out with Genoa velvet and trimmed with gold lace. The curtains were made of green and yellow silk. Jane curtsied to the cheering crowd then took her seat with a show of determination that impressed everyone. 'Having received an affectionate farewell from several around her, she stepped into the car with firmness, and an unmoved countenance, and took her seat amid the most enthusiastic cries of "Bravo!" and loud clapping of hands,' reports *Bell's Weekly Messenger*. Jane called out for someone to tell her parents what she was doing and triumphantly picked up a flag.

At 4.30pm Harris gave the word and they rose a little way. Then they stopped. This was one of his innovations. The extra-long fourth rope was deliberately left in place to give the crowd a good look at the floating balloon for a few minutes. This alarmed not only the spectators. Jane was seen clinging to the side and almost losing her seat as the car rocked sideways. Then the last rope was released and they 'ascended most majestically' with 'Mr. Harris and his fair and courageous companion waving each a flag from the car.' After precisely six and a half minutes they floated out of sight.

Like so many of the first female aeronauts, Jane felt an instant affinity with the air. She always maintained she 'felt extremely delighted with the ascent, and not the least dread', but when the balloon entered a cold cloud she suffered a severe fit of the shivers. Thomas took out some brandy, saying, 'Dear girl, don't let your heart fail; we shall sup together all well.' She took the small glass, no doubt wishing she had listened to the women who told her to wrap up warm. Having reassured the girl, Thomas pulled out his watch and said they had been up for a quarter of an hour and it was time to descend. He asked her to hold the valve line while he put his watch away and that was when things went spectacularly wrong.

Jane caught hold of the cord and held on tight but Thomas had made a terrible mistake. It was the wrong valve line and when he realized it was too late. He cried out, 'Good God, the gas is bursting through!' and Jane promptly fainted. The assumption was that Harris had handed her the wrong line, accidentally opening the large experimental valve. Too late he saw the gas escaping from the balloon in a great gust, leaving them to fall from the sky like a stone. Jane did not even manage to finish her warming tipple before blacking out, the brandy spilling down her white dress. How much of the sickening plummet Harris was conscious for and whether he tried to cushion his young passenger with his body, no-one ever knew. Jane, at any rate, lay mercifully senseless as they hurtled towards the earth.

Down below a gamekeeper called Anthony Geary was standing under an oak tree with his gun when the air shook with an almighty roar. He heard 'a loud rumbling noise as of thunder' and looked up just in time to see the deflated balloon whistling towards him, a mere length of two trees from his head. The *Examiner* reports:

'Almost instantly it struck against the tree about forty yards from him, carrying away a branch: it was then driving very rapidly in an elongated form, when Geary put down his gun and laid hold of the car, which was partly covered with the balloon, then nearly emptied of gas.'

Jane and Thomas had crashed down in Beddington Park on the Surrey estate of Anne Paston Gee. The gamekeeper lifted the balloon silk covering the wreckage, frantically searching for the source of the deep moaning he could hear. It was coming from Jane. She was lying across the back of Thomas, who was doubled up and clearly dead. She managed to ask, 'Where am I?' as she was lifted out and laid on the grass. The people of nearby Carshalton heard the terrific rumble as the empty balloon flapped and rushed to where they saw it fall. Someone grabbed a cushion from the car for under Jane's head and Geary ran to Mrs Gee's mansion for water and harts-horn (a remedy for fainting) to rub on her temples. Local doctor John Wallace arrived 20 minutes later and saw immediately that 'to attempt to restore life in Mr. Harris was useless'. The man's neck was black and oozing blood from a gash and his ribcage was horribly smashed in. Thomas was beyond help and Jane looked in a very bad way. Those who tended her felt certain she was fatally wounded and the doctor suspected spinal damage. Though she had no visible wounds she was concussed and groaning in pain.

By now hundreds of people had gathered at the crash scene. Jane and the body of Thomas were taken to a nearby pub called the Plough. She was put to bed and the doctor treated her by letting blood. The Surrey coroner was sent for and as they waited for him to arrive from Kingston, Jane rallied sufficiently to answer a few gentle questions. She remembered nothing of what had happened after her sip of brandy and Thomas's cry of terror as the gas began to flood from the balloon. 'During this time Miss Stocks was in a state of insensibility,' according to one report. 'She remembers passing through clouds, some of which appeared as bright as silver, and others white as snow, but has no recollection of the latter part of the descent.' Thomas had told her not to be alarmed because they were going to descend, she explained, and 'she had not taken the least alarm, but she thought Mr Harris seemed [to] be alarmed.' The last thing she remembered was his distinctly alarming shout, 'Oh, God, look out!' The rest was a blank.

The corpse of Thomas and the injured Jane lay in rooms side by side at the Plough while a dozen or so miles away their friends grew uneasy in the Eagle. Thomas had promised to be back within two hours. There was no sign of the carrier pigeons he had taken to bring word of his landing. His wife declared that he must be detained by some hospitable person near where he landed. Maybe the wind had taken him further than he predicted. Thomas, she insisted, was safe and celebrating somewhere and she left with her daughter around midnight. His friends were not so sure. A cutting from the Major B. F. S. Baden-Powell Collection reports, 'The time was anxiously looked for, and the crowds were waiting inside and out to welcome his safe arrival; but when the time elapsed, and hours passing and no intelligence whatever arriving of the safety of the adventurers, a gloom seemed to pervade the assembled party.'

More than five hours after the balloon set off an eyewitness to the crash galloped up to the pub 'and gave secret information to Rossiter of the death of the intrepid young man.' Desperate for it not to be true, Thomas's uncle set off immediately to see for himself. The hours dragged by and Jane's father turned up to find out what was happening:

> 'About half past four on Wednesday morning, the father of Miss Stocks appeared at the gate of the Eagle ... and made anxious enquiries after the fate of his daughter. Some of the committee, who were waiting up for the return of those who had gone in a chaise and four to Beddington to ascertain the truth or falsehood of the report of the fatal event, answered him with proper caution, and he went away to his work apparently satisfied.'

As dawn broke the atmosphere in the tavern was tense. The gloom intensified with each tick of the clock until finally:

> 'One of the gentlemen drove up to the gate of the Eagle, and jumping from the chaise, was met by the eager inquiries of the gentlemen waiting; his feelings overcame him, and bursting into tears, he could only say, "it is too true!" and sunk upon a seat.'

At 8am the news was broken to Mrs Harris that Thomas had not landed safely. She was a widow, her husband killed the day after his thirty-second birthday. Jane's mother set off for Beddington as soon as she heard that her daughter, too, looked likely to die.

Back at the Plough, it was pandemonium. Amid the uproar coroner Charles Jemmett swore in a jury of respectable locals and at 4pm, he opened the inquest. It took three hours to piece together what had happened.

First Jemmett and the jury trooped upstairs to view the corpse and then they came back down to listen to the witnesses. Geary the gamekeeper described the crash landing as 'it "flobbed" down in a lump and did not rebound' before he found the casualties. The doctor explained he found Jane 'in a very low state, scarcely able to speak, but not senseless; there was no wound upon her, but she complained of severe pain in her back, her stomach, and legs.' Jane's dress was torn to pieces. A bone from her corset had absorbed the impact and snapped clean in two. It was graphic evidence of how Jane's own bones had escaped such a fate. Her flimsy dress was in shreds but her stays had saved her.

Fellow aeronaut George Graham took the stand and said that having two or three valve lines meant they were bound to get tangled. 'He was firmly of [the] opinion that the fatal result was caused by the construction of the valve,' according to the *Public Ledger and Daily Advertiser*. The jury agreed and the coroner recorded a verdict of accidental death.

The stunned father and younger brother of Thomas took a seat in the bar and mulled over the tragedy with Jane's mother. The father said he tried to talk Thomas out of 'building a machine for his own destruction' but had been told to mind his own business. The relatives were forced to find room where they could because the tavern was packed. Not only was the inquest underway, people had come from miles around to see what was going on. The normally sleepy Beddington found itself at the centre of a sensational disaster. Once the immediate crisis was over, locals were keen to bag a souvenir. 'So great is the demand for pieces of the tree against which the balloon struck, that it has been found necessary to station two men near it to prevent its being literally torn up by the roots,' reports the *Public Ledger and Daily Advertiser*.

They also wanted a good look at the mangled corpse, according to *Bell's Weekly Messenger*:

> 'On Wednesday morning the tavern where the body lay was crowded in the inside, and surrounded outside by persons from the neighbouring villages and towns. Many were admitted to take a view of the body of the deceased, which had not been stripped, but had been laid on a bed in the same situation as when taken out of the car.'

In the next room Jane tossed and turned, crying out from pain and nightmares, no-one believing she would make it. The doctor said she was in danger, the rector paid a visit and papers including *The Morning Chronicle* did not hold out much hope:

> 'Miss Stocks passed Wednesday night in a very bad state, continually moaning. She says it is too much for her to bear, and is continually praying to God to relieve her. She often says she is afraid her recovery is impossible. ... She awoke from a very short slumber, in the greatest fright, fancying herself in the balloon.'

Everything pointed to Jane following Thomas to the grave. However, the young lady with the delicate frame was a lot tougher than she looked. By some miracle – maybe her corset, maybe the chivalrous act of a doomed man – Jane fell from the sky and survived. She began to revive, sipping tea and even making it out of bed so the sheets could be changed. Before long she appeared considerably composed and her fever subsided. By the time a hearse arrived to take the dead aeronaut back in to London, Jane was feeling much better. Then she dropped a bombshell. 'At three o'clock in the afternoon Miss Stocks was considered quite convalescent,' says the *Morning Advertiser*. 'She converses freely and cheerfully, and has said more than once that she would ascend again in a balloon, were an opportunity to offer.' The ordeal had not put Jane off ballooning. On the contrary, it had made her famous.

The funeral procession for Thomas Harris set off from his home near Tottenham Court Road and walked to St James' burial ground. A man carrying a plume of feathers walked ahead of the coffin, Thomas's wife and eight-year-old daughter followed behind with a few close friends and family. The widow composed herself until almost home. Then she heard distant cheers for her husband's friend George Graham ascending in another balloon and it was all too much to bear. The sound 'revived her extreme grief' and she stumbled home in tears. The heartbroken Mrs Harris is usually conveniently airbrushed from history. The press noted at the time that she was a tragic figure. Not only was she left without a husband to support her and the child, but had 'lately quitted the horrible recesses of St. Luke's madhouse.' The afflicted and forgotten wife did not hold the appeal of the death-defying young adventuress. The idea that Jane and Thomas were lovers – engaged, even – was necessary to the romantic legend that later grew around them, especially overseas. There were certainly rumours about their real relationship in Britain, but they only caught hold across the Channel. A dramatic late Victorian drawing called *Mort de Harris* shows Jane leaning out of the balloon car, hair flying and arm reaching helplessly towards Thomas falling through thin air to certain death. Rather than the more realistic scene of her fainting, him panicking and both crunching messily into a tree. The drawing was one of a 10-card set commemorating the first century of ballooning that now sits in the Tissandier Collection in the American Library of Congress. The arresting, if fanciful, tableaux of Jane and Thomas features alongside France's own tragic heroine in *Mort de Mme Blanchard*. Like the famous picture of the three aerial travellers Mrs Sage, Mr Biggin and Mr Lunardi in the imaginary clouds almost thirty years before, *Mort de Harris* owes more to art than actuality.

The kindly aeronaut was obviously concerned for his young passenger but once he had given her a nip of brandy they had bigger problems than the cold. When the wrong valve opened Jane fainted and Thomas panicked as 'the balloon descended about a mile, coming perpendicularly to the earth with great swiftness,' as *The Gentleman's Magazine* put it. Maybe he did try to break her fall, but it is doubtful he had time as even the ballast he might have thrown over to slow the descent was still in the car (as were the stunned carrier pigeons).

Jane's story rewritten as romantic tragedy appealed more to the gothic imagination, summed up here in 1869 by *Harper's New Monthly Magazine*, an international title published in New York:

> 'Harris, to give greater *éclat* to the spectacle, invited a young woman to whom he was engaged to be married to accompany him. The departure and the ascent were accomplished without any difficulty; but when high in the air the cord communicating with the valve at the top of the balloon, used for discharging any excess of hydrogen, or the valve itself, became disarranged, so that Harris, after opening it when he had reached the proper altitude, in order to prevent any farther ascent, found, to his consternation and horror, that he could not close it again. Of course, as the gas continued to issue from the opening, the balloon descended with greater and greater rapidity every instant. Harris threw out all his ballast, and every thing else that he could lay hand upon, to arrest the descent. He took off his own and the lady's outer clothing, and threw it over. All was in vain. He finally concluded that by throwing himself over he might save her, as the balloon might perhaps have buoyancy enough left to sustain the weight of one. He accordingly kissed her farewell, and leaped into the air. She saw him go down, and immediately fell fainting into the bottom of the car.'

A far prettier story than the real one. The fairytale of Jane and Thomas is introduced with what may be a disclaimer, the magazine suggesting it 'belongs rather to the realm of sentiment and romance than to science and philosophy.'

The truth was always more terrible for the young survivor. Jane put on a very brave face after her accident but the reality was she took a long time to recover. *The Cambrian* reports that two months after the crash Harris' balloon committee met 'to consider upon the means of relieving the necessitous condition of this female, who, so far recovered as to be able to walk, is likely for a long period to be a burden to her poor parents'. Thomas's uncle had recently taken his courage in both hands and ascended in the restored *Royal George* from the Bedford Arms in Camden Town to raise money for the widow. Now kind Rossiter wanted to help Jane. The silk monster that fell from the sky flapping like thunder was an object of morbid curiosity. Rossiter proposed they put the balloon of the ill-fated aeronaut on exhibition for a few days in the gardens of the Bedford Arms and encourage visitors to make a donation to the cause. It was a good plan and adopted 'amidst loud applause'. People had torn down the tree Jane crashed into and queued up to gawp at the corpse of her dead hero. Now they turned up to take a good look at the girl who lived. 'Numbers thronged to see it, or, with more probability, to see the unfortunate girl, who was present. She looked cheerful; but her countenance was pale, and her frame weak.'

Against all the odds, and with the support of the ballooning community, Jane returned to the clouds. One year after the infamous accident Jane set off in a balloon from Leeds with the most successful aeronaut of the nineteenth century, Charles Green. They ascended from the Coloured Cloth Hall in Leeds and came down a little over half an hour later in a village near York. As ever, she displayed remarkable grit, even when they descended amid a violent storm of wind and rain. Any real thunder can only have been a horrible reminder of the catastrophic moment when the *Royal George* valve opened and she blacked out. *The Intelligencer* notes, 'She maintained the greatest self-possession during the whole voyage and her intrepidity does not seem in the least impaired.'

George Graham also felt an obligation towards both his friend's widow (he promised Mrs Harris a third of the proceeds of an ascent following the crash) and the young survivor of his fatal last flight. George visited Jane shortly after the accident, saying he would take her on another balloon trip if she wanted to go. When Jane finally took up the offer two years later it was to accompany his wife, Margaret. Mrs Graham was only a year or two older than Jane and already embarked on one of the longest careers of all the balloonomania belles. George was still the most famous person in the family but as the century progressed, Margaret would become a superstar in her own right.

The June day that Jane and Margaret shared a balloon car in 1826, however, did not go well. Jane's horrible accident allowed her to stay in the exciting world of showbiz balloons, but the price was forever being paraded as the girl who cheated death. One report marvels that two women were flying alone, but defines them by their relationship to male pilots. Mrs Graham was wife to the celebrated aeronaut and Miss Stocks 'the companion of the unfortunate Mr. Harris at the time of the lamentable excursion by which he lost his life.' The ascent was held in the tea gardens of White Conduit House in Pentonville, but for disaster prone Jane it was third time unlucky. Margaret Graham was a much sturdier professional and a dab hand at working a crowd. She appeared wearing a white dress with a violet bonnet and pink cloak with a yellow lining, ready to ascend in style. Unfortunately the inflation took a lot longer than expected because the day was again marred by a thunderstorm. Frail Jane decided to sit it out with friends over a cup of tea but this was a mistake, as Mrs Graham made very clear in her own account. She was ready at 6pm but there was no sign of Jane:

> 'I was sent for (the arrangements being complete), from a lady's house in Warren-street, where Mr Graham had previously placed me and Miss Stocks. I accordingly entered the ground and took my seat in the car, where I remained a full 20 minutes before we could find Miss Stocks, (who not being aware that every thing was ready, had gone with some friends to take tea).'

When Jane appeared, she took her seat opposite Margaret but looked a lot less composed than the furious pilot in the pink cloak. Jane had wasted valuable time and everything was out of sync. Believing the balloon was ready George had set off on horseback to get ahead of the women, and had to double back. He had left the safety valve open to help Margaret with taking off. It was a windy day and while she waited for Jane the balloon was buffeted around, leaking gas:

> 'The oscillation of the machine caused a great deal of gas to escape, and when, at length, Miss Stocks took her seat, it was

found that there was not sufficient ascending power to carry both of us. Mr Graham accordingly requested her to relinquish her seat.'

The cup of tea had cost the endlessly unlucky Jane her place and Margaret set off without her.

A consummate performer and skilled aeronaut, Margaret was also a superb self-publicist. Nothing was ever less than a nail-biting drama in the interviews she gave to the pressmen who would visit her at home for tea and a good story. Jane walked dejectedly away while Margaret was mobbed at the last minute by fans. When she finally took off it was touch and go whether she would clear the buildings, she told reporters.

> 'The car became entangled with the coping of a house; but by pushing my foot against it, it was disengaged, and I then passed down a street, the car as low as the second floor windows, and the monstrous machine swaying from one side of the way to the other. I now anticipated immediate death, and nothing can exceed the exertions of the people in the street, and at their windows, to arrest its progress; but they failed, and I desired them not to alarm themselves for my safety – that I trusted in Providence, that nothing serious would befal me.'

She threw out everything except the seats and eventually rose out of danger. People reached up from the steeple of an Islington church in an attempt to shake her hand as she floated by. Then everything was delightful for a short while before a gust of wind made her plonk down among some beans in a garden. Then she rose again to finally come down in a field where 'to my delight, the first person that caught hold of the car was my husband.' Lurching along would become Margaret's signature style but on this day, it must have seemed like a one-off bumpy ride. She was invited to the home of a kindly couple in Newington Green for refreshments while George and a friend sorted out the balloon to take home. He had endured quite the stressful day himself and there was more to come:

> 'They were surrounded by a set of brickmakers and others, who, instead of rendering them any assistance, took a delight in injuring the property as much as possible; one man in particular, cutting the balloon with a large knife … The

balloon was with difficulty placed on Mr. Adam's gig, but was captured by the mob and almost cut to pieces.'

Margaret explained the reason for their fury.

'The attack was caused because Mr. Graham would not give them more beer, he having already presented them with 16 gallons.'

After a pitched battle, 'the machine was recaptured.' At 10pm, Margaret returned to north London safe and well:

'with a sincere hope that my next ascent will be still more gratifying to my friends and the public, as they may be assured that ascending with a balloon is more pleasing to me than any other amusement.'

Less pleasing was being sued by the pub landlord for breaching the peace by dropping in uninvited. The heated row over bar bills and balloon slashing was played out in court, much to the amusement of the press bench. The *Evening Mail* reported how George, 'his fairer half' and their lawyer 'made an excursion (not an aerial one)' to the police court in Old Street. The landlord sent his able daughter and some minders and the ranting began. The pub demanded another £5 for ale drunk by the 'immense number of bricklayers' who followed George to the pub, plus damage done to the property during the fighting. It transpired the landlord had tried to hold the balloon hostage until the aeronauts paid up. George hit back with 'complaints both loud and deep' about the damage to his balloon. The magistrate listened patiently to 'a warm and rather irregular discussion' before declaring that he could not interfere in the case.

Jane Stocks, left behind in disgrace, fades from the record after 1826 but Margaret Graham was only just getting started. The ascent was the first solo flight by a British woman, though it was down to her to keep reminding people of that. The plaudits tended to go to male aeronauts. The event showed exactly the kind of bold and pragmatic aeronaut Margaret was from the offset. Nothing fazed her for long. Ditching Jane, kicking roofs to avoid crashing, dodging balloon-slashers and fighting courtroom battles were all par for the course.

Chapter 6

The White-Knuckle World of Margaret Graham

With the heart of a lion and the luck of a dodo, Margaret Graham's achievements were dazzling and her disasters spectacular. During a career spanning four decades under three monarchs, she combined ambition and chutzpah to jaw-dropping effect. From crowd-puller to reporter, the self-styled 'aeronaut to Her Majesty' never paused for breath. There was only one Mrs Graham, unstoppable balloon star of nineteenth-century Britain.

Born in 1804 in Walcot, an area of Bath in Somerset, Margaret Watson was married to the widowed chemist and aeronaut George Graham. He was interested not only in the clouds but the stars above. In 1822, he co-wrote a book on magic, *The Philosophical Merlin,* with an astrologer called Robert Cross Smith who went by the pen name of Raphael. Whether or not Margaret shared George's interest in alchemy and the occult (especially the power of Venus, the realm of lust and love), she shared his passion for balloons. By the time she jettisoned Jane Stocks, Margaret was an adept pilot and gifted entertainer whose gripping accounts of rollicking rides kept the public coming back for more. They also frequently landed her in trouble.

Margaret was a natural aeronaut and only 19 in October 1823 when her career took off, beside George high above her native Bath. By June 1824, Mrs Graham wafted over London as luckless Thomas Harris was being buried below. The *Waterford Mail* notes, 'It is a singular coincidence, that at the moment Mr. Graham's balloon passed over Tottenham Court road, the mourners of Mr. Harris were returning from St. James's burial ground, where they had just deposited the remains of the unfortunate adventurer.' It was the crowds cheering for Margaret and George that Thomas's widow could hear as she crumpled with fresh grief.

The high drama of Margaret's career had begun and when disaster struck in Plymouth in November 1825, it set the tone for decades. One report notes 'the public here have been on the tiptoe of expectation to witness the ascent of Mrs. Graham in an elegant large balloon.' The Grahams ascended from

THE WHITE-KNUCKLE WORLD OF MARGARET GRAHAM

Stonehouse before an 18,000-strong crowd, but were quickly in trouble when the balloon was blown out to sea and landed a mile from the shore. Rescue boats headed for the scene, reports the *Morning Post*:

> 'The balloon was bounding with great velocity upon the surface of the water, appearing from a distance like a large ship, but no car was visible for two or three minutes. In the midst of dire consternation, by a sudden elevation of the balloon, the car, which had been thus dragged through the water for nearly twenty minutes, was luckily discovered; the ropes were instantly seized; and the vehicle, containing Mr. and Mrs. GRAHAM, clasped in each other's arms, in a very exhausted state, was drawn into the boat, and they were thus happily relieved from their most perilous situation.'

The balloon then became tangled up with the boat, injuring two of the rescuers, until crewmen hacked at the ropes with knives and freed it to shoot upwards and float off towards France. Meanwhile 'Mrs G. overcome by the agitation of mind she had undergone, had every appearance of a corpse.'

Faced with such unflattering reports, Mrs G. began issuing her own press releases. She did a lot more during the crisis than droop. A mistress of spin, her thrilling account was snapped up by editors, including at the *Globe*. When it was clear they were heading for a splashdown, 'I at this time put on a cork waistcoat, and at my earnest request Mr G. allowed me to tie a copper life-preserver round his waist ... Our descent now became so rapid, that the rush of air upwards was tremendous, and the noise of the waves seemed to be all around us.' When they hit the water, the balloon car was soon underwater with 'every wave passing quite over our heads'. They kept their nerve for half an hour and while she pays tribute to the rescuers and God for stretching out a saving arm, nowhere is she limp and helpless in the face of danger. Just seven months later she is making history by flying solo over Islington, sans Jane Stocks.

Margaret and George were a formidable couple, working together to build a business on the balloon show circuit. When coal gas used for lighting was found to be a cheap alternative to hydrogen for filling balloons, professional aeronauts grew in confidence and daring. From the 1820s they could fill the balloon quicker, with less danger of bored crowds kicking off, and could afford to fly more often. Hydrogen had more reliable lifting power but was six times more expensive than coal gas. The convenience of connecting a balloon to a gas main slashed the overheads for performers such as the Grahams (though poor quality gas would plague their careers). Margaret made regular ascents. She also had children. She managed to juggle the demands of her growing brood with those of her dangerous career until 22 August 1836, when her luck almost ran out.

The glitzy afternoon began promisingly enough. Another day, another pleasure garden and Margaret had scored a coup with a balloon ride booked for Charles, the eccentric and exiled Duke of Brunswick. The VIP ascent in Bayswater was packed with fashionable aristocrats and A-listers. There was at least one marquis, an earl and a countess, several lords and ladies and a few knights of the realm. His highness was famous for his ostentatious dress and flamboyant manner. For his first ride in a balloon he wore a chocolate coat, dark waistcoat, light trousers and blue silk handkerchief with gold spots. The outfit was topped off with a Quaker hat. Mrs Graham was expecting her eighth child and appeared in an ankle-length cloak of green silk covering her bump, and a cottage bonnet in blue silk. The *Globe* paints a vivid picture of the pomp on show at the party:

> 'About half-past one his Serene Highness arrived at the gardens, accompanied by several gentlemen of his suite. Four of his servants in livery carried an extremely large cloak, a telescope, a scarlet flag, and a large umbrella. Shortly after three o'clock the car, which was a new one, built of cane, and lined with yellow silk, was attached to the netting, and at half-past three o'clock, everything being ready, the neck of the balloon was detached from the gas-pipe, when the stupendous machine was floated to the centre of the gardens, and the car fastened to the top of a large table, round which the company had some time previously ranged themselves.'

Applause rippled through the well-to-do crowd as the dandified duke and the pregnant aeronaut stepped aboard the balloon. His Serene Highness put his hands together in reply though did not appear as serene as all that according to several witnesses, including *The Spectator*. 'His cheeks, which appeared flushed before entering, partook, we thought, of paleness before he left the Flora Gardens.' The German prince managed to master his nerves but whether he did the same on coming down again was the subject of heated debate.

The flight itself was a success, with Margaret busy piloting the balloon and pointing out sight-seeing opportunities to her royal client. The only problem was earache at four miles high. It was the descent that pitched Margaret into another very public argument. When describing the horrific finale to the flight the duke said one thing and Margaret quite another. What was beyond doubt was that as they came in to land on farmland in Brentwood, Essex, the duke left the car and the balloon shot upwards with Margaret clinging onto the side for dear life. Then she fell to the ground. The next day's *Globe* had the first details emerging as it went to press:

> 'From some unfortunate accident, the precise nature of which we have not been able to learn, the car was turned on one side, and both the aeronauts were thrown to the ground, Mrs. Graham from a height, it is stated, of nearly thirty feet, and the Duke just as the car was nearly touching the ground. Mrs. Graham, we regret to state, fell upon her head, and was taken up by those who had run to their assistance from a little neighbouring village, in a state of insensibility, and by some she was believed to be dead.'

His highness, on the other hand, escaped with a slight stunning and a few small bruises. Even his cloak, hat, cap, umbrella and telescope were unharmed, found with the escaped balloon 50 miles from where it took off. Margaret, meanwhile, was in a critical condition. As she fought for her life the duke claimed he had not caused the calamity. In a letter to Captain Currie (a friend of the Grahams who was at the ascent), he blames the accident on a botched landing where they bounced on the ground. As they began to descend very rapidly, he wrote, the grapple iron was not doing its job and Margaret had to prepare him for an emergency landing:

> 'She next inquired if I remembered her informing me the balloon could be converted into [a] parachute, and requested me to observe it was then in that state. I then saw her mount upon her seat and lay hold of the ropes which fastened the car to the balloon. She desired me to do the same, observing we were coming down rather faster than she wished. I followed her advice; ... but I had scarcely put myself in the position required when I felt the car strike with the utmost violence on the ground and overturn the balloon itself, touching the earth and dragging us about 30 yards until it rose again. By the violence of the shock I was thrown head foremost out the car

at the height of about 18 feet, but I contrived to fall upon my hands and escape uninjured. Having gained my feet I had the great grief of seeing Mrs. Graham fall from the car from much higher distance than I had fallen, and, from the apparently lifeless manner in which she lay, I was at first fearful she was killed.'

He was not the only one. By the time George reached Margaret in the farmhouse where she was being tended, he was frantic. She had severe head and lower back injuries. A doctor had her head shorn and bled both her arms, then cupped her temples, which was a treatment involving suction applied to the skin. Inevitably, she suffered a miscarriage. Margaret was bedridden at the farm for weeks, only well enough to go home to Poland Street in London at the very end of September. Meanwhile, the duke's concern for his odd selection of luggage while Margaret fought for her life did not escape notice. The Cuthbert-Hodgson Collection has tongue-in-cheek 'complimentary stanzas' from a newspaper of the day:

'Great Brunswick's Duke, in Mr GRAHAM'S balloon, Resolved one day to venture for a lark, But wisely bargained they should come down soon, As Princes are *too often in the dark!*

'From Flora's gardens, when he rose on high, His want of prudence no one can rebuke; To carry *an umbrella* to the sky Was truly worthy of a *reign*-ing Duke.

'When next he mounts, as cold is past a joke, His Royal Highness has a prudent plan; Besides umbrella, comforter, and cloak, He means to carry up a *warming-pan.*

'Though written when the DUKE was out of breath, His feeling note was to the purpose pat. It told – "A lady's at the point of death – But I, oh heavens! have lost my cloak and hat!"

'Such courage, prudence, gallantry combined, Will make the English folks acknowledge soon
A truly continental Royal mind
Above most others – *up in a balloon!*'

Margaret, too, was less than impressed by the royal version of events. When she finally emerged from her convalescence it was to tell a very different story about the crash. The duke, she insisted, hopped out of the balloon car too early and caused the disaster. 'Mrs. Graham's statement of her late aerial voyages' was published in several newspapers, including *The Standard*:

> 'I saw the Duke of Brunswick step out of the car safely upon terra firma with apparently not the slightest inconvenience to himself. The moment his highness was out of the car, and before I could alight on the earth, the balloon rapidly ascended into the air. I own I felt the situation rather awkward, although I was not at all daunted, and had full possession of my presence of mind. ... After the Duke of Brunswick left the car I kept my hold of the hoop, still hanging to it; but as I was aware of the danger of the balloon ascending too high with so light a weight without the gas being let out, I made up my mind to descend into the car and secure my valve-line, in order to effect my descent as soon as possible.'

Her feet were outside the car, though, so when she let go of the hoop she fell to earth instead.

The scenario was extreme but Margaret could not resist ramping up the drama even further with some dubious claims, notably how far she plummeted and that her clothing acted like some kind of elegant parachute:

> 'I was precipitated to the earth—and here I must distinctly state that I fell more than 300 yards, or 1000 feet; having commenced my fall in perpendicular position, I perfectly well remember that the silk pelisse which I had on at the time became fully inflated with atmospheric air, and prevented the rapidity of my descent, and I was so far conscious as to feel a thorough conviction of my inevitable destruction, and offer up a prayer to the Almighty for the preservation of my husband and dear children.'

She does not remember hitting the earth but the first on the scene had watched her fall and were 'fully persuaded that I was a mutilated corpse'.

Then came the clincher – the duke had not paid a penny towards her care:

> 'In conclusion, I beg to state, in consequence of several erroneous reports, that no persons (with the exception of my husband and

relatives) have visited me at Doddinghurst, or contributed to the expenses to which my unfortunate calamity has subjected me: the Duke of Brunswick, the day after my accident, transmitted to Mr. Graham the amount agreed upon for his ascent, and no other claim has been made upon his Highness.'

Unfortunately, Margaret's habit of embroidering the facts backfired. The *Morning Advertiser* took issue with the more fanciful details and that cast doubt on everything else:

'The extraordinary statement of Mrs. Graham, in her account of her late accident ... that she had fallen from a height of upwards of three hundred yards, or one thousand feet, has created the greatest surprise among all classes, but more particularly among those persons well acquainted with the science of aerostatics, who all concur in the opinion that any person falling from so high a degree of altitude must have been a corpse long before they could reach the earth.'

Jane Stocks had fallen a long way and survived but Margaret's claim strained credibility. Even though she had lost her child and almost died, the paper sided with his Serene Majesty:

'The Duke of Brunswick ... declares, that on the sudden rising of the balloon, after its violent concussion with the earth, he was thrown out of the car head foremost, from the height of full eighteen feet, but contriving to alight on his hands, he fortunately sustained no injury. Having regained his feet, he saw Mrs. Graham in the act of falling out of the car, not at the height of 1,000 feet, but of about 50 yards, or 150 feet; and that, instead of her pelisse acting as a parachute, her clothes were almost forced over her head, and she, consequently, fell to the earth like an inanimate object.'

Bell's Weekly Messenger joined the fray, reporting on the escalating dispute between the duke and the diva. In the duke's corner was the outraged Captain R. W Currie of the Isle of Wight, a sometime customer of the Grahams, whose letter to *The Times* revealed rather more than Margaret would have liked about her rates:

'Mrs. Graham asserts that she has not received from the Duke of Brunswick anything more than the sum agreed upon by his serene highness for the ascent. Now the fact is there was no stipulated sum agreed upon. The duke asked me what I usually gave, when I told him ten pounds or guineas, and the costs of posting to town, which made it about 12*l* [£], with which I said I was convinced Mrs. Graham would feel satisfied, as I had not heard that any more had been given by any of the persons who had accompanied her on her previous ascents. After the accident, his serene highness having expressed to me his desire to present to Mrs. Graham more than the sum before mentioned, and having requested my advice on the subject, I said I thought double the usual amount would be sufficient, but his highness most generously (after I had expressed that opinion) sent Mrs. Graham 50*l*, which amount was mentioned by all the papers of the day, and considered [by] all persons with whom I have conversed on the subject as very liberal.'

His royal highness gave an honest account, according to the captain:

'Judging from the above error of Mrs. Graham, I think there can be no doubt of the veracity of his serene highness's statement as having been thrown out, instead of having quietly stepped out of the car (as asserted by her) at the moment of the descent, especially when is remembered that Mrs. Graham found it necessary to catch hold of the hoop to lessen the violence of the shock. Any one at all conversant with aerostation must be aware that it is impossible to step out quietly, when descending with such rapidity described by Mrs. Graham herself, unless the car was secured by the grapnel. Those persons who witnessed the accident, even from a distance, his highness assures me, felt convinced he must have been considerably injured from the height they saw him fall, and wished him to have medical advice, and be bled to avoid the consequences of the shock. His serene highness, in my opinion, did everything that could reasonably be expected from him, having waited with the unfortunate lady upwards of four hours, and ever since expressed to me his regret for the accident and for her situation.'

THE LOST HISTORY OF THE LADY AERONAUTS

He ended with a swipe at her whole family:

> 'Before I conclude, I will just notice one very foolish account given by Mr. Graham, a day or two after the accident, and to which he signed his name, saying that the Duke stepped safely out of the car, &c., and that Mrs. Wilson, his wife's sister, in Poland-street, would corroborate what he had stated, both being at the time nine miles from the spot where the accident occurred, and Mrs. Graham being at the time incapable of speaking.'

Margaret snatched up her pen and wrote an immediate reply. In a letter to the editor of the *Morning Chronicle*, she claims to have been horribly misunderstood. Her former letter was 'mutilated' so as to convey a different meaning to what she intended. Among other misunderstandings, she denied saying she saw the duke step safely out of the car. It looked very like a hasty attempt to backtrack and drew an acid response from editors. 'Mrs. Graham seems to have been very unfortunate in her communications with the press; but somewhat singular that the same "mutilations," completely altering the sense, should have been made by four or five different papers,' noted one. Claiming to fall from three times the height of St. Paul's cathedral could not really be blamed on a mistake at the printers.

Margaret may have embellished her story a little but there was no denying her serious injuries and the loss of her baby. The arrogant aristocrat was not known for his generosity or forgiving nature and it was a high-stakes fight. Not only was the indignant duke fabulously wealthy – he wore diamond-studded underwear – he relished a legal fight. He was actually living in exile after being deposed by his brother in Brunswick. Considered a tyrant while in power, he bridled at any and all criticism in London and elsewhere. A grudge he nursed about an article in the *Weekly Dispatch* when he was chased out of Brunswick became the basis of a British libel law that survived until 2013. He was rich enough and paranoid enough to ruin the Grahams.

Margaret cut her losses, dusted herself down and went back to her balloon. With one cause célèbre only just dying down, she was back in the papers almost immediately. "Serious accident to Mrs Graham..." began the headline in *The Morning Chronicle* of 22 May 1837. It was a report of her ascent from the gardens of a Marylebone pub called the Yorkshire Stingo with her husband and a man from the Surrey Zoological Gardens:

THE WHITE-KNUCKLE WORLD OF MARGARET GRAHAM

> 'The descent of the balloon took place under most frightful circumstances, and it is most providential that the whole of the persons ascending in it were not destroyed.'

Blown off course by a gust of wind, the balloon had hit an iron suspension bridge near Reigate and pitched Margaret and George out of the car and into a hillside:

> 'Mrs. Graham was in an almost insensible state, and bleeding profusely from the head, but Mr. Graham appeared to have received very little injury.'

The quick-thinking man from the zoo threw himself to the bottom of the car to avoid falling out. The balloon floated another mile and came to rest in a field. According to the newspaper, the crash landing followed a familiar path. The furious landowner put the balloon in a barn (with two guards) and refused to hand it back until he was paid compensation for a trampled crop. Next day Margaret was 'very considerably worse'.

This was not good for the Grahams. Margaret was all for spicing up her performances with the appearance of danger and some first-hand descriptions of her derring-do afterwards, but it was beginning to look like she did not know what she was doing. Even though this was her third ascent that week, her reputation was at stake. Rather than rest, she had to put the record straight. She managed to get a letter to the editor in time for them to run it below the news story, admitting they could not say how authentic their account was but it was from a trusted source. 'In justice, however, to Mrs Graham, we annex a letter which we have received from her, and which gives a very different account of the occurrence.'

Margaret was 'much surprised and hurt' to arrive back in London to learn of the 'very erroneous reports which are in circulation respecting my late descent'. She did not want her friends, relatives or the general public to run away with the idea that she had gone and fallen on her head again. On the contrary, 'I did not receive any injury except a slight sprain in my ankle'. The balloon had been impounded, true, but only until the owner of the field (another pub landlord) returned home. Then he was kindness itself. He 'readily delivered up the machine' and told his men to help pack it up for bringing back to London.

This may have been pure spin or it may have been a spirited struggle to get the facts straight when Margaret was, however you looked at it, quite an accident-prone aeronaut. Throughout her career she defended herself against any and all criticism in the press. The majority of her ascents proved her great expertise as an aeronaut. She knew what she was doing but when things did go wrong, they went wrong in spectacular fashion.

The intrepid duo was back on the road by October 1837, for a West Yorkshire ascent from Piece Hall in Halifax. Despite rain and hail holding up preparations at the elegant cloth-trading centre, the courtyard was filled with paying spectators and the surrounding hills packed with those watching for free. Even local notable Anne Lister, subject of BBC and HBO drama *Gentleman Jack*, recorded watching the Halloween ascent in her famous diary. Anne writes that 'ab[ou]t 4 1/2 p.m. A- [Ann Walker, her 'wife'] and I and the serv[an]ts all saw Mrs. Graham in her balloon (w[a]s to asc[en]d at 3 p.m. fr[om] the Piece hall) ov[e]r Hipperholm – might be 400 or 500 y[ar]ds high?' But it wasn't Margaret in the balloon. She stepped down at the last minute, according to the *Halifax Express*: 'The roughness of the weather, and the lateness of the hour, then induced Mr. Graham to make the ascent himself; not thinking it prudent to permit his wife to go, under such circumstances.' The real reason was a paying punter had turned up and only two people could ascend. This second person in the balloon with George was Halifax optician Mr. J. Aked Metcalfe, according to the paper, while 'Mrs. Graham, who had followed in a chaise, joined the party at Leeds, where they were taking tea at the Griffin Inn.' Metcalfe had persuaded friends to pay for and secure his trip and the Grahams never refused hard cash. Margaret wasn't the only no-show. 'Mrs. Graham and the monkey did not go up as announced in the bills...' remarked the *Leeds Times*. Like other aeronauts, she occasionally included a simian special guest in the performance.

By 1838 the Grahams had patched up the row with Captain Currie. At the age of 34, Margaret was prepared for a summer of hard graft with the balloon, but had no idea how much fresh calamity would unfold. She had already chalked up dozens of ascents. Her bookings schedule was gruelling and the strain was beginning to show, not least on the equipment.

She could not have chosen a more high-profile event for the next debacle, the coronation of Queen Victoria. London was packed on 28 June 1838 and Margaret was calling herself 'aeronaut to Her Majesty'. Every theatre, hotel, pleasure garden, pub and street was thronged with people enjoying the festivities. That meant plenty of witnesses to Mrs Graham's latest mishap. She ascended with Captain Currie from Green Park, just after the royal salute to mark the crown being placed on Victoria's head.

Margaret floated over London landmarks – Trafalgar Square, Horse Guards Parade, St Paul's cathedral – before she began descending rapidly towards rooftops in Marylebone Road. She had intended to land in a park

Does my bum look big in this? Dedicated followers of late eighteenth-century fashion.

The Lunardi Bonnet: all the rage in 1784 among fans of Italian aeronaut Vincent Lunardi.

Saucy Georgians: satirists delighted in mocking the craze for balloons.

COUNT ZAMBECCARI's BALLOON.

Which was to have taken up Himself, Rear Admiral Sir Edward Vernon Kn.t and Miss Grice, from Tottenham Court Road, but not having time to fill the Balloon sufficiently, Miss Grice, was obliged to get out: after this it ascended with Sir Edward and the Count, about 4 o'Clock, and descended near Horsham in Sussex, 36 Miles distant, in one Hour, March 23.d 1785.

Count Zambeccari and Sir Edward Vernon sailed in an air-balloon from Tottenham-Court Road to a place near Horsham, thirty-five miles distant from London, which they performed in one hour.

The moment 'Miss Grice was obliged to get out' by Count Zambeccari before ascending from Tottenham Court Road in March 1785. *The Royal Aeronautical Society (National Aerospace Library)/Mary Evans Picture Library*

French actress and dancer Rosine Simonet became 'the first female aerial traveller in the English atmosphere' on 3 May 1785. *The Trustees of the British Museum*

Actress, aeronaut and lady of letters Letitia Sage claimed the title of first Englishwoman to fly on 29 June 1785. *The Royal Aeronautical Society (National Aerospace Library)/Mary Evans Picture Library*

How rude: The Parachute or a Sage Lady's Second Experiment by caricaturist Thomas Rowlandson in 1785. *The Royal Aeronautical Society (National Aerospace Library)/Mary Evans Picture Library*

Come up and see my etching: Lunardi lampooned in *Rambler's Magazine*.

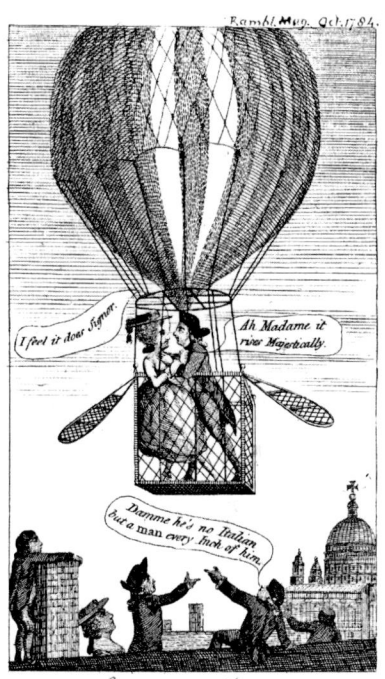

Pioneering pilot and first female parachutist Jeanne-Geneviève Garnerin entertains French spectators in 1802.

Sophie Blanchard, feted by all France, came alive when she took to the air – but died when she mixed hydrogen and fireworks in 1819. *The Royal Aeronautical Society (National Aerospace Library)/Mary Evans Picture Library*

MORT DE HARRIS (1824)

Fanciful version of the 1824 tragedy over Surrey that left Thomas Harris dead and Jane Stocks famous.

MRS. GRAHAM'S
FIRST ASCENT
SINCE HER ACCIDENT!!

Surrey Zoological Gardens,

The Season at these Gardens will commence on
THURSDAY, 27th of APRIL, 1837,
Being the Celebration of the Birth-Day of
Her Most Gracious Majesty,
Patroness of the Gardens, with a
GRAND
AEROSTATIC FETE,
WHEN
Mrs. GRAHAM,
THE ONLY FEMALE AERONAUT IN EUROPE,
WILL MAKE HER FIRST
BALLOON ASCENT
(Since her most unfortunate Voyage with the
DUKE OF BRUNSWICK,)
FROM THE BEAUTIFUL SHEET of WATER,
WHICH ORNAMENTS THESE GROUNDS.

THE SPLENDID BAND OF THE
ROYAL SCOTS FUSILEER GUARDS
Will perform the most popular airs from "Beniowsky," "Fair Rosamond," "Devil on Two Sticks," &c., in the
NEW GRAND TEMPLE OF THE LAKE!!
ADMITTANCE ONE SHILLING.
OPEN FROM TWELVE TILL DUSK.

King, Printer, College Hill, City.

Above and opposite: Mayhem and Margaret Graham: Left to right, back in the basket after one of her mishaps; her balloon on fire in Edmonton, and crashing into a house in Piccadilly in 1851.

MRS. GRAHAM'S BALLOON ON FIRE.—(SEE NEXT PAGE.)

DESTRUCTION OF MRS GRAHAM'S BALLOON, IN ARLINGTON-STREET, PICCADILLY.

Left, Mary Myers, aka Carlotta the Lady Aeronaut who ran a flying empire from Balloon Farm, top, with her husband in Frankfort, New York.

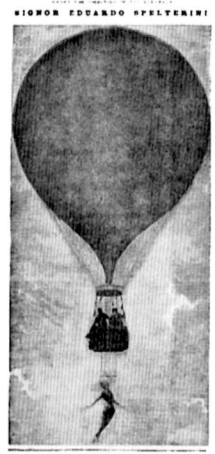

American balloon star Leona Dare took her nineteenth century circus skills around the world.

Mademoiselle Albertina, aka 14-year-old Louisa Maud Evans, who died in a Cardiff parachute accident in 1896. *The British Balloon Museum and Library*

Bumpy ride: Gertrude Bacon and her father John after an 1899 meteor hunt by balloon ended in a crash landing.

Vera Butler shares a basket with fellow founders of the Aero Club, friend Charles Rolls and father Frank.

Vittoria Colonna, Princess di Teano, centre, in the upper crust queue for an ascent with the Aero Club in 1906.

May Assheton Harbord ready to fly her balloon Valkyrie during the Edwardian resurgence of balloonomania.

One of My Most Exciting Ballooning Experiences, according to May Assheton Harbord in *The Wide World Magazine* in 1909.

Map happy: actress Charlotte Granville, centre, found fame on the London stage before heading for early Hollywood.

East End girl: Elizabeth 'Lily' Cove who toured as 'Leaping Lily' in the early 1900s. *Steven Wood*

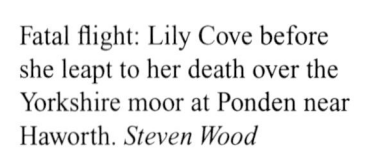

Fatal flight: Lily Cove before she leapt to her death over the Yorkshire moor at Ponden near Haworth. *Steven Wood*

Price of fame: poster for Lily Cove's Haworth leap and the service sheet for her funeral.
Steven Wood

Sky sailor: Dolly Shepherd in 1904, sporting her first uniform. *The Dolly Shepherd Trust*

The flying suffragette: Muriel Matters in 1909.

but had no choice but to let down a rope and call out for help. A young builder called John Fley, up from Devon for the coronation, rushed forward and grabbed the rope. The balloon netting caught on the roof of a second-hand clothes shop and dislodged coping stones crashed down onto the heads below. John received a terrible blow and a gentleman's servant called Wilson was also 'severely hurt on the head, and conveyed in a state of great suffering to Middlesex hospital'. Wilson recovered, while 26-year-old John Fley took two weeks to die. His father travelled up from Devon to tend John in hospital and, 'though with a heavy heart, had satisfaction of administering comfort to his only child in his last moments.' Across the hospital in the boardroom, an inquest was opened into his death.

When the adjourned inquest reconvened in late July it was not a hearing the Grahams could bluff their way through. This was not a red-faced publican claiming an unpaid bar tab, this was an investigation into a death directly related to Margaret's handling of the balloon.

First witness up was Edward Smith of Wigmore Street. He said on the day of the accident the balloon snagged on the roof of his house and tore before it headed towards the house in Marylebone Lane and pulled off some stones. Fley was in the act of taking hold of a rope when a stone fell on him and threw him to the ground. 'I do not think that the parties in the car saw the accident; but it is my belief that the balloon was in a most rotten state,' he said.

Then Margaret took the stand, reports *Bell's Weekly Messenger*:

> 'On nearing Marylebone-lane she saw the people running in all directions towards them, and waved her hand for them to keep aloof, and threw out part of the line on the top of a house, as also ropes attached to the car, and called to the people to hold but not pull them; they unfortunately did so, and she saw deceased fall, but could not say that he had hold of the rope.'

She was positive that her balloon was not torn and did not leave any bits dangling from Mr Smith's house. Whereupon he handed her four yards of silk and she was forced to admit it was from her balloon. She then produced her own portion of torn fabric and claimed it came from the balloon of rival aeronaut Charles Green. Green was present and asked to take a look at the oiled skin. It did not come from any of his balloons, he said. On that note he took the stand and gave a withering assessment of the Grahams and their operation. They used shoddy kit that was prone to failure. 'In his opinion the specimen produced as being part of the Victoria balloon was entirely unfit for such purpose, the silk being of too flimsy a nature. He would not have allowed his wife or anyone belonging to him to have gone up in such a balloon. Gas of an impure nature would be likely to render a balloon speedily unfit for use.'

The coroner recorded a verdict of accidental death with the balloon a deodand, or instrument of death. John Fley's body was taken back to south Devon by trading boat, his friends gathering on the beach to receive him home. Thousands of people crowded the funeral where he was remembered as 'kind and charitable to all who required it, who had been known to take his shirt from his back and his shoes from his feet to give to those in distress.' Rushing to help was in his nature and trying to rescue Margaret Graham cost him his life.

Margaret, of course, carried on climbing into her balloon car with the unfounded but utterly unshakable conviction that she would step back out alive. Ballooning was her livelihood and she was keen to take her children into the airy realm. More than a quarter of a century after her first flight she launched a new novelty on the public. Handbills appeared across London announcing, 'First ascent at night attempted by a female!' They showed a red and white balloon emblazoned with 'Mrs. Graham' in giant letters and the lady herself gamely waving her Union Jack in a moonlit sky. It was on 26 July 1850 at the Vauxhall Gardens and she took her daughter with her. Miss Graham was a natural and Margaret was full of pride:

> 'I cannot omit noticing the extraordinary admiration of my daughter Alice ... at the astonishing view of London, at midnight, being the first and only attempt by females to conduct the management of a balloon at night, and so much pleased am I with the nerve exhibited by those of my daughters who have hitherto accompanied me (four in number), that if on trial I find the others of equal spirit (which I doubt not), I feel disposed (God willing) to ascend with my seven daughters at the Great National Exhibition of 1851.'

As the summer progressed she introduced more of her children to ballooning to test their mettle. On her fifty-fourth ascent, from Bayswater, she took three of her daughters and her eldest son and was delighted to see they had that spirit. The effect of the view on her son and the one daughter who had not flown before was 'almost electric', much to Margaret's delight, and 'the exclamations of surprise and astonishment equal to any I have ever heard emanate from persons possessed of nerve that have accompanied me'. One thing was certain, the fearless Mrs Graham had raised a fearless brood.

THE WHITE-KNUCKLE WORLD OF MARGARET GRAHAM

There was plenty to be frightened of in her line of work. After her successful ascent with Alice, another night flight ended with her balloon in flames. 'Mrs Graham was severely scorched on the face and hands, and part of her clothing was destroyed,' says *The Illustrated London News* in August. Despite this she once again endured her injuries long enough to give her own account of what happened. Flying alone because she had 75lb of fireworks on board, she took off from Chelsea and endured a hard landing in Edmonton.

Fireworks and gas balloons were a dangerous combination but it was not the pyrotechnics that caused the inferno:

> 'I at length touched the ground, and the wind still increasing, was carried over several fields, where the grapnel took a firm hold in [a] ditch; and for half an hour I continued shouting as loud as I could for help, but to no purpose. Meanwhile, I kept the valve open to its full extent, rolling about all the while, the car at times completely turning over, and giving me plenty of trouble to retain my hold. At length, police constable 305 came over the fields to my assistance, and held on to the car. For at least twenty minutes I had no other help; but, at length additional assistance arrived, and I continued emptying the balloon. Upon walking round to see if the valve was open, a man indiscreetly came behind me with a light, which coming in contact with the escaping gas, instantaneously ignited, giving forth volume of flame which resembled the dome of St. Paul's on fire: the effect of the sudden combustion of from 8000 to 10,000 cubic feet of gas was terrific.'

Lady aeronauts emptying gas balloons do not need male rescuers who strike matches. The balloon was new and had cost a lot of money to fit out, said the newspaper, which also ran a large illustration captioned, 'Mrs Graham's balloon on fire'. People were invited to help Margaret by donating to one of two bank accounts opened for the purpose.

The appeal must have helped because she was soon back in a balloon with George, but no-one seemed surprised when their ascent the following year to mark the Great Exhibition also ended in bandages. Luckily Margaret had changed her mind about taking her seven daughters when they ascended from central London because they were in trouble almost immediately. The historic exhibition of technology from around the world was held in the Crystal Palace, the prestigious venue built to house the event in Hyde Park. Given their track record, having the Grahams fly their balloon anywhere near a building constructed largely from huge plates of glass was not the wisest plan.

'As the balloon approached the Crystal Palace great fears were entertained for the safety of a portion of that building, and of those who were inside,' says a report in the Cuthbert-Hodgson Collection. Fearing they were about to shatter the most famous new building in the British empire, Margaret and George tipped all their ballast overboard onto the palace roof. People on the ground scattered in all directions, 'At this time the grappling irons were within a few feet of the summit of the transept, and if a hold had been obtained a vast mass of the building must have been torn away.' As it was, the glasshouse escaped with only a broken flagpole. Which is more than could be said for the home of Colonel North in Arlington Street, Piccadilly, a few minutes later when the out-of-control couple smashed through the roof, taking down neighbouring chimneys as they went. Police found 'a frightful spectacle' with the balloon car jammed between the remains of two chimneys and the Grahams thrown from their seats and lying on the roof looking very dead. Once again, however, the resilience of Margaret and her husband bordered on the miraculous. They were carried to a doctor's house and though 'alarmingly contused and lacerated' they were deemed not about to die. The patched-up pair were taken home in a cab by a police officer. Patching up the apoplectic colonel's house would cost £300.

It was another extremely high-profile disaster. One Charles S. Swain decided to catalogue her catastrophes under 'Mrs Graham again!' in a letter to the editor of the *Morning Advertiser*. Cue another almighty public fight in print, where both sides are best served in their own words:

> 'We have the old familiar name again heading a fresh tissue of accidents and singular escapes. My object in troubling you is to know how long this celebrated heroine is to peril her own life and endanger others? It is not a year ago since her balloon was ignited, down by Tottenham, and herself scarified by the explosion. On coronation-day she "effected a discent,' [*Sic*] in Marylebone-lane, killed two poor creatures, and most desperately wounded others. The Duke of Brunswick's escapade also is fresh in memory; in addition to which "the new and splendid balloon" caused serious riots and loss of property at Birmingham and Welchpool not long since. I think this amount of adventure is enough to satisfy any *one*. We will rest contented with Mrs. Graham's present renown, and vote her intrepid at

once. But shall we have more of it? Are our brains yet to be dashed out by coping stones and falling stacks of chimneys, because Mrs Graham can't manage a balloon? Magistrates and police laws forbid any man to drive over, or run you down; then why is an adventurous female to be suffered to make herself a martyr with impunity, and knock our housetops upon the passers by whenever she can get "an engagement" to do so? Be good enough to satisfy me on this head, for I cannot satisfy myself.'

The letter hit a nerve. She and George were recovering from nasty injuries, besieged by pressmen and now had to read a report of the accident as no more than could be expected. Margaret was taking no prisoners. She fired off her own letter to the editor, starting with the fire, moving on to coronation day and revisiting the very sore point of the Duke of Brunswick:

'I have not the pleasure of knowing who or what Mr. Swaine [*Sic*] is, but from the untruth and acrimony of his statements I conclude he is some paid hireling, or one of those disappointed "would-be reporters," who intruded themselves yesterday at my residence, one or two of whom made the remark "that if I could give account to one I could give a later one to another." This was in answer to the information that Mrs. Graham had sent down an account to one respectable individual, and she could not be troubled for any more. Be this as it may, in justice to myself allow me follow your correspondent through his various assertions. In the first place, he says, "It is not year ago her balloon was ignited down Tottenham, &c." Pray Sir, does this prove my incapacity to manage a balloon? The night was a tempestous dark one, and pouring in torrents, I nevertheless ascended (having pledged to the public to do so), and descended safely; it certainly was a long time before I received any assistance, although shouting as loud as possible, and the lights from the Tuns Inn, Edmonton, were perfectly perceptible to me, but my grapnel having providentially taken fast hold, I went no further in distance. After the lapse of half an hour I had the pleasure of hearing a voice requesting me to come over the hedge, but as I could not do so, the welcome owner of that voice crossed to me—this was policeman Hillier, 305 N division, who remained upwards of twenty minutes before any other assistance arrived, though he was springing his ratttle as often as the rolling of the car would allow him the opportunity, and who very singularly remarked, after the remnant of the balloon was packed, "Lord grant, Ma'am, they had left you and I to finish it." In justice to this man, I cannot refrain mentioning one circumstance which highly redounds to his credit, and the force to which he belongs. On my reaching the inn above-named, after the burning of the balloon, I discovered that every thing I had in my pocket had been shaken out, by the constant rolling of the machine whilst on the ground,— amongst other articles, 46s. 6d. in silver. I made known my loss to the policeman, who advised me to say nothing to any one but the landlord and landlady, and after he was off his beat or duty in the morning, he would search for it. On my husband going down next morning, this same Hillier returned him 28s. in silver, though the place had been ransacked before he got there. Now, Sir, the ignition was perfectly accidental, but where was my want of management of a balloon upon this severe night?

'Your correspondent next says, "On Coronation-day she effected a descent in Marylebone-lane; killed two poor persons, and most desperately wounded others." This is not true. On the day named, myself and the late Captain Currie ascended from the Green Park, at two o'clock, the sun shining resplendently upon the balloon, consequently the gas was expanded to its extent, which to aeronauts is not at all desirable, inasmuch, as the air cools, the gas condenses, and becomes less and less buoyant. We remained up nearly two hours, but not a current, high or low, could we find to waft us from the metropolis; and after expending all our ballast we were compelled to descend upon a house in Marylebone-lane. One countryman, in his eagerness to render us assistance, climbed up the front of a house, and laid hold of a coping-stone, which gave way, and the poor fellow fell with the stone. He was taken to Middlesex Hospital, where he remained about three weeks; and in evidence before the Coroner it was stated, that when brought there he was in a state of inebriation, which ultimately caused erysipelas to take place, and death ensued. I am sure I have more regretted the death of this man than I think your correspondent would, or could, under any circumstances do.

There were not two men killed, nor any one most desperately wounded, as Mr. Mallilieu, of the police force, can prove, should that gentleman still belong to it. Charles Swaine next proceeds to say, "the Duke of Brunswick's escapade is also fresh in memory." I can tell your correspondent if it is not in his, it is in mine; the balloon was safe upon terra firma, and whilst I was calling to a man on my right in the field, his highness (inadvertently, I am certain) stepped out on my left. I need not tell you, Sir, the result of losing the weight of a man; if Charles Swaine is ignorant of the sudden effects of buoyancy, you are not. Where was want of judgment exemplified here? With regard to the new and splendid ballon (which, I presume, he means the one with which I and my husband ascended on Monday) having caused riots in Birmingham and Welchpool, I only beg to assure you, Sir, that the balloon was completed late in the last summer, and the only places at which any ascent was announced in the provinces, were at Gravesend, in presence of the Lord and Lady Mayoress, the Corporation of the city, and vast assemblage of spectators; from Porchester Castle, Hampshire; from Bury St. Edmond's, Suffolk; and from Woolwich. To any other place it has not yet been taken, neither have I seen the places, named by Mr. Swaine, for many years; but if you, Sir, think a detail of the misfortunes occasioned to the now living aeronauts by deficiencies of gas at various places, would be acceptable to your general readers, I will with pleasure meet Mr. Swaine, and enter into a copious detail of the disappointments occasioned by all; and am happy to say, that to the satisfaction of yourself, or any other respectable editor, I shall come off victorious. With regard to knocking out brains, if your correspondent has suffered the loss of any by a balloon descending upon a house (and I am sure in his case the loss would have been a calamity, if ever so trifling a portion), will he good enough to say by whose balloon it was occasioned; as mine is not the only one that has fallen on a house coping and chimnies. With regard to my management of a balloon, I would refer to many living gentlemen for their decision as to my ability, amongst whom are Jas. McTaggart, Esq., who has ascended twice with me, also with Messrs. Green, and the late Mr. Gale; Sir Francis Hopkins, Bart.; Mr. Gregory, the late

M.P. for Dublin; Mr. Court, late colonel of the Lumber Troop; Mr. Mazzucchi, Mr. Bertenshaw, of Shrewsbury; Messrs. Rogers and Tunnecliffe, of Leeds; Captain White, and about 20 other gentlemen and ladies, including Captain Elliot, R N., who accompanied me from Vauxhall Gardens, upon the occasion of her most gracious Majesty's birthday. I really must apologise for troubling you at such a length, but feel certain, as you have given insertion to your correspondent's letter, you will also to mine. The public, as well as yourself, Sir, will look with the same opinion, I feel convinced, at such an unmerited, dastardly attack being made upon a female, the mother of a large family, and at so trying a moment as the present.'

Dastardly, it was, *dastardly*. Only then did Margaret allow herself to collapse back into the pillows to recuperate. It is noticeable that she blames John Fley for his own death, as a drunk who dislodged the stones himself and went on to die of a skin infection. This may spring from unreported details at the inquest, or a guilty conscience. Either way, she certainly did not kill *two* people. One was unfortunate, two really might have been carelessness. Mr Swain was delighted with getting a rise, so to speak, out of the aeronaut and wrote another letter to the editor, accusing her of being high-handed about the press and anyway, aerostation was a dangerous waste of time.

Margaret, always a woman to be reckoned with, was now fit to be tied. Her usual articulate and lightning-fast response begins with a defence of her relationship with the gentlemen of the press. It is a fascinating glimpse into how a nineteenth century celebrity looked after the press so they looked after her, always finding time for a briefing over a cup of tea whatever time she arrived home from work, exhausted:

'Many of those gentlemen I have known for years, and after returning home, at two or three o'clock AM., after an ascent and descent, will acknowledge that I have remained up at my own residence an hour or two very often when I found them waiting my return, and over an early cup of tea supplied them with the information they required, as to place of decent, &c. &c. I did not apply the term "paid hireling" to the respectable class of men alluded to, but I said, I concluded *he was a paid hireling,* by whom I leave him to guess, *or one of those would-be reporters,* who do not know when they call upon an individual (even though that one is the property of the public) how to conduct themselves in a gentlemanly manner.'

She demands details and evidence after Swain implies a passenger died from brain fever after a ride in her balloon. Then she tackles his criticism of her ability head on. She is loved by charities all over the country for her fundraising ascents. If Swain will 'ascend with me willingly,' the proceeds will go to 'a fund for the benefit of aged and decayed respectable reporters of the press of this country, than whom a more deserving or enlightened class of men does not exist.' She is understandably vexed that he only highlights her misadventures when she has an impressive record of managing a balloon in tough conditions. How come a solo flight to mark Queen Victoria's public entry into Windsor when 'the rain poured down in torrents' somehow 'did not prove my ability to manage a balloon.' Then she gets to the nub of the matter. If he hated ballooning so much, why did he save up all his scorn for her?

> 'If Mr. Swain's intention is only to provide for the public safety, why did he not attack aeronauts of his own sex, when reverses have occurred, and loss of life ensued, or descending upon house tops and taking off coping stones? Such opportunities have been afforded him, but for some sinister design he awaits an opportunity of attacking a female. Perhaps he thought he could do so with impunity.'

That was enough for now, decided the newspaper. 'With this letter the correspondence between Mr. Swain and Mrs. Graham must close.–EDITOR' Mr Swain had to abide by the veto and content himself with equally barbed letters on other issues of the day. The caustic correspondent had not finished with Margaret, though, and confidently awaited her next mishap.

Margaret is every inch the wronged Victorian diva defending her name, although behind the fury lies genuine fear. George was 66 and had been seriously injured in the accident. He had a gash to the head, broken breastbone, fractured collarbone and various other injuries. Margaret suffered nasty cuts to her head and face but their livelihood now depended even more heavily on her. Though often fighting a rearguard action against her critics, Margaret was a resilient woman. She had to be, she had a big family to feed. With George an invalid, her relentless workload demanded great mental and physical strength. The demonstrable danger would have lead many in her position to retire from the profession before it killed her.

Instead she doggedly carried on, year in, year out, showing a huge amount of aptitude and quick-thinking, for all her accidents. Whatever scars and aches she carried from the falls and fires, flight never lost its hold over her life.

It seems George never fully recovered from the injuries he sustained in the Great Exhibition crash and that was his last recorded flight. Margaret soldiered on, ascending with a male passenger in Dublin in 1853 only to suffer, as the *Dublin Evening Mail* puts it, a 'series of disasters, which have eventuated in the almost entire destruction of the balloon, and in the serious hazard of the lives of the lady and gentlemen adventurers...' In an all too familiar scenario, the balloon failed to reach a safe height and careened along at roof level, knocking off coping stones and demolishing chimneys. Margaret remained impressively cool (it was not as if she had not been here before) when the car caught between the gables of a double roof:

> 'The excitement amongst the people in the streets was considerable; crowds rushed towards the spot where it was expected the balloon would fall, and few dared to hope that either of the aeronauts could escape fatal injury.'

Police and friends rushed to help, tearing the balloon to release the gas. 'After immense exertion Mrs. Graham and Mr. Kennedy were rescued from their perilous position, and the remnants of the balloon secured.' The Irish fans praised her courage and presence of mind throughout. Another day, another crazy accident, another set of bruises. It was all taking its toll. The Dublin bookings had been exhausting and the damage to the balloon led to more problems later in the year. In November Margaret was in Manchester County Court, embroiled in a row over a failed booking where the balloon would not inflate, no matter how much gas was poured into it. Margaret was forced to say why, according to *The Manchester Courier*:

> 'In cross-examination by Mr. Saunders the lady admitted that the balloon had been broken and torn very much at Dublin by coming in contact with some chimney pots.'

Which is putting it mildly. Then came what sounded very like one of Margaret's tall tales. 'A Captain Kennedy accompanied her upon one of her ascents, and he bowed to the lady of the Lord Lieutenant who was in the gardens below them, taking off his hat and bending his body, and that had the effect of bringing down the balloon.' The judge examined the balloon, saw all the inadequate patches and ordered Margaret to pay up.

After that, she appears to have retired. As the 1860s dawned the Grahams both appear in the census as aeronauts but their flying days appear to have been over. By then Margaret was 57 and the couple lived in Eastcheap, a street near Monument, with their son and two daughters. George and Margaret worked side by side for more than four decades. They flew together, crashed together, faced down their foes together and battled on with their balloons through every kind of adversity. They studied the stars and the doings of Venus and had nine children. Exactly when Margaret finally said goodbye to the sky is not clear but she died aged 60 in 1864, on the 26th anniversary of her coronation day crash. Having escaped death so often from tumbles, tree branches, chimneys and fires she died quietly at her London home in Upper Thames Street. The cause of death was dropsy, the general term for severe fluid retention that could have been caused by a number of things, ranging from liver disease to heart failure. Despite her phenomenal career as a professional aeronaut, Margaret's occupation was reduced to 'wife of William George Graham, a chemist' on the death certificate. She didn't even get a headstone to mark her glorious life. Impoverished in retirement, she was buried in a pauper's grave at Abney Park Cemetery in Stoke Newington, where George joined her three years later, aged 82.

The amazing Mrs Margaret Graham might have always flown on a wing and a prayer, she might have caused death and destruction along the way – while resolutely never accepting the blame – but she always survived to ascend another day. Considering the sheer number of scrapes she managed to extricate herself from and the many horrible injuries she sustained (she must have had the face of a prize fighter) the fact that she lived into her 60s is remarkable. She was Britain's pre-eminent female aeronaut of the nineteenth century.

The predictable glee with which Charles S. Swain took up his toxic pen again after Margaret's crash in Dublin irked the distinguished fellow aeronaut Henry Coxwell. In August 1853 he wrote an elegant defence of both his misjudged colleague and of ballooning itself. It serves well as a final tribute to her courage and persistence. It was written, as ever, to that great conduit of balloon-based feuds, the editor of the *Morning Advertiser*:

> 'The Parliamentary debates have ceased to occupy their accustomed lengths in your interesting columns; but, as if to compensate your numerous readers for the oratorical loss sustained, Mr. Charles S. Swain, your great correspondent

on ballooning, publishes his first epistle this season, and, with a degree of zeal no less than impetuosity, rushes at Mrs. Graham on the housetops —where, instead of displaying that chivalrous gallantry which we all admire in the noblest portion of creation, he proceeds (shall I say with malice aforethought?) to precipitate the fair *voyageur* to the very dust, and, with sundry blows fiercely dealt by his angry pen, well steeped in gall during the summer months, to goad the unfortunate lady while yet on the ground, and then to recall and array all her past professional accidents in methodical and business-like order, with the intention, it would appear, of annihilating Mrs. Graham with one fell swoop ... Mr. Swain, like Mrs. Graham, is evidently not tired of ballooning; he has merely retired to a quiet place of ambuscade—not, however, without spreading his web to catch the first unwary fly. The gossamer wings of the aerial traveller no sooner foul, than down pounces Mr. Spider, and labours to carry off the prize. On more than one occasion I have seen a fly escape a spider, and revel in free air, whilst the latter hung suspended and disappointed. Mrs. Graham, too, has made a safe passage since her unsuccessful trip in Dublin, that she has risen above a recent misfortune. Now, Sir, in plain concise terms, I contend, that all Mr. Swain can convince us about aerial travelling is, that, like all other modes, it is dangerous. Who denies it? But, admitting the dangers which ever accompany, more or less, a temporary absence from our firesides, whether by balloon, boat, or rail—admitting this, is that sufficient warrant for those oft-repeated and laborious attempts to slight aeronauts and ridicule the journey *in nubibus* [the clouds]? Your intelligent readers must be the best judges; but I have notion that some few of the writers on this subject are averse to observe less-gifted fellow-creatures so far above them; and that, as a natural consequence, because there are few coaches, and they have no taste for balloons, they rail.'

Chapter 7

Queens of the American Clouds

When balloons arrived in America, balloon riots were not far behind. As the nation's first female pilot watched New York's finest in a punch up with her howling fans, there was no debate. Balloon madness was in full swing and if the mob did not get what it wanted, a lady aeronaut needed to know where the back doors were. In the 1820s the magnificent Madame Johnson had her work cut out on the cloudy frontier. The founding mother of female flight in the States was either an American or an international woman of mystery. She was only ever described as Madame Johnson and the lack of a first name was all part of her mystique. What *was* recorded was her landmark flight from New York in 1825, when she led women into the United States sky. The rioting came later.

The early aeronauts often assumed French names regardless of where they were born, though everything points to Madame Johnson hailing from France. She flew the French and American flags and knew the Blanchards in Europe. Both Sophie and Jean-Pierre were long dead from balloon disasters by 1825, so clearly Madame Johnson was not easily discouraged. At 5pm on 24 October she became the first woman to fly in America. The place was Castle Garden, a fort transformed into a fair ground and now part of the Battery. It had only recently gone from being a military base ready (but never needed) to keep the British out of Manhattan during the War of 1812 to a relaxed open-air entertainment venue. It was a good place for America's first female aeronaut to make a little history.

'Madame Johnson, handsomely attired, made her appearance, amid the huzzahs of thousands,' reports the *Ladies Museum*:

> 'In two or three minutes from the time of her entrance into the area of the Garden, she was seated in her car, and with the American and French flags, and a graceful inclination of her body, she saluted the respectable thousands who occupied

the seats and walks which cover the arcade of this spacious promenade.'

To prevent the balloon hitting the arch over the arena, the cord-bearers climbed the main stairway:

> 'and when it was committed to the mercy of the heavens, the ascent was not only rapid but highly interesting; and the gazing multitude for some minutes was motionless, and gave way to expressions of the most intense solicitude as to the fair object who had thus jeopardized her life by exposing it in so frail a machine.'

Thirty thousand people watched her float away and remained rooted to the spot until 'the Balloon was apparently reduced, from its distance, to a mere black speck, resembling, in size, the crown of a hat.' The first female pilot in America touched down in a salt marsh on the Brooklyn shore, just before reaching the ocean. She was driven back to the city in a gig, arriving at 9pm. 'After changing her attire, she repaired to Castle Garden, where she was received with the warmest congratulations.'

Madame worked from the outdoor venues springing up around Manhattan. Like Vauxhall in London and the Tuileries in Paris, they were perfect for a bit of ticketed balloonomania. Three years after her first ascent she was working out of Niblo's Garden, the exclusive new haunt on Broadway. Niblo's was an upmarket venue where prices were steep and the clientele discerning. It would become the hub of the city's theatreland and on 23 July 1828 it was already a prime location for wealthy New Yorkers in search of amusement.

Unfortunately, the well-heeled ticket holders inside got more of a show than they bargained for when the hoi polloi that gathered outside to watch for free went on the rampage. A problem with the gas supply meant Madame had to release the insufficiently filled balloon without being on board and the mob outside the gates had to be quelled by watchmen (early police).

Balloon riots had always been the dark side of balloon mania and disappointed New Yorkers were no exception. Madame Johnson dusted herself off and set up an ascent for later the same year in Philadelphia. She even held out for more money, cancelling the show in front of the crowd until her demands were met. The proceeds at the gate would not even cover her costs. There was no riot, there was a pay rise and she pulled off a perfect performance on 27 October.

A colourful account of the ascent reveals more about prevailing attitudes to women than their demonstrable abilities in the air. A reporter from *The Ariel* joined the crowd moving towards the ascent at the Liberty Inn, where 'the grounds were covered with a dark, humming mass of human beings' looking forward to Madame's 'second grand aerial ascension'. The aeronaut was well underway with inflating the balloon, which is not described as readers would have seen it for themselves, apparently, plus 'our inability to do it with the use of proper terms.'

The balloonist, however, knew every inch of her kit:

> 'In an incredibly short time from the commencement, all was ready. Madame Johnson entered the enclosure, beautifully attired; her plumes waving, and with a smiling countenance, took her seat in the car. We watched her features pretty intently – and she looked perfectly calm and collected. The ropes were then severed and with the strength of a tiger released from his cage, the majestic object rose in the air. A shout of congratulations burst from the spectators, as the intrepid Aeronaut waved her flags from her perilous seat.'

She rose swiftly, until 'her banners had faded to little white atoms, and the Balloon itself seemed but a diminished little globe, swaying about in the changeful atmosphere, and reeling in the abyss of heaven.'

Her skilful ascent was impressive so it is a shame the reporter imagined a pathetic figure with no choice but to fly for a living:

> 'As we gazed at the little dark object, we could not but reflect how great must be the necessity which could thus impel a woman, with all the meekness of her nature, thus to jeopardize her life in a manner, which, did her situation permit she would gladly relinquish.'

The writer gets quite carried away with what he assumes is going on in Madame's mind:

> 'We thought what contending emotions of anxiety and uncertainty were revolving in that immortal mind, thus pending

between us and Heaven! – Isolated from the world – above and beneath her the abyss – and the fearful fluctuations of the atmosphere to encounter in a descent round which so many dangers clung! Doubtless much of this *was* felt; – and as we thought of the conflicts of that "human heart, with its dreams and sighs," – of the yearnings which must possess it for herself, and her fatherless children – and the fantasies which so rapid and perilous a flight must create in the strongest brain, we could not but ejaculate a wish, that the exertions of a mother for her offspring thus so clearly shown, might be directed into a safer and more agreeable channel.'

Whether there were any fatherless children at the event or they were simply supposed to exist somewhere is hard to tell. *The Ariel* describes itself as a literary and critical gazette, so this perhaps accounts for the flight of fancy over the simple facts. Those being that Madame, working mother or not, had staged another successful solo ascent. There is no evidence of a meek nature and if she was not fazed by rioting New Yorkers, it is difficult to believe she clung quivering to her perch yearning to be released from her unnatural profession. No female aeronaut ever described her thoughts in the air as those assumed to be 'doubtless' here. Neither did they ever report feeling forced into a balloon car by cruel fate. Other theories did the rounds as she voyaged happily above. 'One thought Madame Johnson's motives were more for fame, and to be "the observed of all observers," than for the sake of her children.' Lady aeronauts were no stranger to disapproval or mockery and a punster weighed in with, 'Madame J. was at present *above* his reproaches; that she stood *high,* and was beyond the reach of his animadversions.'

Female ballooning was a slower burn in America than in Europe but once La Johnson lifted off there was no going back. Madame floats out of the record with her plumes waving but if anything like fellow pioneers, adventure would always be a way of life.

When Lucretia Bradley bought a beat-up balloon called *Vesperus* from touring aeronaut John Wise, she, too, was driven by bold ambition, not tragic necessity. Wise was famous for bursting balloons and also for selling them on to trusting amateurs. Despite the dubious quality of her hundred-dollar purchase (even Wise felt a pang about selling it to her) Lucretia was all ready to risk it at Easton, Pennsylvania, in January 1855. The car looked good, even if the balloon did not. It was decorated with gold and silver tassels and long ribbons of red, white and blue. On either side were flags in the same ribbon trimmed with silver stars taken from a vintage fan that belonged to her grandmother. Lucretia stepped aboard, a novice aeronaut wearing a red velvet skirt covered with more of grandma's stars. What happened next was so unforgettable that she could recall the whole story for an interview in her seventies.

'I rose with perfect calmness and great velocity to a height of over two miles, my whole feelings being those of indescribable tranquility and gratified delight,' she told *The Courier-Journal* of Kentucky in 1898:

> 'There was no perceptible breeze until I reached the highest point of my voyage, directly over the Delaware, when four heavy currents struck my balloon on all sides with equal force. Finding my balloon full, I opened the valve three times in succession, and while letting off gas as fast as I could, the balloon at the same time rapidly emptying itself from the mouth, a very strong undercurrent forcing up the mouth of the balloon caused a roaring like the ocean in a heavy storm, followed by a noise like the discharge of a cannon and a sudden fall of about a hundred feet.'

The patched old balloon had burst but Lucretia did not panic. Lucretia did not, in fact, feel worried at all:

> 'I then looked up and saw the balloon all shattered, with the exception of two pieces, one being about one-eighth the size of the balloon. One formed a parachute on the top of the network and the other a sail at the side. These bore me off eastward. The wind rocked the car violently at the time and for ten minutes succeeding. Knowing my situation, I had no feeling of fright or anxiety whatever, but tranquilly trusting in that same Almighty power I always loved to trust, I prepared myself in the best possible manner I could for my descent, believing I should land safely.
>
> 'I threw out my sand and grappling iron, placed myself firmly in the car in an upright position, my hands extended clasped the handles on each side. I alternately looked on each side and admired the grandeur and beauty of the scene, in fact I spent ten minutes singing a song of praise to the Creator of such a scene of beauty and sublime grandeur.'

THE LOST HISTORY OF THE LADY AERONAUTS

In this impressive manner Lucretia descended rapidly to earth and landed with a tremendous thump in the middle of a New Jersey clover field. She had been in the air for thirty minutes, twenty of them after her balloon had burst at two miles high. This might have put some people off ballooning, but not Lucretia:

> 'I afterward built another balloon and stationed it at Elmira. N. Y., during the State Fair. I spent there $3,000 in building a scientific machine to manufacture gas on an improved plan.'

John Wise, relieved that she survived his duff old balloon, always considered Lucretia one of the most heroic women in America. In fact, he said, determined women in general were more daring than men. Despite her substantial spending on kit and research, lighter-than-air flight was only one of Lucretia's interests. As a well-known phrenologist, attempting to understand the mind with measurements of the skull, she lectured and published theories based on charts of the body. She was good friends with fellow pioneering medic Dr Mary Walker. Mary was the only woman to work as a battlefield surgeon in the Union Army during the American Civil War. She was derided for her habit of wearing comfortable male clothes but sheer bravery, skill and time spent as a prisoner of war won her the Medal of Honor. Mary fought for women's rights all her life and endured a decade-long battle for a divorce. Lucretia was part of her freethinking circle and the doctor hosted the aeronaut's unconventional wedding to artist Algernon Hubbell, a union that celebrated the marriage of equals.

By the middle of the nineteenth century, ballooning belonged to the barnstormers. Flashy travelling aeronauts were everywhere and women were often an intrinsic part of the show. Nothing could compete with the intoxicating mix of glamour and genuine danger the balloon girls trailed into town. America was soon awash with professional aeronauts travelling the states with sensational sideshows and exotic stage names. Their lives were, naturally, full of ups and downs. Mademoiselle Emma V., for example, had good days and bad days. *The Daily Green-Mountain Freeman* in February 1848 reports a splash landing in Louisiana:

> 'M'dle Emma V., a female Aeronaut, has made several successful balloon ascensions at New Orleans lately. Her last

ascension however did not end very agreeably, as she came down plump into the river, where she got a most thorough ducking.'

Happily, she had her dignity back by December, according to the *Daily Crescent*.

'A second ascension took place on Sunday week in Baton Rouge. Miss Emma V. ascended beautifully ... and after an aerial voyage of about twenty minutes, descended about one mile from the place of starting. The weather was beautiful and clear, and the balloon passed over the centre of the town, giving a full chance to all our citizens of witnessing the intrepidity and bold daring of this female aeronaut.'

As impressive acts go it was hard to beat the Connecticut trapeze artist known as Leona Dare, whose chosen soubriquet was Queen of the Antilles (she had Mexican roots). She was a formidable woman with formidable talents, not least the 'iron jaw' act that brought her worldwide fame. Sometimes she was taken aloft holding on by her teeth to the bit attached to her trapeze. Other times she lifted fellow acrobats into the air using her iron jaw. An *Indianapolis Sentinel* report from the summer of 1872 describes her first ascent in the circus of Joel E. Warner with her trainer turned husband, Tommy Hall:

'Warner has actually persuaded a young and beautiful Spanish girl, named Leona Dare, who does marvellous feats upon the trapeze in the circus, to make balloon ascensions. The trial trip was made on Thursday morning at a point about nine miles southeast of our city. The balloon was duly inflated, and at a quarter to eight was cut loose, and the fine-formed Leona, in circus clothes, dangling downward from the trapeze bar, holding in her teeth a strap which encircled the waist of Tommy Hall, her companion for her very first voyage in the air, left *terra firma*. Everything was still as death, and it was observed that Hall weakened a little, but the plucky "Queen of the Antilles," Leona, was perfectly cool. Just as soon as they left the earth Leona commenced spinning Hall around until it made us giddy. After this performance, and about three hundred feet in the air, they commenced their hifalutin performances, known in show language as the double trapeze; and almost everybody who has attended the circus can imagine much better than we can describe their various evolutions and gyrations.'

Leona landed laughing and asked the compere, 'How was that for high?' She became an international star and was especially popular in London and Paris. Like many celebrities, Leona saw her private life played out in the papers. In 1879 her marriage to Tommy had broken down and they were fighting for custody of a custom-built trapeze in a British court. Leona appears to have walked out on Tommy and the judge, Mr Justice Denman, found the whole matter a hoot, according to a press report from June of that year:

> 'Leona Dare ran away, her husband followed and found that she had gone to Paris. The only remark that the learned judge had to make was, "That's the effect of a man teaching his wife to fly," whereupon, we are informed, there followed much laughter.'

The late-nineteenth century fashion in flying circuses was for parachuting women. Ladies leaping from balloons were all the rage and any outfit that could boast a skydiving showgirl was on to a winner. Though they became sought-after stars, their real identities were elusive. Amid the impressive titles and stage names, ones acquired at birth could get lost in the mix. For example, the first name of the Mrs Van Tassel who threw late 1880s Los Angeles into uproar is a mystery. The confusion stems from her husband's legal wife being Clara Coykendall, other reports of a lady barnstormer called Jeanette Van Tassel and Parker running a troupe of aeronauts, including a daughter Jenny and sisters called Valerie and Gladys Freitas, who all used his name.

Whatever her first name and relationship to the pilot, the tenacious Mrs Van Tassel who launched herself out of a balloon on the fourth of July 1888 certainly made her mark on the city of angels. As soon as the couple announced the parachute jump, LA fizzed with a heady mixture of excitement and fear. Knocking over the ex-mayor's chimney during rehearsals did not inspire confidence and there were calls for the police to stop the lady balloonist committing suicide on a national holiday. 'The Chief took the writer's view of the matter,' reports the *Los Angeles*

Herald, 'and ordered Detective Tom McCarthy to be on hand at the time appointed for the ascension and unless Mrs. Van Tassell gave her word of honor not to make the leap, to prohibit her from going up in the balloon.' Charged with the unenviable task of grounding the balloon, the hapless detective told Mrs Van T that women were not allowed in balloons and it was a men-only amusement. This merely served to make the Van Tassells take off before lawmen could ruin the fun. 'The hardy aeronaut and his wife heard of what the Chief was going to do, and they decided to get heavenward with all possible speed.' The parachutist, pilot and a leading local balloonist cast off in a tearing hurry, leaving the thwarted LA police department staring upwards in fury and everyone else wondering why the balloon was in the air three hours earlier than advertised. The madcap escape simply added to the drama and an angel appeared over the city as promised, though locals argued into the night about whether they had seen a living lady or a stuffed dummy. By the following day, eyewitnesses had silenced the doubters and 'Mrs. Van Tassel was the recipient throughout the day of a storm of congratulations from numerous admirers.' Such touch-and-go drama never failed to appeal. Women who flouted convention in the name of dangerous entertainment were in demand. While balloonists outran the cops into the sky, Annie Oakley promised sharp-shooting thrills at ground level with Buffalo Bill's Wild West Show.

The risks for the aeronauts were very real. Aliss Ruby Deveau was billed as Queen of the Clouds when she worked the southern states. The German-born teenager worked as an actress in a travelling vaudeville troupe before ballooning beckoned in 1892 when she was 15. She saw a parachute display in Memphis, Tennessee, and applied on the spot. She clocked up 175 skydives over the following three years until, barely 18, she broke her back crashing into a chimney in Ontario, Canada. The young queen was forced to retire from the clouds and retrain as a legal stenographer.

Stars of the 1900s such as Tiny Broadwick were the last generation of stuntwomen to begin their careers in balloons and end them in aircraft. She too was a feisty 15-year-old when she began life as a parachutist. Georgia Thompson earned the name Tiny Broadwick from being 4ft 8ins tall, weighing 85lbs and being dressed like a baby doll by manager Charles Broadwick, who posed as her father. Tiny, from North Carolina, looked like a little girl jumping into the wide blue yonder. In fact, she had been married, widowed and was working in a cotton mill to support herself and her baby by the time she volunteered for the carnival in 1908. Balloons looked a lot more fun than the twelve hours a day she had worked in the mill since she was eight years old. So began her career as a diminutive daredevil and in 1913 near San Diego, California, she became the first person in the world to parachute from an aeroplane. Her only regret, she admitted as an old lady, was being born too early to walk on the moon.

One balloonist outdid all the sky-going sisterhood. Of the early aeronauts, none was more adept or adaptable than the balloon farmer of upstate New York, Mary Breed Hawley. She was born in 1849, married photographer and inventor Carl Myers in 1871 and settled on 'Carlotta, the Lady Aeronaut' as her name for the top of the bill. Like many male aeronauts, her husband adopted the title of 'Professor' but had more justification than most. He ran the test grounds and workshops at their homestead, Balloon Farm in Frankfort, New York. It was named for its peculiar appearance, with rows of semi-inflated balloons lying in the fields out front as if waiting to be harvested. The Myers were industrious and well matched, working together to master the sky. Mary made her mark with daring displays in the air and Carl built their balloon-making business on the ground.

Mary's technical expertise and uncanny ability to read the high winds meant she was seldom pitched into the kind of catastrophes that plagued her counterparts. Her claim to be the queen of the air was well earned, though she almost came a cropper in the stormy September of 1880 at a fair in Norwich, New York, just two months into her flying career. 'A lady aeronaut's narrow escape' was reported in *The New York Times*, after Mary 'found herself in rather an unpleasant situation before she reached the end of her ride.' She had reached a height of two miles and travelled for two miles before the weather intervened:

> 'Encountering a cloud of rain, she threw out ballast, and everything in the basket, but the balloon became heavy from rain, and, descending, dragged up on the top of a basswood tree 80 feet high. A party of men who were out hunting discovered her perilous situation, and proceeded to the rescue, which was no slight task. A long ladder was procured, and upon ascending the tree it was found necessary to cut limbs from it, and the lady was with difficulty rescued, after remaining in the tree-top for an hour and a half, in a drenching storm.'

The incident was the nearest Mary ever came to joining the sad roll call of aeronauts who died in (parachute) harness. Instead it became a gripping story with a happy ending for her memoirs, *Aerial Adventures of Carlotta; or, Sky-Larking in Cloudland*. The notable omission from newspaper reports was her leading role in effecting her own rescue. The landing was frightening, but she kept her head:

> 'I was just beginning to think the world had somehow got loose and lost itself, when, through an opening in the mist, the earth suddenly jumped up at me, and I found myself swiftly driving at a few feet elevation over a woods several miles in extent.'

She threw her waterproof, rubber boots and carrier pigeons overboard in a bid to rise clear but the balloon 'bounded rapidly across the tree-tops, with "a hop, skip and a jump;" the basket collecting leaves, twigs and acorns at every plunge, till an immense bass wood tree, looming high above the forest, threatened to wreck craft, crew and cargo.'

Mary cast her anchor and the grapple caught on two branches, stopping her from plunging on but leaving her a long way from safety. 'The air ship was at anchor, in sight of land, – but there was no little boat to go to shore!' The balloon was stuck 20ft from the tree trunk, 80ft from the ground and more than two miles from the nearest house. All Mary could do was sit tight and call for help. Luckily, she was heard by puzzled hunters who were answering her calls without looking up. Eventually one saw her and burst out laughing, asking whether she could not have found a taller tree to land in. Mary took immediate charge, sending for an axe, a saw, some ropes and the best climber in the area. He duly arrived but declared it an impossible climb.

'I said it *must* be done, and sent for a long ladder, meanwhile employing other men in cutting down six smaller trees below the balloon, so that it might be safely lowered,' she recalls. The climber ascended the ladder but again quailed at her plan, which was to saw through the branches holding the balloon. With admirable restraint, she patiently persuaded the men that it would work:

> 'When it was found that I purposed sawing off these two limbs they all said it could not be done, as they were very large and would come down on me and kill me. I said I had a plan to prevent that and would take all the risk if they would obey orders.'

Her cool command of the situation won through. She directed the ropes being arranged so they were tied around the two branches in such a way that just before each was sawn through, the men could heave at the rope and ensure they landed harmlessly on lower branches to one side rather than Mary. Then the ropes were used to lower the basket to the ground, branch by branch. After two hours dangling precariously from the tree in a rainstorm, Mary was safe:

> 'We were all much fatigued, and glad to shake hands together, as we felt quite like old friends. The men said they never knew a woman who could engineer a job so well before, but I guess that may be that they never before caught one "up a tree!"'

The following Spring Mary gave birth to a daughter and the new member of the ballooning family was named Elizabeth Aerial. Mary did not take much maternity leave, climbing back into a balloon in Hamilton on the fourth of July 1881, then hopping onto a train to meet Carl in Utica for the second ascent of the day. They were home for the baby's bedtime. Carlotta the lady aeronaut was soon in demand across America and Canada and in 1886 she claimed a record for the highest ascent in a balloon filled with natural gas. Though difficult to prove, she rose to 21,000ft (almost four miles) from Franklin, Pennsylvania.

With two or three ascents a week through the 1880s, she had her performance down to a fine art. The 4 July gig on Coney Island in 1888 was her 'three hundred and fifth trip skyward' and the 150,000-strong crowd was 'in high feather', according to the *New York Times*. The aeronaut 'wore a yellow dress, with trimmings of old gold' and 'sailed merrily over the big elephant, threw out a bag of sand, and waved a big handkerchief furiously.' Sometimes she spiced it up by pretending to be an old lady stealing the balloon in front of flabbergasted spectators.

The kit was key to her reputation for reliability despite a punishing schedule. Carl developed a sturdy, lightweight balloon with a flexible coating that could be emptied quickly, folded down small and bundled into a bag for quick exits. The lady aeronaut, meanwhile, developed and patented a nimble balloon car. The floor was suspended from a ring by netting and could be tilted to steer. In this way, she could control her descent like a surfer. The ingenious basket was also easy to collapse and pack and weighed just 7lbs.

Some of Mary's biggest coups came from her intimate understanding of air currents. She could ride the air like a bird, navigating her course with the shifts in the wind. Staring into the sky before ascending she would read the clouds and predict her route, sending a carriage ahead to pick her up. Her knack of knowing her exact destination never ceased to amaze and won her a reputation as 'mistress of the winds'. It also won a famous bet in 1888 when she proved she could predict her precise course in her balloon *Zephyr* from Brooklyn to Jersey City via the Battery, Brooklyn Bridge and New York City Hall.

Mary never rested on her laurels and was fascinated by balloon engineering. She was always experimenting with faster, more controlled flight using innovations such as a screw-sail and a rudder kite operated by hand as though sailing in a boat. Her secret weapon was the Flying Dutchman, a collapsible sail she swore by but never advertised. This command of both the air and her equipment gave her an enviable safety record. The *Harmsworth Magazine* noted that she was 'an aeronaut of no mean ability ... and not a single accident has occurred.'

When Elizabeth Aerial (known as Bessie) was three she became the world's littlest lady aeronaut. Mary planned another fun ride when Bessie was seven. Instead it was one of the rare occasions when skylarking went awry. Mary got her ballast sums wrong and they landed in a steep-sided lake near Syracuse. Luckily the little girl named for the sky was every inch her mother's daughter. She climbed onto a log with the anchor rope, waded ashore and dragged the basket and her mother to safety. After that, Bessie preferred working behind the scenes as a test pilot on the farm. Her favourite balloons were invented by her father and in 1903 she demonstrated the ingenious sky-cycle at the St Louis Exposition, navigating the hybrid balloon's course by means of pedal power. According to *Pearson's Magazine*:

> 'the last proof was shown of the flying machine's complete control by its operator – a seventeen year old girl, daughter of the inventor – flying with the machine through a maze of columns and festoonery in the large exposition building crowded to the doors with thousands of amazed spectators.'

Mary spent a decade as Carlotta and retired in 1891 after around a thousand ascents, the most successful balloonist in America. She was 42 and happy not to have starred in any horror stories. For the next two decades, she concentrated her talents on the research at Balloon Farm. The Myers mansion was a hive of activity between 1889 and 1910. Carl patented the tough fabric coating and his strange crop was in demand everywhere from meteorology stations to the army. His most startling experiments involved exploding balloons to make it rain. When they finally decided to put their feet up, the USA's first couple of the air went to live with Bessie in Atlanta. Mary and her husband shared a passion for balloons that made them money and made them happy.

The pioneering women of America loved a frontier and ballooning gave them plenty. Adopting personas as big as their ambitions, every performer from Madame Johnson to Tiny Broadwick laid claim to the freedom of the clouds. Over a sensational century they put their courage to work as they looked down on cheering crowds from New York to Los Angeles. Little wonder they claimed to be the queens of the sky, of the air, of all they surveyed.

Chapter 8

Champers and Hampers ... How the Other Half Flew

No-one captures the sheer thrill of ballooning quite like pioneering English aeronaut, author and journalist Gertrude Bacon. As a liberated lady adventurer, she revelled in one airborne escapade after another. While fellow Victorian ballooniac Jules Verne wrote novels such as *Five Weeks in a Balloon*, gung-ho Gertie simply shared the fabulous adventures she enjoyed in real life. Every heart-stopping moment in the clouds was captured in vivid accounts and fabulous photographs that held readers of her books and articles spellbound. Through her writing and public speaking, have-a-go Gertrude brought ballooning to the people. Born into an enlightened and well-connected family that allowed her to follow her interests, she never lost her boundless enthusiasm for 'sky-sailing' through a wondrous 'cloudland'. An indefatigable fan of flying who loved to bag a first, she spent a lifetime notching up a series of landmark achievements. Though the first woman to fly in an airship, the first passenger in a seaplane and the first Englishwoman to fly in an aeroplane, her early ballooning adventures remained the benchmark for everything that followed.

When bouncing baby Gertrude arrived in Cambridge on 19 April 1874 she was named after her mother but caught the ballooning bug from her father. The Reverend John Mackenzie Bacon filled her childhood with exciting stories about ballooning and star-gazing that launched her towards a career in the clouds. Gertrude was part of an educated and accomplished clan. Great-great-grandfather was sculptor John Bacon and the family tree boasted at least one bishop and the military commander who invented khaki uniform. Her uncle Harry was known as 'Lumsden of the Guides' after the elite corps he raised in the Punjab and clothed in local dust-coloured – 'khaki' – cloth. Her scholarly father was known as 'Bacon of the sky' for his work as an astronomer and aeronaut and Gertrude grew up among the nineteenth century luminaries who often visited their home.

When she was a toddler, poor health forced the reverend to give up university tutoring in Cambridge and ship the family to the village of Cold Ash near Newbury. Her father threw himself into his scientific research and good works among the poor and young Gertrude watched how the other half lived. In her autobiography *Memories of Land and Sky*, Gertrude describes the poverty she saw among the 'Berkshire yokels', pondering on what counted as happiness from a position of upper class comfort. Farm labourers were quite content with their lot, she concluded with patrician certainty, 'their lives were hard, their food scanty, their clothes deplorable, their cottages too often the merest hovels. But were they happy or content?' Emphatically yes, she avers. 'They lived as their forefathers had done and they knew and expected no otherwise.'

Gertrude, of an altogether different class, had every reason to expect a good deal more out of her life. The comfortable Bacon home in its own nine acres was also her school. Her father believed in learning through curiosity rather than a formal curriculum. His main occupation was that of scientist and philanthropist, only ever undertaking temporary clerical duties, and he took charge of the education of Gertrude and her younger brother Fred. The reverend considered that being able to carve and speak in public without looking an idiot were invaluable life skills. So they were for a future adventurer and celebrity speaker. When young Gertrude wasn't getting to grips with a goose at the family table, she was delivering little speeches to the household. Audiences never fazed Miss Bacon, the great teller of tales.

Gertrude was devoted to her father from the first. No-one, she wrote in *Memories*, ever had 'a more implicit trust, a more adoring admiration, a more whole-hearted affection than I had for the father who was parent, teacher, comrade, guide, philosopher, and friend in one'.

One review of Gertrude's memoirs sums up her father's role as enlightened mentor:

> 'They were companions rather than children, and allowed to take part in the experiments and the adventures of a father, whose active brain was ever in advance of his day and generation.'

Her father fed her relish for a rattling yarn with *The Arabian Nights* at bedtime and *Robinson Crusoe* when she learned to read. But far and away her favourite stories were the ones he told of cloudland. The reverend's fascination with ballooning stemmed from his father being a college friend

CHAMPERS AND HAMPERS ... HOW THE OTHER HALF FLEW

of Robert Holland, the barrister who bankrolled the 500-mile flight to Nassau in Germany in 1836. Gertrude soaked up every word. One day, Bacon of the sky promised his devoted daughter, he would take her on a balloon voyage too.

Gertrude came of age during the belle époque, an era of European history later considered a golden age of discovery and scientific advancement (known as the gilded age in America) before the First World War. The 1890s and early 1900s were a hectic time of human exploration. The sheer joy of discovery was everywhere. For Gertrude's generation, the world was awash with new inventions and scientific advances just waiting for a test run. These were the best of times for a young writer able to bring every thrilling new experience to life in exquisite detail. Armed with her talent, education and family entrée to every social and scientific circle, Gertrude was perfectly placed to become a maven of early flight. By the age of 24, her twin passions were firmly in place. She loved an adventure and she loved a good story. She also quite liked showing off and absolutely nothing fitted the bill better than taking to the air in a beautiful big balloon.

In 1898, the reverend finally kept his promise to take her on a trip to cloudland. Gertrude started as she meant to go on – with a commission to write up the adventure for the best-selling *Harmsworth Magazine*. Her talents as a storyteller more than matched the stories she had to tell and 'A Girl's Balloon Journey Over London' began in suitably dramatic terms. 'A few weeks ago a telegram was put into my hands containing two words only, "Come along."' She did not need to be asked twice. The invitation was to join her father on the balloon trip from Crystal Palace in London piloted by Stanley Spencer of the professional piloting dynasty, who, as Gertrude put it, almost had 'right of way in the skyey realms'.

Despite a bumpy take-off Gertrude felt nothing but wonder as she floated over the capital city for the very first time. Drinking in every sight and sensation she relayed the extraordinary novelty of a bird's eye view for her readers, crossing 'the gleaming Thames that wound so sinuously through the maze and tangle of streets, lost in haze as it crept towards the sea, and dazzling in its brilliance.' Landing was another ordeal rendered in page-turner prose by Gertrude the gonzo journalist. The giant red and yellow silk balloon a 'dying monster' that 'struggled hard' as 'half a dozen lusty harvesters' raced to the rescue from surrounding fields, closely followed by people in carts and on bicycles. Gertrude was sold. Wild rides and crash landings were exactly the sort of girl's own adventure she was born for. Her brother also enjoyed ballooning but it was Gertrude who was another Bacon of the sky. She only knew that for certain, though, after taking off on her maiden flight. As well as flasks, notebooks and blankets she had climbed into the basket at Crystal Palace carrying a secret fear. One she had hidden for years.

'Wildly keen as I was to go aloft, a horrid, unconfessed dread was ever at the back of my mind,' she admits in her autobiography:

> 'I knew I abhorred a height, that up a lofty building, or at the edge of a cliff, my legs become, even now, as cotton-wool and my heart sinks down to my very heels. What would it be like to look down from hundreds and thousands of feet? Should I be ignominiously reduced to sitting with tight-shut eyes, howling, at the bottom of the car?'

To her enormous relief, it only took a few seconds to realise that being high in a balloon did not bother her at all. Before long she was looking down from miles up without a single qualm. The highest ascent she ever experienced was with her father and another Spencer brother, Percival. The trip from Woolwich began in fog and almost came to an abrupt end when the trailrope caught in a tree near a Hertfordshire railway station. An obliging porter shinned up the oak and released them. The wet mist was still weighing them down and when all the ballast was gone Percival decided to whip out a knife and cut the rope free, shouting to the poor porter to ship it to London as they shot straight up and burst through the clouds to a height of three miles.

Even the reverend had never flown so high and Gertrude looked around to see what the altitude was doing to everyone. Apart from singing ears and faces of greenish-white hue they were all smiles. When Spencer suddenly announced he could hear a cow, though, she worried for his brain until the moos reached them all and it was duly noted in the reverend's record of acoustic findings. Then came a less amusing shock. They began to descend, speeding up until they 'were simply tumbling down our three miles aloft.' Never, however, was Gertrude without her stiff upper lip. 'Mr Spencer,' she writes, 'explained the situation and its somewhat exciting possibilities.' In a nutshell, these were that the usual way to arrest such a hurtle towards the ground was by the hurried dumping of ballast and a good long tailrope to cushion the landing. Both were long gone, so that was out.

The quick-thinking Spencer captains never failed Gertrude (or their other upper class clients) and Percival wielded his knife once again, cutting the lower ropes so the bottom half of the balloon collapsed upwards and formed a sort of parachute to slow their fall. They still plunged into the clouds at uncomfortable speed and there was nothing for it but to sacrifice some of the reverend's heavy scientific equipment. It was tossed overboard 'with a pang as to possible heads below' and with great relief they spied a soft landing ahead, finally coming to rest in a water meadow near Oundle. The only witness, Gertrude records, was 'one mildly astonished old rustic.' Maybe one day his path crossed that of a railway porter and they traded tales of the day eccentric gentry almost fell on their heads.

Gertrude's life became consumed by ballooning as she joined her father on ascents designed to gather data and conduct experiments, usually to do with weather or sound. By the closing years of the nineteenth century balloons were largely the preserve of showbusiness and the Bacons were determined to return them to scientific service. Though she shared a certain disdain for working balloonists who set up solely to entertain, Gertrude was far from averse to enjoying the limelight herself. She simply could not get enough of going aloft and never tired of the sheer drama of it all, even when one early ascent went terrifyingly wrong. The dangerous voyage that helped make Gertrude a celebrity could easily have killed her or put her off ballooning for life.

Instead she relates 'A Lady's Meteor Hunt Above the Clouds' for *The World Wide Magazine* with her signature brio intact. Her sex, according to the magazine, made the whole episode even more eye-popping. 'That the person who went through the following exciting and well-told adventure is a lady renders the narrative doubly interesting' is an introduction that reflects attitudes towards female achievement that balloonistas were adept at confounding.

Mid-November 1899 was ringed on Gertrude's calendar as the Leonids meteor shower that usually happens every 33 years. She and her father were determined to watch the celestial show from a ringside basket above the clouds. Once again they enlisted a Spencer – Stanley complete with gold-trimmed naval cap and jacket – to take them aloft. The balloon was courtesy of *The Times* newspaper and fitted with a one-use rip valve rather than an ordinary open and close one. It meant the gas would not leak if they had to stay in the air a long time to see the shower, but also that tearing a hole in the silk could only be done when low enough not to simply fall out of the sky.

They elected to take off at 4am, departing from unprepossessing Newbury gas works with the hope of catching what star gazers promised would be 'the height of the brilliant heavenly shower.' Even at that time of the morning, there was no shortage of well-wishers and helpers to see them off. Sandwiches, lamps, rugs, coats, cameras to catch the shooting stars and scientific equipment for collecting any actual stardust were bundled on board before the intrepid Gertrude hopped on too. Stanley lifted off, the crowd cheered and they were heading towards the inky sky.

At first there were plenty of wonders to see as they burst through the thick cloud cover and into a beautiful 'fairyland' where Gertrude reports, 'The moon was of a strange, tawny, copper hue; and round her was a large and glorious halo of brightest prismatic colours, weird and wondrous, but supremely lovely.' Unfortunately, the 'sea of snow-white cloud' and celestial silence could not distract forever from the fact that there was no meteor shower to be seen. The night sky was not as promised by fellow astronomers. They glimpsed just one shooting star before the balloon began to sink back into the clouds.

Suddenly they had more to worry about than an astronomical no-show. They were sinking too quickly and Stanley worried that they had already jettisoned too much ballast. He managed to stabilize them at 3,000ft, long enough to resume scanning the skies for the much-trumpeted meteor shower. A distant church bell tolled 6am and dawn began to flood the sky. Now they had the opposite problem, they were climbing too high. Worse, they could not tell where they were and strained their ears for clues. By Gertrude's account, all three aeronauts kept their heads. Even when her father looked over the side and lost his cap from his head, they simply laughed and watched him replace it with a huge knotted hankie to lighten the mood ('the knots hanging down in unbecoming fashion about his face').

Then came a terrifying sound – a steamer's siren. They were heading over the sea and did begin to panic, but in a dignified way. They formed a little SOS note-writing chain gang. Gertrude grabbed red and black pencils and wrote 'URGENT! Large balloon from Newbury overhead above the clouds. Cannot descend. Telegraph to sea coast (coastguards) to be ready to rescue,' and signed them Bacon and Spencer. John folded them into neat three-cornered notes, Stanley wrote 'Important' on the cover for good measure and threw them over the side. The operation was more a stoic attempt to keep them occupied than one with any real hope of working. The paper pleas, Gertrude discovered later, disappeared into the Bristol Channel or onto Welsh mountainsides.

Then they huddled in the corners of the 6ft by 3.5ft basket, the Bacons tactfully leaving Spencer to write what they assumed was a farewell letter to his wife and baby daughter. Gertrude frankly admits to falling into a mood of 'wrath and rebellion'. No fit of the Victorian vapours for her when she was staring death in the face. She sums up her feelings as, 'How cruel, how unfair, to catch me like this and kill me slowly, as a rat in a trap, at my age!'

Goodbyes penned, rage at cruel chance accomplished, the trio turned back to practicalities. Pulling the rip valve was out of the question. They grimly agreed it would be better to hope for rescue if they splashed down in water than be smashed to pieces plummeting from such a height. The stranded sky sailors took doleful photographs of one another and the clouds and pondered their fate.

Suddenly, after ten hours aloft, the aneroid (air pressure meter) showed they were finally beginning to sink and through the breaking cloud Gertrude saw, to her enormous relief, fields and roads, not the killer deep. Stanley sprang into action, negotiating the landing amid the fag end of a gale. Gertrude and her father hung on for dear life as the basket bounced and crunched across the ground. Eventually they came to a painful halt, Gertrude's arm broken and her father's leg gashed and bleeding. Then the shouts of rescuers were heard. They had landed in Neath, South Wales, just a mile and a half from certain doom over the Atlantic. The whole near-death experience in search of an invisible comet did not dent her enthusiasm. It was all grist to the Gertrude writing mill. As American journalist Norah Ephron was to remark more than half a century later, everything is copy.

Scientific ballooning went hand in hand with the family fascination with astronomy and for Gertrude, the late 1890s were one star-gazing adventure after another. She was an original member of the British Astronomical Association and joined the British Association for the Advancement of Science. The Leonids were a dangerous disappointment but a total eclipse of the sun was a dead cert. When she wasn't earning her sky legs, Gertrude was voyaging across the world 'corona-hunting'. She joined her father on three celebrated missions to observe and record an eclipse. The first was to Norway in 1896 where for once Gertrude was not entranced by the clouds, obscuring as they did the main event. She had more luck in India the following year, practising changing her photographic plates with closed eyes. By the third expedition – to America in 1900 to see the eclipse in North Carolina – Gertrude was processing through New York as a leading lady in a celebrity circus, thronged by newsmen. As they were delivered to their Southern hosts like visiting royalty, there was a sudden reminder of cloudland. The astronomers mistook fireflies for a meteor shower, Gertrude writes, like the 'display we had pictured but never seen, the night we hunted Leonids above the clouds.'

THE LOST HISTORY OF THE LADY AERONAUTS

The twentieth century dawned just as 26-year-old Gertrude was getting into her stride. Her class and connections always smoothed the way but the place she carved among aeronautical pioneers was what made the history books. Her mission was to be in the thick of it, reporting on the adrenalin-fuelled adventures of the age – her own, mainly.

It is little surprise that Gertrude was among the first liberated ladies to get behind the wheel of a motorcar (snapped driving the family Benz in 1899) but even this could not compete with whizzing through the air. In 'Ballooning as a Pastime' in *Badminton Magazine* of January 1903, she holds forth on its popularity as a practical and fashionable mode of transport.

Owning a balloon, she predicts in her article, will become as popular as owning a motorcar. With recent land versus air experiments proving that a balloon can easily outdistance the fastest car or yacht, flying wins hands down as *the* mode of transport for ambitious travellers of the future. There is just enough 'spice of daring and adventure' involved to hook anyone. 'No-one,' Gertrude says, 'is ever known to be content with one balloon voyage.' She certainly wasn't and in a 12-page paean she sets out to 'arouse in the reader who has never yet made a sky voyage some sense of the delight of such an experience'. In her usual upbeat style, Gertrude takes the reader on an imaginary (and therefore absolutely perfect) voyage.

No travel agent's pen could beat hers for 'the wild, boyish enthusiasm of the aeronaut, no matter how experienced, when he finds himself aloft in that boundless realm, floating free in the blue vault or amid matchless scenes of fleecy cloudland, the wide expanse of earth beneath folding itself in vistas of beauty past description.'

Going aloft became an all-consuming passion. 'For a number of years in my twenties I lived in an atmosphere of balloons and ballooning,' she says. Everything about being an aeronaut fascinated her, from the mechanics of the moment of take-off to the rough and tumble landing. She captures the rush in *Memories of Land and Sky*:

> 'The plunging, heaving folds of the rising silk; the fixing of the ring and car, the swaying ropes between which one bundles anyhow into the basket, the "weighing" of the balloon as bag after bag of ballast is passed out until the correct lifting weight is reached. "She'll lift now!" "No she won't!" A shattering crash back to earth. "Another bag out!" Another crash; another bag. "Now we're off! Let go!";

CHAMPERS AND HAMPERS ... HOW THE OTHER HALF FLEW

Gertrude thrived in the generation that witnessed the birth of powered flight and was uniquely placed to experience the engineering evolution of balloons into airships, then the arrival of the aeroplane. She gloried in being a guinea pig in any new machine and hers was the first female hand in the air to try out a powered balloon.

She became the first woman to ride in an airship when her obliging friend Stanley Spencer invited her aboard the cigar-shaped yellow Spencer Airship No. 3 in Shrewsbury in the summer of 1904. They caused a sensation by almost crashing into the crowd on take-off and narrowly missed landing under a steam train when landing. Of course, such scrapes only added to the fun for the intrepid writer. When Gertrude recounted her experience in 'A Lady in an Airship' in *Cassell's Magazine* she was chuffed to claim another feather for her cap:

> '"First in the world" to accomplish a feat, no matter what that feat may be, is a much coveted and highly esteemed honour. It is one, moreover, which daily becomes more difficult to secure when the whole earth is ransacked for new sensations and fresh achievements of every kind. I count it, therefore, as a piece of rare good fortune that I can boast myself the first woman to make a "right away" voyage in that invention of the future, an airship.'

Gertrude was so bowled over by the powered dirigible that she predicted it would dominate twentieth century transport:

> 'Possibly before I die airships will be even as motor-cars are now. The heavens will be darkened with the multitude of their sails. Aerial policeman [sic] will regulate their flight and teach them the rule of the road in skyland. Cheap summer tourist tickets will be issued to the North Pole, and winter ones to the Sahara, and we shall have airship costumes, airship periodicals, and airship ailments. It is satisfactory to reflect that when these days come I, as a white-haired, tottering octogenarian, may still mumble, "Ah! My children, but your old Granny was the first woman to go [on] an airship voyage!"'

Her vision is uncannily close to the truth, of course. Except it would be aeroplanes that would rule skyland, as she was soon to discover.

As her career as the scribe of the skies gathered pace, Gertrude's family life underwent a series of upheavals. Her mother had died in 1894 and in 1903, her father married again. His second wife was Stella Valintine from Goodwood and she gave him another girl. How losing the spot as her idol's only daughter made Gertrude feel she does not say. But the reverend died only months later, on Boxing Day 1904 and this time was sad and anxious, 'the home was being broke up and lives resettled.' He had suffered episodes of poor health all his life and was only 58 when he died.

Gertrude took refuge from her enormous grief in her career, writing about the lighter-than-air world he taught her to love. In 1905, just months after his death, she published *Balloons, Airships and Flying Machines*. In the chapter on the origins of ballooning Gertrude recounts how an illustrious thirteenth-century Bacon, Roger, the philosopher known as Doctor Mirabilis, worked out that a sphere of very thin metal might float upwards if filled with 'ethereal air'. She also relates the story of Hollond, the family hero behind the Nassau balloon. Her grasp of both history and engineering again served to bring ballooning to a wider public. Her skill was to convey the story of earliest flight with a clarity that appealed to everyone.

She presented a specialist paper to the Aeronautical Society of Great Britain shortly after she became a member in December 1905. Her father had promised to present the paper, but after his sudden death Gertrude used his notes to write 'The Acoustical Experiments Carried out in Balloons by the late Rev. J. M. Bacon.' Her audience included the American showman turned aviator Samuel Cody, at that time an instructor at the Royal Engineers' Balloon School at Aldershot.

The lengthy and complex study of air currents and their effects on sound at altitude was then published in *The Aeronautical Journal* in January 1906. The Aeronautical Society was founded in 1866 and from the start admitted women on an equal footing. Though at first designated as associate members, the rules stated, 'Ladies may be admitted as associates upon the same terms as Members, and subject to the same rules.' In theory, British women had the vote in matters aerostatic more than sixty years before they could all vote in parliamentary elections. A woman did not join, however, until 1874 when the first female name appears on the list of members. A popular and benevolent lady of the manor in Staffordshire, Ethel Bourne of Hilderstone Hall near Stone was an associate. She used her real name for the society but the pseudonym Evelyn Burne for writing her romantic novels, *Storm-beaten and Weary* and *Spectre Stricken*.

CHAMPERS AND HAMPERS ... HOW THE OTHER HALF FLEW

By 1909 the rules stated simply, 'Ladies are eligible as Members.' As long as they could afford a guinea a year in fees, they could apply to join. The society was set up with the express purpose of furthering the cause of ballooning as a scientific endeavour rather than a fairground attraction. The first annual report of 1866 notes that professional aeronauts 'have exhibited for gain that which is known, without adding to our knowledge at all adequate to their many opportunities for observation.' Gertrude, Ethel and others signed up because they were deeply interested in the science and potential of flying. The world's oldest aeronautical society was created to help inventors and to pool knowledge through its meetings, lectures and publications. Its open door again put British balloonists ahead of their time with their respect for female contributions.

A year after her paper to the society, Gertrude revealed a work even closer to her heart, a biography of her adored father. *Record of an aeronaut, being the life of John M. Bacon* was published in 1907. In the touching preface Gertrude sets out her intention to tell the story of 'my father's brave life'. He had won the admiration of his peers but she wanted to capture the kindly essence of her hero too. 'Besides recording his aerial adventures, it has also been my endeavour to represent him as the broad-minded, many-sided, loveable personality he was, and paint him as he appeared to those who knew him best.'

When her father died she thought her sky-sailing days were over but a few months later she made an ascent with her brother in France. Their pilot was Charles Levee and Gertrude relished the refinements of a continental balloon ride compared with one at home. The luxurious basket had a seat and there were different coloured ropes to operate the valve and ripping seam. Where the Spencers simply heaved bags of ballast overboard, Levee delicately scooped and weighed the sand before sprinkling it over the side, she observes, like a chef. They set off a little west of Paris and drifted for a hundred miles over the city and Versailles, then the spires of Normandy, enjoying a long conversation about their shared passion for all things airborne.

Ballooning soothed Gertrude's soul but after the death of her father she succumbed to the fever sweeping through her flying circle. American brothers Wilbur and Orville Wright succeeded in flying the first aeroplane in 1903 and Gertrude was gripped by the unfolding drama. She wasn't alone and as the race for the sky gathered pace she was once more in the thick of it. The first decade of the twentieth century passed in 'a dream of aviation' for Gertrude. 'I thought of nothing else,' she writes and commissions included an interview for *Pearson's Magazine* with Samuel Cody, the first to fly a plane in Britain.

By now Gertrude had earned her place as a member of the airborne elite as much for her own merits as her birthright as a Bacon. Her role as eyewitness and chronicler chimed with the free-for-all spirit of inventors and test pilots. Whenever Gertrude put pen to paper the result was riveting and in 1911 she was hot off the press with *How Men Fly*. Though the book jacket features a woman and the author is female, the title seems to exclude her entire gender. Her father had used 'every boy' to also mean 'every girl', she once declared (possibly optimistically) and seems to simply follow suit. As she proved time and again, it was never only men who knew how to fly.

Gertrude's reputation, connections and sheer brass neck secured her a couple of new firsts in this brave new world. She became the first Englishwoman to fly when she pleaded for a ride at the first aviation meeting in Rheims in 1909, taking to the sky squeezed in beside French aviator Roger Sommer. She was the first seaplane passenger when she hutched up behind Herbert Stanley Adams in *Waterbird* to whizz across Windermere in 1912. A regular at Brooklands aviation ground in Surrey, she enjoyed weekends as part of the inner circle that gathered in the Blue Bird shed café. She took a flight there with Douglas Graham Gilmour in the monoplane dubbed the Big Bat and fitted in looping the loop in a biplane at Hendon.

Then came the First World War and with it a brutal end to the sky as playground. Gertrude plunged into war work with the Red Cross, a far cry from the jolly japes of her younger days. Brooklands teabreaks with aviator chums were replaced by harrowing encounters with shell-shocked and terribly wounded young men returning from the trenches.

In August 1902, the German inventor Count Ferdinand Graf von Zeppelin had exchanged letters with Gertrude's father about his airships. During the war Zeppelins became a nightly source of terror and in 1917 one dropped a bomb that landed in Gertrude's garden in Greenwich, shattering every window in the house. She never stopped writing and lecturing, though, storing up stories and publishing *All About Flying* in 1915.

When the war ended in 1918, women were granted the vote from 30 and Gertrude exemplified the emancipated woman. She certainly worked hard to educate her contemporaries about the central role women had played since the birth of ballooning. In 1919, she wrote a piece for *The Weekly Telegraph* headlined 'The First Woman in the Clouds' where she relates the story of a 'humble, nameless old widow woman from next door' who used her 'quicker feminine brain' to suggest how the Montgolfier brothers could get a paper bag to fly. 'They say that a woman was directly responsible for the invention of the first balloon – that is to say, the very first means that ever carried mankind aloft into the clouds,' Gertrude writes. 'If this indeed be so (and the tradition is well authenticated), then the sex may well take the adjective "flighty," so often hurled at them in disdain, not in its opprobrious sense but as a simple statement of fact!'

She brims with admiration for the female aeronauts who came before, from Letitia Sage to Sophie Blanchard:

> 'When one considers the social conditions of a hundred years ago, the sheltered lives that women then led, the customs and conventions that hedged them round, and the tremendous obstacles that lay in their way should they attempt the unusual and daring, it is proof of the lure of the skies for the female sex, that they achieved so great a share in early aeronautics.'

Her conviction that women were made to fly only grew stronger and in the same year she told *The Daily Chronicle*:

> 'David sighed for the wings of a dove, but I will stake my life that Eve wished for them first! And because of this very yearning of theirs, if for no other reason, women take to the air as ducks to water.'

She was writing from the heart. Almost always outnumbered by the men who shared her passions, she reminded readers that women had always been part of the high-adrenaline, ground-breaking world of the aeronauts.

Gertrude's gumption extended to giving anything a whirl, especially if there was an engineering breakthrough involved, but ballooning was always her yardstick. Whatever the challenge set by herself or her editors, she called on the skills she learned in cloudland. She climbed bell towers and bridges with her camera to recreate the balloon-eye-view. When she went half a mile down a Cornish tin mine it was as a mental match to her three miles aloft. Deep below the streets of London watching the construction of a tube line she knew to swallow to relieve ear pressure. And when she donned a heavy diving suit for an experimental dip in a submarine engineers' tank it was to compare conditions underwater with those in the air.

THE LOST HISTORY OF THE LADY AERONAUTS

Her days up in the air, deep under the ground and bobbing about in a Waterloo diving tank were crammed into her autobiography in 1928, the year women finally won equal voting rights. Her popular style did not impress everyone, though. One reviewer in *The Yorkshire Post* sniffs, 'Miss Bacon gives a chatty rather than a literary account of fifty odd years of adventurous life…' before conceding, 'There has been no lack of incident in her chameleon career as balloonist, flier, eclipse-hunter, journalist, diver and lecturer.'

It is unlikely Gertrude lost much sleep, busy as she was with legions of fans packing out her talks the length of the land. She was in great demand as a public speaker, giving lively lectures to anyone and everyone, Borstal boys or female prisoners; the mentally ill or miners. Gertrude was a born crowd-pleaser. In 1902, she had fought hard to be allowed onto the Lecture Agency books alongside her father. Women lecturers, she was told, were 'mostly cranks' but she proved them wrong after stepping in to fulfil her father's bookings after his sudden demise. By 1906, one report of a lecture in Leeds introduces her as 'perhaps the most distinguished aeronaut in the world.'

Her memoirs safely filed, 53-year-old Gertrude cheerfully set off on another adventure – going from Miss Bacon to Mrs Foggitt. When love bloomed it was not with a balloonist, but Yorkshire botanist Thomas Jackson Foggitt. Gertrude's great hobby was flower hunting and she had been a member of the Wild Flower Society since 1901. The race to find rare blooms in Britain was great fun and she bagged her botanical first like all her others, around three thousand feet above sea level. She struck green gold on an organized hunt in the Scottish highlands in 1923, sharing the glory with botanical illustrator Lady Joanna Charlotte Davy. The women found themselves on a foggy and boggy mountainside where they stumbled on the pretty blue flowers of the bristle sedge, a grass-like plant seen in the Alps but never recorded in Britain.

Gertrude and Thomas enjoyed a society wedding at St Mary Abchurch in London in early 1929. Her brother, by then Professor Frederick Bacon, gave her away and she cut a dash in a dress of golden brown satin and an ermine fur, along with a little of the old lace her grandmother had worn on her own wedding day. She carried orchids and orange blossom, with a little niece for bridesmaid and the grandson of her old flower-hunting friend Lady Davy as pageboy. Gertrude moved to her new husband's home town of Thirsk but he died just five years later. Doughty Gertrude soldiered on, her unquenchable quest for experience an antidote to widowhood. At the age of 64, she was still in demand and never very far from the headlines. She met a glider pilot at a radio studio and talked them into taking her for a spin. Before long she was swooping over wild moorland with the Yorkshire Gliding Club. She had a ball, she told a local paper. 'They said I must not mind being shot into the air like a rocket or banking at an acute angle for losing height when we were coming down,' said the venerable queen of cloudland. 'Those I found were the most thrilling parts of the trip.'

Gertrude's gusto remained undimmed. Her delight just as pure as when she was cloud-sailing over Victorian London. She died in December 1949, at the age of 75. Always larger than life, Gertrude seldom spoke of death – except to celebrate a near miss – but she did once share her hope that ballooning offered an actual glimpse of heaven:

> 'I feel again the quick rush past of the treetops, so swift as to be almost instantaneous, and hear again the ringing cheer that dies so suddenly away, and the new world, so strangely silent, so still, so fresh and glorious, into which, all in a moment, we plunge. I have felt it many times since then, but always with the same rapture and always with the same flashing thought: "Will it be like this to die?" – the quick silence, the sudden peace and calm, the glory?'

Gertrude was a respected member of the scholarly branch of aeronautics, maintaining her fascination with the mechanics of flight through her membership of the Aeronautical Society. However, that did not prevent her from enjoying the champers and hampers of the proto jet set. The irrepressible Miss Bacon was among the upper-class women who could afford to enjoy ballooning purely as an exhilarating pastime. They did not have to drum up a crowd, flog tickets or flash a bit of leg. They were not required to grab a monkey or risk their necks with a parachute to be an aeronaut.

When a renewed burst of balloonomania grabbed the Edwardian upper crust, ladies who lunched also flew for fun. Fired by fashion as much as by curiosity, high society women always took to the air with a select audience, careful to look their very best and always packing a few luxuries to enjoy once aloft. Where a modern picnic might consist of a few sandwiches and a bag of crisps, amateur aeronauts dined on champagne and game.

Society bible *Tatler* paraded a host of high-born fans in an article on the balloon mania that surged afresh through the early 1900s:

> 'Women took up telephones, drove motors as soon as their worser halves, and have now gone in hot and strong for balloons and aeroplanes.'

Heirs and heiresses flocked to the Aero Club, the social and sporting hub for better off balloonists. Founded just eight months into the reign of Edward VII, it was the brainchild of Vera Butler, the most influential female balloonist of her day. Her first ascent was with her father Frank Hedges Butler, the drinks tycoon and leading light of the Automobile Club. She drove a Renault and when a motoring trip had to be cancelled (the car caught fire), Frank consoled her with a balloon ascent. On 24 September 1901, they were joined by family friend Charles Rolls, the founder of Rolls-Royce, and the pilot was Stanley Spencer. Sipping champagne five thousand feet above Crystal Palace, Vera came up with the idea of the Aero Club. She was going in hot and strong for balloons and the club was born the same day.

As a contributor to Frank's *5,000 Miles in a Balloon* of 1907, Vera makes it clear that a woman's place is in the sky. A founding member and its first lady, she notes the Aero Club was 'mixed' from the outset. 'Ballooning ranks as one of the most delightful and exhilarating pastimes of the twentieth century in which women can share,' she writes:

> 'What can appeal to a woman more than to rise for a season above the petty discontents, annoyances, and ambitions of the daily round, into an atmosphere of sure beauty and serenity, which somehow or other seems usually to alter one's whole point of view, and is, therefore, wonderfully restful and refreshing? I have never been able to see why women should be incapacitated from sharing in the delights of aerial navigation. Their imagination is said to be keener and more receptive than that of men. Therefore they should be able to enjoy the fascination of the sport the more keenly.'

Frank's book is a love letter to his 'dear old balloon' as aeroplanes roared into centre stage in the story of flight. His ballooning question and answer page gives only practical advice, including what to wear. Men should wear ordinary golfing or outdoor clothes. 'For ladies walking costume, with motoring hat or toque [bonnet]. Large headgear, such as picture hats, are a nuisance.' Vera, suitably attired, enjoyed flying with impressive insouciance, describing how she passed the time flying solo on her fifteenth ascent:

> 'It was a very lonely voyage, without even a momentary glimpse of land or sky ... Luckily, with a copy of the *Car* to read, and a luncheon basket to investigate, I spent the time comfortably enough.'

Vera had been raised as an adventurer. Like Gertrude, she was the beloved only daughter of an enlightened father. Having lost another little girl when she was a baby, Frank doted on Vera. He was a bon viveur and inveterate globetrotter and where he went, Vera went too. They climbed Mont Blanc when she was 16 and went to Paris for her first motorcar in 1900. When he introduced her to fellow balloonatic Charles Rolls they hit it off immediately. Though seen together so often they were assumed to be a couple, Vera and Charles were instead great friends. They shared a love of racing cars and balloons but not romance and were to be found speeding along country roads (once running into a horse and trap near Barnet fair) or taking part in balloon versus car races. Ballooning allowed men and women to meet on equal terms and Charles enjoyed the friendship of Vera and the other ladies who shared his passions. In 1904 Vera married Hugh Iltid Nicholl, a captain with the Bedfordshire Regiment, but remained friends with Charles until his death in an aeroplane crash at Bournemouth in July 1910.

The scientifically-minded and long-established Aeronautical Society was irritated by the claims of the brash young Aero Club. An entry in *The Aeronautical Journal* of January 1903 advises Vera's friends to get their facts straight. 'It has lately been stated in public that the present Aero Club was the first institution in this country to organize club balloon ascents. This is an error.' Victorian amateurs, all 'ardent balloonists in the cause of pleasure and sport', got there first:

> 'Therefore, this country, years ago, set the example in the formation of balloon clubs, as it did in the formation of aeronautical societies. By all means let the rising generation have their balloon clubs, but in their historical allusions let them not forget those who have piloted the way before them.'

THE LOST HISTORY OF THE LADY AERONAUTS

A civilized division of Britain's airy realm came in May 1909, when it was formally agreed that the Aeronautical Society would be the paramount scientific authority on aeronautical matters and the Aero Cub the supreme body in all matters of sport.

If the society was for scientists, the club was for thrill seekers. A notable aero clubber was May Constance Assheton Harbord, almost always referred to as the Hon Mrs Assheton Harbord. The honourable mister was Edward Harbord, younger son of Lord Suffield (the Assheton also fell from his ancient family tree). Born plain May Cunningham she married the Australian lawyer Arthur Blackwood in 1885 and suffered the loss of their only child, who died young. Arthur expired unexpectedly in April 1905 and just eight weeks later May walked down the aisle with Edward at a low key Chelsea wedding. May loved fast cars and balloons, just like everyone else in the Aero Club. She was finally where she belonged, in the wealthy and adventurous world of Vera, Frank and Charles. Charles in particular enjoyed her company, sharing the same kind of camaraderie that he did with Vera. When May was not behind the wheel of her own Rolls-Royce she was busy in her balloon.

She cut such a dash through high-flying society that an entry in *Every Woman's Encyclopedia* of 1912 focuses exclusively on her aerostatic honours:

> 'It was quite by accident that Mrs. Assheton Harbord became one of the most daring lady aeronauts of to-day. In 1906 she went to see off some friends who were making a balloon ascent, and at the last moment they suggested that she should go with them. She went, and when she returned to earth once more it was an enthusiastic aeronaut. Since then [she] has made nearly two hundred voyages, owns her own balloon, and has been entertained by the members of the Aero Club in token of their appreciation of her pluck and skill. She has made four voyages across the Channel, and has had a number of thrilling escapes, notably when the car of the balloon, which was her own, on reaching the Continent, bumped on the ground, owing to a storm, and threw out its unlucky occupant. "I can claim, therefore," humorously remarks Mrs. Harbord, "to be the only woman who has landed on the Continent on her head."'

CHAMPERS AND HAMPERS ... HOW THE OTHER HALF FLEW

Needless to say, Mrs. Assheton Harbord 'is pretty and petite, and possesses a charming taste in dress'. She also had a taste for an Aero Club aeronaut's certificate and in April 1912 became the first British woman to be granted one. May wrote about her exploits. In 'My Most Exciting Ballooning Experiences' in *The Wide World Magazine* of September 1909 she describes crossing the channel in her balloon, the *Valkyrie*. She and her pilot, Charles Pollock, set off from Battersea gas works and at 2,000ft the weather immediately turned ugly:

> 'At half-past ten we found ourselves in a stiff squall which made the balloon sway from side to side just as if it had been hit by some heavy object. These somewhat terrifying oscillations occurred through the envelope of the balloon and the car striking two opposite currents, and, in consequence, we had considerable difficulty in keeping inside the basket – an experience which is far from pleasant when you are several thousand feet from the earth and know quite well that there is no springy net waiting to catch you if you are thrown out.'

They hung on and an hour later eventually saw the twinkling lights of the fishing boats at the coast. Crossing the Channel was the least eventful part of the voyage but as they neared the French seaside town of Le Touquet:

> 'the inky darkness of the night suddenly changed into light, so intensely brilliant that it completely dazzled us. We were passing through a storm of sheet lightning, which illuminated the car, hoop, and neck of the balloon as if by electric light, and when I touched the ropes my gloves seemed to be alight with phosphorescence – a strange effect indeed!'

Once through the lightning, the darkness returned, so pitch black they could not even see each other as they hurtled along at fifty miles an hour. Vertical air currents 'drove us swiftly upwards and then brought us down like a log' and 'the wind whistled and howled in the most mournful fashion.' Then, still one and a half thousand feet up, crash! Pollock guessed they had hit a mountainside. 'Our tail-rope then began to catch somewhere below, giving us a series of shocks like miniature earthquakes.' They offloaded ballast but the heavy thuds continued. There was nothing for it but to take their chances and land. She crouched low in the car as he released the valve and they fell towards who knows where:

> 'Indeed, for all we could tell we might have been descending into anything – a fiery furnace, a swiftly-running stream, a thickly-populated city.'

They discovered soon enough they were heading for trees. Pollock deployed the ripping panel but a gust of wind caught them and almost overturned the basket. May clung on:

> 'We were swept through the trees at such speed that, on a dozen occasions at least, I thought that nothing but a miracle could save us from being thrown out, as all the time the basket was performing antics of the most grotesque and alarming kind. Now its sides were parallel with the earth; now it seemed to do a most effective somersault; now it righted itself. Crashing into heavy branches, rebounding off the trunks, and skimming lightly over thick foliage, we were dragged headlong – the tail-rope sometimes getting entangled, sometimes dragging aimlessly along as if it were wondering what part it was supposed to play in ballooning, and why it was there at all.'

Eventually the balloon snagged on a tree, came to a sudden halt by a clearing 'and sank gently down to earth like a tired-out bird which finds at last a haven of rest.' At dawn they trudged through the forest until they found a woodcutter's cottage and organized a rescue.

Exciting as that all was, May still counted the most thrilling five minutes of her life as an ascent the year before with her aeronaut friends Princess di Teano, Lord Royston and Jacques Faure. They set off from Paris aiming for Germany and ended up in Holland:

> 'A strong gale was blowing when we started at six o'clock in the evening, but in spite of the rain and wind we resolved to attempt the ascent, although several friends tried to deter us, as we hoped that by rising above the clouds, with a little luck, even if we did not find a comparative calm, we might at least escape the discomforts of a drenching, pouring-cats-and-dogs night.'

CHAMPERS AND HAMPERS ... HOW THE OTHER HALF FLEW

They shot up to four thousand feet, still enveloped in cloud, and were blown north easterly at seventy miles an hour, 'which, of course, is a tremendous speed, though, if one crouches down in the cage and shuts one's eyes, practically no movement whatever can be felt'. There was no time to relax when the North Sea hove into view:

> 'Something had to be done. There was no time to discuss calmly what one ought or ought not to do; so, inwardly blessing its inventor, we turned our attention to the ripping-cord, and M Jacques Faure, timing the psychological moment with wonderful accuracy, half ripped the balloon. Down, down, down we went. And as we descended I began to wonder – you know how, in anxious moments a thought flashes across your brain with lightning-like rapidity and vanishes almost as quickly – whether we should reach the earth before we got to the sea ... it conveys exactly what I felt during those three hundred intensely exciting seconds'.

Faure had pioneered the new ripping cord and it saved them from drowning. The balloon, almost in half, 'collapsed like a bird in full flight shot on the wing, quite close to the dreaded sea.' The rough touchdown gave May a chance to debut her favourite joke:

> 'As it came down, however, the car turned completely over, throwing Princess di Teano and me out on to our heads; so I think we have every justification for our claim that she and I are the only women in the world to arrive in Holland with our feet pointing towards the heavens.'

The rain was still lashing down and they staggered to a nearby house, hoping for shelter. Their garbled pleas in many languages failed to impress the occupant who refused to let them in. They trudged for two miles through 'a budding typhoon' until they reached a friendlier house:

> 'There, however, we fortunately met a courteous douanier [customs officer], who showed us to a little inn, spotlessly clean, where Princess di Teano and I rested in a room with two dear little beds hung with the whitest of curtains.'

Not much had changed about balloon landings since Elizabeth Thible and Letitia Sage crashed down wherever the wind had taken them in the

1780s. For May too, the gain of the landmark voyage outweighed any pain incurred in achieving it. They had travelled a record-breaking 240 miles in four hours:

> 'I think it is the exception rather than the rule for anyone to say good-bye to nerves unless they have actually been badly hurt in an accident. True, when I landed in Holland on my head I was hurt "some," as the Americans say, but then the accident had the saving grace of creating a new record which completely healed any pain that I felt at the time. So I never count that undignified arrival as an accident.'

May's roomate also shared her thoughts in print. Vittoria Colonna, the princess of Teano in southern Italy, was already a familiar face in the society pages. She was named after her ancestor, a sixteenth-century poet and great friend of Michelangelo. In the tradition of the balloonomania belles, Vittoria was a flamboyant and determined character. Based in Italy but often in London, her husband the prince was a big game hunter.

'She is not royal but belongs by marriage to one of the noblest houses in Italy,' according to *Tatler*. 'And – this may account for her pluck and daring – she is, although an Italian by birth, yet on the maternal side an Englishwoman ... She dresses to perfection and her jewels are marvellous.' One portrait in *The Bystander* of 1907 shows her in a column dress and miles of pearls. Headlined 'Of Rome and London' she is described as 'The beautiful Anglo-Italian, grand-daughter of the late Lady Walsingham, who is well known as a sportswoman and a lover of adventure.' She certainly was and despite falling on her noble head from time to time, that year Vittoria defended ballooning's safety reputation to an island race. 'The first thing that strikes one after becoming a convert to ballooning is the extraordinary ignorance of everybody in general concerning the sport,' she says in 'The Pleasure Balloon' in *Strand Magazine*:

> 'To begin with, an idea firmly rooted in the human mind is that whichever way the wind is blowing, and at whatever rate, you must immediately and inevitably be carried out to sea and drowned; the only other alternative is that the balloon should burst in mid-air, and that forthwith you are landed in fragments on Mother Earth. There seems no middle course available.'

CHAMPERS AND HAMPERS ... HOW THE OTHER HALF FLEW

Those old enough to recall Margaret Graham's many mishaps and contemporary witnesses to fairground accidents took some convincing. Vittoria, however, made a good case. 'Balloons do not burst through pure contrariness, and only a suicidally-inclined aeronaut would tie up the neck of his balloon and thus court disaster'. Clearly accustomed to having many such conversations, she ticked off all the arguments for avoiding an ascent:

> 'Of giddiness I know nothing, having never experienced it, either when ballooning or otherwise; but as to seasickness I can speak with assurance, for if anybody was likely to feel it in a balloon I should be the first sufferer. No, it is all comfort and peace and perfect rest.'

She does admit to the odd discomfort when landing, 'but people who can't stand a bump should stay at home in a comfortable arm-chair.'

Vittoria experienced a sense of unending freedom in the sky that brought her joy. 'The world is stretched beneath you as a large unrolled map of which you cannot see the corners.' Her favourite voyages were high above the clouds, where 'the magic charm of ballooning grips you in full, and you feel in another world and another life.' Her poetic descriptions belie her insatiable love of balloon flight and why she found its critics so irritating:

> 'Some of the effects are marvellous; every cloud has a different colour and a different shape. I have seen some purply-blue ones lying perfectly horizontally across the sky, and great, spiked, craggy, white ones coming down on the top of them, for all the world like the glaciers of Spitzbergen descending to the sea. Then little detached white clouds, like small icebergs, would float across the darker mist, completing the illusion perfectly. The balloon would sail round the edge of some huge, solid-looking mass, that offered such delightful peeps of smooth stretches, mysterious caverns, and untrodden heights that one longed to anchor in one of its many little bays, and land in this wonderful new country to explore its beauties.'

Little wonder ballooning was referred to as the cloud-cult under yet another fashion plate of Vittoria to mark another balloon event in another edition of *The Bystander*. This time draped in velvet and furs, she is identified as the aeronaut:

> 'Who ascended with Viscount Royston in Mr. C.F. Pollock's balloon in the recent "cloud race" from Ranelagh. The Princess is a daughter of the Duchesse di San Arpino, and is closely related to well-known British families. She is very popular in Rome. The cloud-cult is Society's effective retort on Father Vaughan and others, who are so fond of denouncing its inclination towards the lower regions.'

Who knows what Vittoria got up to in Rome but Father Bernard Vaughan was a catholic priest in Mayfair who gave a series of famous sermons, including one on the wicked ways of smart society women.

Vittoria pursued balloon sport with a single-minded passion. Once she had a taste of flying she could not get enough. Though all the society balloonists were photographed looking demure in full-length gowns and capes, they were fully prepared for an undignified moment. The princess looked less than regal when she was dragged across a muddy field when a ripping line failed:

> 'the jerk on hitting the ground having made me lose my hold, my left arm and right hand got caught between the car and the ground, and in this unpleasant position I was dragged across a ploughed field, with my face only a few inches above the ground.'

When not enjoying semi-religious raptures high above the clouds, Vittoria loved tailroping, travelling along at a steady 200ft or so thanks to the tailrope dragging along the ground below. That brought its own problems, especially when people assumed she wanted to land. 'A good deal of shouting is necessary to explain that is not your intention, and some individuals get quite huffy at the idea that you do not wish to alight in their field.' A giant rope crashing through a person's garden could also provoke quite a large degree of huffiness:

> 'The long, wriggling line of rope does no damage in the open country, but over houses and flower-beds it is a different matter, and it is often wiser to sacrifice a little ballast and rise above other people's chimney-pots.'

CHAMPERS AND HAMPERS ... HOW THE OTHER HALF FLEW

'Ballooning for Ladies, Society's novel week-end method of recuperation' in *The Lady's Realm* of 1906 gives readers a quick history lesson. The editor points out that female fascination with flight began in the 1780s. The Edwardian craze echoed Georgian balloonomania well over a century before. 'Ballooning, once more a fashionable pastime, has always held an extraordinary fascination for women from the time of its first inauguration.' Balloons 'took the entire fancy of the smart set of both sexes in London town by storm, and it became the rage, whilst London dandies complained that their view when ballooning was vastly impaired by the monstrous unsuitable coiffures of their fair companions!'

Now anyone who was anyone was up, up and away with Vera, May, Vittoria and co:

> 'The eyes of all London have again been lately fixed, in the most literal sense of the word, on the exploits of the plucky little band of lady balloonists, all members of the Aero Club, whose frequent ascents into cloudland formed one of the chief sensations of the past season. Princess di Teano, the Hon. Mrs Assheton Harbord – wife of Lord Suffield's son – Miss Moore-Brabazon, Miss Maxwell-Heron, and Miss Granville, the talented actress, who have each made a number of ascents, are amongst the most fearless and enterprising of the lady aeronauts, and their enthusiasm for the newly revived and fashionable sport shows no sign of abating, despite the fact that Miss Granville at least has already had several rather too exciting experiences in the matter of rough descents; whilst on one occasion, when going up from the Crystal Palace, where the Aero Club holds a meeting every Thursday afternoon during the season, the anchor caught in the top of a high elm-tree, and with it, of course, the car to which it was attached.'

Charlotte Granville was an enthusiastic member of said plucky little band. After a few dicey moments dangling from the elm, they landed:

> 'Miss Granville's coolness much delighted the onlookers, who gave her a cheer on finding out that, nothing daunted, she was about to start gaily off again, and this she accordingly did, managing, by a stroke of luck which hardly occurs once in a hundred times in ballooning, as she laughingly explained, drop

down into the garden of a friend's country house some twenty or thirty miles from town, just in the nick of time for tea.'

Fast cars were all part of the frolics, when drivers:

'having first watched their friends' ascent in a balloon and ascertained its intended direction, fling themselves post-haste into their motor-cars ... and chase madly after it in the arranged direction. In this pastime Miss Granville also excels.'

For Miss Granville (her stage name), the benign coverage of balloon jollies was a balm after the details of her failed attempt to end her miserable marriage to Robert Synge made lurid headlines in 1900. Her petition for divorce from the retired infantry major for desertion and adultery had readers riveted for weeks. Her counsel argued that she only took to the stage when her husband was stationed in India and did not send home enough money for her and their son to live on. When Charlotte discovered something about 'his health' from another woman she stopped having sex with Robert. He went to lodge with a Miss Hooker and was caught helping her make their bed by the chambermaid. Charlotte was denied a divorce because in the dying days of the Victorian era, having sex with his landlady was not deemed unreasonable.

Charlotte worked her way to a better life instead and her career went from strength to strength both on stage and in balloons. She moved from London's West End to become a star of the Broadway stage in New York and later, the silver screen in Hollywood. There was a nasty shock waiting for her across the Atlantic, however, when she made arrangements to carry on ballooning. As in the divorce courts, sometimes it was hard to be a woman. The 1911 headline 'Aero Club Bars Her Out' in *The New York Times* reveals the English actress was refused membership of the Aero Club of America. Unlike the British and French clubs, where she was an active and welcome member, the American club secretary wrote, 'I beg to convey my regrets that the club does not at this time admit lady members.' To which Charlotte said simply, 'How perfectly stupid!'

Charlotte had a lot in common with her contemporary, the great French actress Sarah Bernhardt. Sarah also took to the air to escape the headaches of a tempestuous lovelife and demanding career. She was a frequent flyer and wrote the whimsical story *In the Clouds: Impressions of a Chair* (from the point of view of the balloon seat) about a voyage over Paris with her artist friend, Georges Clairin.

CHAMPERS AND HAMPERS ... HOW THE OTHER HALF FLEW

Aero Club sporting events at Crystal Palace or the polo grounds at Ranelagh and Hurlingham drew gents in top hats and tails and ladies with parasols, the whole scene looking more Ascot than aerostation. Balloon races and midnight supper parties in the sky became a feature of the social season. Violet Dunville, whose family built the Royal Irish Distilleries in Belfast, won the Hedges Butler Challenge Cup for long-distance racing three years in a row. In February 1906, Beatrice Brewer became the first woman to cross the Channel by balloon. The three-hour trip included a picnic at seven thousand feet and a race with a steamer. 'Sausage Rolls In Mid-Air' announced the *Eastern Evening News*:

> 'In crossing the Channel the equilibrium of the balloon was so well maintained that the voyagers were able to enjoy a meal consisting of sausage rolls, cake, and champagne. As the strange meal was finished, the cross-Channel steamer Onward ... was sighted below, and the race between the balloon and the turbine boat for the French shore afforded considerable excitement to the aeronauts.'

Beatrice and her fellow balloonists beat the boat to France by five minutes.

Competition among Aero Club members for its many cups and records was fierce. The wealthy belles of the belle époque lived a world away from women who took to the air to earn a living with spangles and parachutes. They could concentrate on sporting achievement and the honours that brought. In gilded balloon circles before the First World War rich ladies much preferred a breathless adventure to a sedate afternoon. They often packed champagne but absolutely never needed smelling salts. 'All can choose their own day and its consequences,' wrote the gutsy and glamorous Princess of Teano, 'the so called "ladies' day" with its calm pleasures, or the record-breaking gale with its indescribable excitement.'

Chapter 9

Of Pluck and Parachutes

The one word that follows the balloonomania belles down the decades is *pluck*. They were, to a woman, very plucky people and none more so than the parachutists who went up by balloon and down by the seat of their scandalous pants. Though invented as a safety device, for more than a century parachutes were purely for astonishing the punters. Parachutes spelled danger and no matter how many people spluttered in the press and parliament about morality and motives, the skydiving divas were unstoppable. If watching a plucky woman floating off in a balloon was exciting, imagine seeing her jump out of one on purpose.

When Sophie Blanchard's balloon caught fire over the rooftops of Paris in 1819 she could have survived if she had packed a parachute. So wrote her great rival Elise Garnerin in a letter to the editor of the *Quotidienne*:

> 'There was no doubt but that if Madame Blanchard had been furnished with a parachute, which on unfolding itself would have been separated from the burning balloon, she would not have fallen victim to this useless experiment.'

Harsh but possibly true, though parachutes were by no means an especially safe option for the early aeronauts. Far more women would die suspended from a sheet of silk than ever met their end in a balloon basket.

Sophie had been implacably opposed to using a 'chute, despite her husband Jean-Pierre Blanchard using his own version to escape a burst balloon in 1793. Elise's uncle, the equally publicity-driven French aeronaut André-Jacques Garnerin, was the first to incorporate parachuting into his show. Leonardo da Vinci famously imagined a parachute in his sketch of 1485 but it was the balloonists who made them real. On 12 October 1799, Garnerin's pupil and future wife Jeanne-Geneviève Labrosse became the first woman to leap into the blue.

OF PLUCK AND PARACHUTES

Jeanne had no qualms about introducing her cat to skydiving three years later in a publicity stunt during a tour of England. It was not the first or last poor animal to be put to work on a parachute. Blanchard dropped nameless dogs, cats and squirrels but the most famous performing pet was the monkey of English aeronaut Charles Green in the 1830s. It is debatable whether Jacopo was ever quite the sane and happy primate he had been before he was tipped over the side of a basket to flail towards the earth as entertainment, but this was a long time before an animal rights movement could have stepped in to object.

Madame Garnerin's cat was dropped overboard in August 1802, according to press reports in the Major B.F.S. Baden-Powell Collection of Aeronautical Cuttings:

> 'This evening Mr. and Mrs. Garnerin ... ascended from Vauxhall in a balloon; which rose about 7 o'clock, and was distinctly seen for 54 minutes, when it had attained an height of 6000 feet. M. Garnerin had taken a cat with him in a basket, which came down from this stupendous height in a parachute with perfect safety.'

This does not seem to have been the impression of horrified onlookers. To mollify the cat lovers of London who rushed to the spot where it landed near the Thames at Millbank, the Garnerins sent a light-hearted letter from Tom Cat of Poland Street to the press, titled 'The Cat's Account'.

> 'Brought up under the care of Madame Garnerin, I may be said to have been nursed in the very bosom of aerostation, and to have breathed nothing but the pure air of oxygenated gaz from the first moment of my birth. Hearing of my mistress's intended ascension, and having learned, from my master's late experiment, the turbulent nature of the English atmosphere, I who had been a quiet spectator of her aerial flights in more peaceful skies, determined on sharing the danger of her new voyage.'

Not a very cat-like sentiment, but it goes on,

> 'The very first moment I found myself buoyant, I felt disposed not to be an idle spectator, but to take an active part in the boat. Madame Garnerin, however, near whom I was seated, in a neat

wicker basket, patting me gently upon the head, and smiling irresistibly, said it would be of dangerous consequence and requested me to sit still. Ever obedient to the call of beauty, I complied, and instantly began to pur a little tune, to prove at once the placidity of my temper, and the total absence of all fear and apprehension.'

Which was just as well, as quite soon after that the cat basket was hooked onto a parachute and dropped overboard by his beautiful mistress:

'Every eye was turned from the balloon and fixed upon me, and several ladies swooned, fearing I should fall into the river... You can have no idea of the crouds that ran from all sides to offer me their assistance. They rushed with so much impetuosity that they tumbled over one another into the ditches.'

Thousands escorted the crazed cat back to the address tied round its neck (there was a guinea reward), while 'the others were busily employed tearing the parachute to pieces, with a view to prevent me from ever exposing myself to a similar danger.' Still, a breathing showbiz cat was a successful showbiz cat and in 1815 the new family parachute passed to Elise Garnerin, four years before she wrote the letter pointing out Sophie Blanchard's 'useless experiment'. Like her arch rival, Elise was feted across France and often made high profile ascents in Paris. She, however, would come back to earth by parachute, as in this report of a jump over the Champ de Mars in 1816:

'Mademoiselle Garnerin entered a very magnificent car, affixed by a rope twenty feet long to a parachute, above which was the balloon. The whole then rose majestically in a westerly direction. When about the height of 1200 feet, the lady cut the rope, the parachute unfolded itself, and the descent took place slowly, and without the least concussion. Mademoiselle Garnerin alighted near the Barrier of Gross Caillou, and quite close to the River. The young lady went through the business with great *sangfroid*, and received the testimonies of satisfaction of the numerous spectators assembled. A great number of gentlemen on horseback preceded the young aeronaut on her return to Paris, and among the company was the Duke of Wellington.'

OF PLUCK AND PARACHUTES

Sangfroid and *plucky* often went together in admiring reports of parachute adventures. Unfortunately, these qualities were not always enough to stave off disaster. Elise (also known as Elisa and Lisa) made around forty parachute jumps at home and across Italy, Spain, Russia and Germany, with her share of spills including a splashdown in a river in 1818. She could not swim and was saved in the nick of time by two boatmen. Elise retired at the age of 36 after fifteen years in the air, and lived into her sixties. A long retirement was not something many later lady parachutists lived to enjoy.

By the time ballooning marked its first century, parachutes were integral to the barnstorming belle's repertoire. The earliest parachutes resembled umbrellas but by their late Victorian heyday they were frameless and foldable, and therefore portable. The French invented aerostation and ran the most successful teams across the world. Earlier in the century a family of acrobatic aeronauts headed by Eugène Godard (no relation to Sophie) and including his wife, sister Eugénie and cousin Fanny, took parachute shows around the world. In Britain the French dominated the flying circus scene, and Auguste Gaudron became one of the leading operators in the country. In the Spring of 1891 he married Marina Spencer and she helped build the business, sometimes making parachute jumps herself. The Spencers were the influential balloon makers and professional aeronauts who worked with everyone from the skydivers to the Aeronautical Society and, later, the Aero Club.

Britain in the 1890s and 1900s was packed with parachuting women. Sundays were the day for travelling and railway stations teemed with aeronauts who bundled their balloons and bags into steam trains and headed for their next gig. It was a small world and most skydivers knew each other, often working together. Entertainment committees could not get enough of plucky girls who guaranteed a good turnout with their death-defying displays, though the cruel truth was that for some, no amount of nerve or verve could keep them defiant forever.

Leaping lady aeronauts promised bank holidays and gala days to remember. They kept quiet about the chance of taking part in that old favourite, a balloon riot. Marie Merton was booked to make a sensational drop from the clouds over Gloucester on August bank holiday 1894. The show was organized by Percy Chavasse, who worked for the Birmingham-based aeronaut George Philip Lempriere. The plan was to rise to 12,000ft in her balloon *Skylark* and parachute back but the headline in the *Gloucester Journal* said it all, 'Friendly Society Fete a Ballooning Fiasco: Disgraceful Conduct of Spectators.'

Marie had never had an accident and in 1891 set a record by jumping at 15,000ft. As so often, it was a poor supply from the gas works that scuppered the show. A day of bank holiday drinking might also have played a part. After nine hours the balloon was not fully inflated but the crowd was restless. Marie climbed onto her seat at 8.30pm and attempted to take off. She only made it a little way before coming down again in the crowd. The balloon was dragged back and she tried again and again. It was no use, there was not enough gas to lift her free. The fiasco gathered pace as 'hooting was freely indulged in, and a rush was made towards the aeronaut and her aerial conveyance.' Within seconds the balloon was torn and the gas flooded out. 'Matters then became lively' as the hooting hooligans surrounded Marie and made for manager Percy. They escaped after he floored one of his assailants and six policemen attempted to protect the balloon. For half an hour, the Friendly Society mob made 'ugly rushes' at the *Skylark* with penknives before being beaten back by beleaguered bobbies. The holes hacked in the balloon proved the final straw for the shaken showpeople. 'Both Miss Merton and Mr Chavasse were much upset at the occurrence, and the latter said if the crowd had refrained from injuring the balloon he would have given a free display on the following day.' As it was they took home their bat, ball and what remained of their balloon.

The case that shocked Victorians the most was that of little Louisa Maud Evans, a 14-year-old from near Bristol. She worked at a local fairground but when Auguste Gaudron's balloon show came to town she was lost. Claiming to be 20, she persuaded him to take her on as 'Mademoiselle Albertina'. Gaudron needed fresh talent and in the competitive world of show ballooning, bravado and fake identities could get a girl a long way. So little Louisa from Bristol pretended to be grown-up Mademoiselle Albertina, complete with fictional flying CV. A fatal combination of her single-minded bluffing and Gaudron's selective blind eye led to her ascending from Cardiff Exhibition into the blustery sky of 21 July 1896 – for the first and last time. The waving mademoiselle seemed set for success as she climbed high and then leaped out over the city. 'Her performance was watched by thousands of persons, and to all appearances everything was successful as she came down slowly and steadily,' ran one report. But appearances were deceptive. The doomed girl was heading for the Bristol Channel, landing a mile and a half from shore. A witness with a telescope saw her hit the water on her back and she appeared lifeless as she sank beneath the waves.

Cardiff went into shock. Wild stories circulated for three days. She had been picked up and taken away by schooner or was inexplicably in hiding. The truth was simple and sad. She had drowned. Another 14-year-old girl on an evening stroll to find driftwood found a dead body instead, near the mouth of the Usk. 'It put an end to all surmises, and destroyed the last faint shadow of hope which, despite all evidence, still lingered in some minds,' according to one report. She was wearing a cork lifebelt but the parachute was never found. Louisa's bruised body had been 'tossed in the eddying currents and races and shoots of the Severn estuary for full 70 hours' before being washed up onto the shingle near Nash lighthouse, 'within sound of the harsh death-song of a clanging bell-buoy.'

More gothic horror was relayed by the *South Wales Daily News* reporter who drove Gaudron to view the body laid out in a church belfry:

> 'With the aid of a lighted candle the corpse is seen lying on a bier set against the west wall of the tower. It is very slightly swollen considering the duration of its immersion in the water, and there is a placid expression on the face. The short upper lip exposes a perfect row of small white teeth, but the lower teeth are not visible.'

Her jaw was tied with a handkerchief by locals. They also gave her the dignity of closed eyes and arms folded over her chest. They could not disguise her injuries, though – the torn scalp, the mutilated flesh on her head and arm, the long bruise on her neck – or the state of her clothing. 'The girl's bodice is open, displaying a frilled under-garment, and the corsets, folded, are resting under the left arm on the breast.' There are tiny gold hoops in her ears, but no rings on her fingers. 'As the body lies here it is incredible that it is that of a girl not yet fifteen years of age.'

Gaudron was castigated for allowing such a young and inexperienced girl to go alone into the sky. He said Louisa had lied about her age, followed him to Wales from Cornwall and pestered him to be a parachutist. The stories Louisa told to become Mademoiselle Albertina were exposed one by one at the inquest. She was not 20 years old, she was not an experienced balloonist, she had never made a parachute jump before and most tragic of all, she could not swim. Gaudron does not appear to have told the whole truth either, especially about whether he encouraged her to come to Wales after the Westcountry shows because he had just lost his star performer. Alma Beaumont left after an argument over money ten days before the Cardiff booking. When Louisa claimed to have been a balloonist in Dublin, going by the name Grace Parry, Auguste took her word for it. 'She said that for the last four years it had been her only ambition, and that she had a cousin who made parachute descents,' he told the court. 'If she had said a word or turned colour at the last minute I would have stopped her going up,' She was not his servant, he added.

On the day of the tragedy, Gaudron believed the wind was blowing away from the sea but suggested she take a lifebelt, 'for you never know what happens.' If she did land in water she should unhook herself from the parachute and wait for a boat. But, it emerged, there was no boat. Providing one was not his job and the boatman that set off in the event was a good Samaritan. Recruitment, training and safety checks seem lacking now but were all pretty standard for aeronauts of the time. What was different about Louisa was her age.

If she had followed Gaudron's instructions on when to jump, she would have been okay. Instead, she panicked. 'A young girl going up for the first time would probably hesitate and might be alarmed,' said the coroner, 'and every moment of hesitation would increase her danger. The result was that she got further and further up in the clouds, and when at last she did jump she was too far out and landed in the water.'

The coroner delivered the verdict with a devastating rebuke:

> 'The jury have decided on a verdict that the deceased was accidentally drowned in the Bristol Channel on Tuesday last whilst descending from a balloon, and they are unanimously of [the] opinion, Gaudron, that you displayed great carelessness and want of judgment in allowing so young and inexperienced a person to make such a perilous ascent and in such weather as prevailed on Tuesday last, and they wish me to censure you and to caution you against allowing anything of the sort to occur again.'

With so many accusing eyes upon him, the aeronaut broke down. 'Gaudron burst into tears at the mention of his name, and turning his face to the wall near which he was standing, sobbed audibly.' Still only 27 himself, the showman would be involved in more parachuting tragedies but the story of Albertina was one no-one could forget. She was buried in Cardiff cemetery and her grave was tended. She was just a star-struck child and the terror of her final moments made her a poignant case. The mystery of her parachute remained unsolved. The answer, thought the dogged *South Wales Daily News* reporter, could lie with Alma Beaumont who worked with Gaudron for three years prior to the tragedy and quit just before Louisa

OF PLUCK AND PARACHUTES

tried to fill her shoes. The unanswered questions gripped Victorian readers' imaginations like a new Sherlock Holmes mystery. 'Alive or dead, conscious or unconscious, why did Mdlle. Albertina, literally enclosed in cork, sink so suddenly in the waters of the Bristol Channel, and how, and where did she part with the firmly fixed parachute?' asked the newspaper. Alma agreed to be interviewed at her home in London.

Alma was the opposite of Albertina, a seasoned professional famous not only as a 'thoroughly courageous' aeronaut, but also as a champion high diver and tobogganist. She had chalked up 33 balloon jumps for Gaudron and made her name around the country. She left after he refused her a pay rise but was still working with him in Devon and Cornwall just before the move to Wales and remembered the pretty, obsessed girl. Alma's expert opinion was that the cords of Albertina's parachute were twisted and she fainted from being whirled around on the descent. She also wanted to know whether the quality of the cork in the vest had been tested since it was found.

As to the missing parachute, she was baffled. 'That is a complete mystery to me,' says Alma. The rope fastenings swelled in water and a soaked parachute would drag the rope tight. 'I can never believe she released herself from the hooks after she struck the water. I am an expert and an exhibition swimmer, and even I could not do it.' Alma was speaking from experience, having had a splash landing herself. She could not account for how the poor child had lost her 'chute. Privately, the American knew that so often it was just dumb luck. Gaudron had shocked the inquest when he candidly admitted that there was no real training for parachutists. 'There is no experience whatever necessary; any one can do it.' The rest was down to pluck, wind and chance.

The agile and petite Alma (5ft tall and just 6st) knew that only too well. She crashed onto a roof in Aberdeen, landed in a tall elm in St Austell, became tangled in a water chimney lightning conductor near North Shields and almost drowned in the Clyde before she retired. Though these were not the things that gave her the heebie jeebies, according to an unrelated account in the *Sunderland Daily Echo*:

> 'What a mystery is a woman's bravery. Miss Alma Beaumont, an American lady, is a daring aeronaut, who last night, at North Shields, ascended fifteen thousand feet in the air clinging to a hoop affixed to a balloon. Thence she made a drop to the earth, trusting life and limb to what is called a parachute, but is only an umbrella. The first rush down is so rapid that it takes away

her senses, which do not return until the opened parachute imposes a check. Miss Beaumont is not afraid to do this time after time, yesterday's being her sixteenth essay. Yet she was in mortal terror last night because in the field where she must alight there were some cows, and like all women who are not milkmaids, she has an unreasonable dread of all animals excepting men and cats.'

Gaudron was never mentioned in Cardiff without the ghost of Mademoiselle Albertina in attendance. Reporting his serious injuries from a burst balloon during an ascent in Ireland a few weeks after the scandal, the South Wales reporter remembered both his eerie calm when he saw the dead girl and his words as he walked away:

'The occurrence at Enniskillen serves to recall an observation made by Gaudron on leaving the belfry of Nash Church, where lay the bruised body of Mdlle. Albertina. He had viewed and examined the corpse with singularly calm demeanour, and it was only as the door of the belfry was again locked, and Gaudron was threading his way amongst the tombstones in the village churchyard, that he huskily remarked to our reporter, who had driven him in from Newport, "I suppose that will be my fate some day."'

This was the fear all aeronauts lived with, though seldom voiced in public. They could only hope to be among the lucky ones. On bank holiday Monday in August 1895 Alma Beaumont appeared in the same editions with another London aeronaut, Adelaide Bassett. Alma's balloon in Slough was damaged during inflation and would not lift. 'After considerable time had been spent in an endeavor to secure an ascent the balloon suddenly exploded, and a huge mass of flame poured forth,' reports *The Citizen*. Alma was unhurt but the flames burnt a woman's face and took off a boy's hair. Meanwhile Adelaide did not escape her horrifying accident in Peterborough. 'As the balloon ascended from which she was to fall, the parachute was broken by a telephone wire, and, having then no means by which to descend, Miss Bassett jumped from the balloon to the ground, and was killed.' Her speciality was double jumps with her partner Captain Orton, billed as 'a race for life'. He saw her parachute snap when they were about 60ft up and shouted, 'Don't jump Addie!' and was always haunted by knowing she must not have heard the 'don't'.

OF PLUCK AND PARACHUTES

Maude and Edith Brookes were sisters and by May 1902 Maude had been an aeronaut for fourteen years, despite an accident with a torn parachute in 1893 where she damaged her spine. When a booking mix-up meant Maude could not appear as promised in Sheffield on 20 May, her younger sister went up instead. The Whitsuntide carnival appearance at Wednesday Football Ground was arranged by the fist-fighting impresario Percy Chavasse, who managed to keep the switch a secret from the carnival boss. Edith was a speck in the blue sky when the shout went up, 'She's away!' but something did not look right. She was not as high as the day before and seemed to fall from the balloon rather than slide off with control. The *Leeds and Yorkshire Mercury* described how five thousand people watched helplessly as the parachute failed Edith during a sickening corkscrew descent:

> 'As she fell the lady was being turned round and round as if the ropes of the parachute were untwisting, and she was, as a fact, being swung round at the moment she reached the earth. The feelings of the sightseers can be better imagined than described. A low cry of "Oh!" was heard, and then, silent and horror-stricken, most of those in the crowd watched the terrible tragedy that was being enacted. Some, however, could not bear the sight, and turned their eyes from the awful scene, while many women fainted from fear.'

Edith hit the earth at 1,000ft a minute with a stomach-churning thud. She landed on a path just inches from iron railings in Hillsborough Park and the state of the body left no doubt that she was dead. Three days later another crowd gathered, this time for her inquest at Sheffield mortuary, hoping for more revelations. They did not have long to wait. Maude said Edith had died on only her second day on the job. 'She had many times begged to be allowed to take up the work of a parachutist,' Maude told the court. 'She has travelled with me a lot. I always stood in her way, but this season she begged so hard to be allowed to try that at last I consented.' The big sister held out for five years because their parents did not like one daughter jumping out of balloons, let alone two.

Maybe Edith's parachute twisted in the wind, she could not say. 'It is just a chance of Providence' was Maude's only explanation for her little sister's terrible death. Chavasse could only suggest that Edith had a fit or fainted because the parachute for which he bore all responsibility was, naturally, perfectly in order. She had appeared to fall forward and become tangled in the ropes. One witness said Percy untwisted her ropes before her successful first jump the day before, but twisted them on purpose before she went up on the day of her death. He said that was to compensate for windy weather.

The inquest was adjourned and Edith's body was sent home to Liverpool where she was buried the following day. Maude stood with her remaining sister and father at the graveside. They had spent fourteen years fearing Maude would be the one lowered into an early grave then lost Edith in a career lasting 24 hours. The second day of the inquest heard hours of discussion about twisting and untwisting ropes before a more human clue emerged from Mrs Gray, the landlady at Edith's lodgings. She saw Edith after her maiden flight on Whit Monday and before her fatal one on Tuesday. All Edith had drunk on her first day was a glass of wine and she barely touched her breakfast next morning. The pale young woman did not seem at all well but when the landlady asked if she was frightened, she said no. Edith may have been having second thoughts about joining her sister's profession, so exciting from the ground and so utterly terrifying from the air. Having begged for a parachute for years and now posing as Maude, it was too late to go back. Fainting at the crucial moment did not seem too far-fetched. However, just before the verdict was given an almighty row broke out between the carnival organizer William Brown and Percy's boss Lempriere. The promoter insisted he was promised Maude and tricked with Edith and would never have sent up a novice. The balloonist said he was booked only to provide a lady aeronaut. It was the business they call show in the raw. Eventually the jury delivered their verdict. Edith died falling from a balloon when her parachute did not act correctly, probably because she fainted onto the ropes. There was the customary call for such acts to be banned. A week later Maude was back in the air.

People were shocked by each tragedy and the glimpse it gave them behind the scenes of the travelling air shows, but only for a while. By no means all the parachutists came to a sticky end. Hundreds of descents went well and there were enough good times to keep the balloon shows on the road. Balloonomania had filled newspapers with fabulous stories for a hundred years. Add a pair of tights and a parachute and headlines were guaranteed. There were cheerful reviews of the shows that went well, all the gory details of ones that went badly, and a steady stream of calls from editors, coroners, councillors and letters page correspondents for female parachuting to be banned. Every lament pointed out the dark spice of danger that was part of the appeal. The editor of *The Leeds and Yorkshire Mercury* considered that Edith had been 'butchered to make a holiday,' while a letter from 'Disgusted' compared buying a ticket to see women deliberately run the risk of a horrible death to watching the gladiators in ancient Rome and bullfights in modern Spain. 'That they do so in order to gratify a degraded appetite for "sensation" is indisputable.'

Maybe so, but lots of things were sensational, from knife-throwing and high-wire acts to boxing and motorcar racing. That was indeed why people paid to watch them. Audiences have always enjoyed the suspense of seeing stunts performed without a safety net. It provokes admiration and congratulations, not disappointment when there are no dead bodies. Pioneers always take risks. The first flying jobs were always dangerous. The women who wanted to fly just had to take a deep breath and do it. Just as Gaudron had argued at the inquest for Louisa, Maude told the hearing for Edith, 'It requires no practice; you must "do the show." You cannot practise a thing like that ... you may get on all right and you may get killed, of course.' In the end it was all down to providence.

Among the saddest stories is that of Edith Cook from Ipswich. She loved the air from an early age and changed her name almost as often as her balloons and her bosses (she flew for Gaudron and others). The aliases we know about are Viola Spencer, Viola Kavanagh, Viola Spencer-Kavanagh, Viola Fleet and Elsa Spencer. She made more than 300 balloon parachute jumps before learning to fly a plane and becoming Britain's first female pilot in January 1910. In July she made a parachute jump from a balloon in Coventry and providence was looking the other way. Edith was blown into a factory roof. She died of her injuries in hospital and Britain lost a brave aeronaut and pioneering aviator.

Every time a woman rose into the sky beneath her balloon and above a cheering crowd she risked going home in a coffin. It was a choice women were as free to make as men, long before they were even allowed to choose their MP. Some paid for their calling with their lives and some did not. So when two gutsy and ambitious teenaged Londoners chose the same career in 1903, stepping forward for a chance to fly beneath a balloon, neither could know which fate lay in store. How their lives played out in the last days of balloonomania owed as much to the vagaries of weather, human error and split-second decisions as to resilience, planning and courage. They gave their all to the precarious life of the Edwardian lady aeronaut and ignored the doomsayers in the press and dire warnings from their family.

Miss Lily Cove and Miss Dolly Shepherd were young working class women who saw their big chance and took it. Both were plucky... but one was lucky and one was not.

Chapter 10

The Lily Cove Mystery

High above the wild Yorkshire moorland that inspired *Wuthering Heights*, the balloon soared across the summer sky. A golden-haired young woman swung on the tiny trapeze beneath, waving a white hankie and wearing the pretty and practical costume that scandalised and delighted Edwardian England in equal measure. On Monday 11 June 1906, the charismatic Miss Lily Cove was the toast of Haworth. The village – home to the novelist Brontë sisters – welcomed her to its heart and a crowd of thousands stood transfixed by the sight of the 20-year-old Cockney celebrity climbing high into the clouds. What happened next to the tragic young aeronaut was to send shockwaves through the village, the country and the world. There were questions in the House, dark rumours on the street, an outpouring of grief, a flurry of outrage in the press and a warning from the *New York Times* about the implications of Lily's fate for female performers everywhere.

A restless, ambitious young woman of the Victorian *fin de siècle*, Lily was born into a troubled family and escaped into showbusiness. Her given name was Elizabeth Mary Cove and she was born in Hackney in the East End of London on 7 November 1885, a child of the sprawling slums. At her baptism the following April, her father was named as Thomas and her mother as Annie. By the time Lily was seven, she and her father were living with a woman called Margaret. Thomas, a bootmaker, had several partners and later described himself as a widower, so who exactly had the care of his little girl is hard to say. She was enrolled in school at the age of four by her great uncle, George Cove.

The key to Lily's shifting addresses and relationships lay with her family's dark secret. Her father Thomas was a serial sex offender, serving a string of prison sentences for crimes against young girls and women. In 1899 Thomas was sentenced to three months in jail for indecent exposure. In 1903 he appeared at the Old Bailey charged with the indecent assault of a girl aged under 13 and was sentenced to twelve months hard labour in Wormwood Scrubs prison. Thomas went on assaulting women for years to come, earning more hard labour in the Scrubs for indecent assault in 1911 and again in 1912.

There were few opportunities open to a working class girl at the turn of the twentieth century. Most left school before they were 13 and scratched a living in domestic service or factories, working long hours for very low pay with little time off. At the very least Lily must have suffered from the stigma of her father's criminal appetites or at worst, been a victim herself. His first recorded crime against a woman was when only child Lily was 13 and likely to have just left home to go into service. Lily shared her given name with her father's mother and his sister and had already ditched it in favour of another when she began work. Hardly surprising that a girl with such a past would choose a new name for herself. So Elizabeth, daughter of a notorious sex attacker, became Nelly the teenaged nursemaid and servant to a well-to-do family in Hackney – and finally found her true identity as Lily, the daring young starlet of the skies.

Lily's yearning for freedom chimed with the ambitions of the women's suffrage movement. Just a few years after Lily left her home at 170 Bow Road forever, the radical reformer Sylvia Pankhurst set up the East London Federation of Suffragettes at number 198. Pankhurst took her fight for the vote and workers rights to the East End where Lily grew up because it was blighted by some of the worst poverty in England. Lily found work as a servant but when the chance of an altogether more exciting life presented itself, she grabbed it with both hands. Her ticket to complete reinvention came with balloonist and parachutist Frederick Bidmead. The small and wiry performer owned a balloon-manufacturing business and was an associate of Auguste Gaudron on the aeronaut circuit. A popular trick was to ask for volunteers from the crowd and favour any young woman who gamely thrust her hand in the air.

There were balloon entertainments across the East End in the early 1900s, including at Victoria Park and Hackney Down. Lily could have taken her young charges to see a performance and caught Bidmead's eye as he scanned the crowd for recruits. Or she may simply have sought him out and asked for a job. Frederick said she repaired balloons for him before moving on to parachute descents. However their paths crossed, it was the flamboyant Captain Bidmead who introduced the 17-year-old skivvy to a new life as 'Leaping Lily', the glamorous aeronaut. Across town her father stood in the dock at the Old Bailey, guilty of molesting a young girl. For Lily, like so many before her, the urge to run away with the flying circus must have been irresistible.

It was boom time for travelling balloon shows and Bidmead recognized a crowd-puller when he met one. He later described Lily as 'a jolly girl' who 'had a joke and a jest for everyone'. Charismatic, fearless and a fast learner, Lily was perfectly suited to becoming a liberated lady balloonist. Her trademark trick of tearing off her skirt and hopping onto her trapeze wearing velvet tights or beribboned bloomers made her unforgettable. Lily was always described as a friendly and outgoing young woman. She became known for having an exceptionally cheerful disposition and making a host of friends wherever she went. Her ability to charm the audience was as important as her aptitude in the air for drumming up business out on the road.

While French and American male aeronauts often adopted the title of professor, British sky-sailors usually call themselves captain. Captain Bidmead made full use of the dashing addition to his showbiz persona and was the hero of 400 balloon ascents and eighty-three parachute descents. Frederick's many crashes and narrow escapes made headlines throughout his career as he toured galas and fetes around the country. When he joined forces with Lily he was already a veteran of several scary scrapes. Each one fuelled his reputation for sensationally close shaves. In 1895 he fell almost 80 feet before crashing onto a slanting roof and then falling headlong into the street. The topple left him with an injured spine and a long spell in hospital. In another near-fatal fall his parachute failed to open at 3,600ft and he hurtled towards the ground before a gust of wind saved him by slamming him sideways into a stake.

Ominously, trips to Yorkshire often ended a mere moustache whisker from complete disaster. In 1898 the *Wide World Magazine* ran a dramatic interview entitled, 'A Fifty Minutes' Horror, Being an account of the thrilling adventure of Captain Bidmead…' His parachute became tangled up with the balloon ropes and he was dragged along helplessly, crashing 27 miles away in Pontefract. By the turn of the century he wanted to cash in on the craze for female parachute acts. Teaming up was a good career move for both Lily and Frederick. He became her manager and stayed safely on the ground, she escaped her past by taking off in the balloon. Lily began her flying career by jumping with Frederick on a double parachute then graduated to solo jumps, ascending on a simple trapeze. The canny captain chose his pupil well and Lily was one of the most reliable girls that one could desire, he said. She was always cool and did not know the meaning of fear. After two years together he considered her an able aeronaut who knew as much about parachuting as he did. Considering she had never had an accident and he so many, it might be supposed she knew more.

THE LILY COVE MYSTERY

Lily, described in the press as good-looking and well-proportioned, added a touch of gutsy glamour as they travelled around fetes and galas drawing the crowds. She ascended beneath a gas balloon then parachuted down to wild applause and a heroine's welcome. So eight years after his unceremonious crash into a Pontefract hedge, Frederick was back in Haworth on the outskirts of Keighley, West Yorkshire, with someone else taking all the risks – his protégée and star attraction, 'Leaping Lily'.

In the summer of 1906 she accepted an invitation to provide the fabulous finale at the annual Haworth Gala to raise money for the local nurses' association. Organizers needed a headline act to pull in the crowds because interest in the event was on the wane. Nurses made around 70 visits a week to the homes of the sick and relied on fundraising events. It was to be Lily's twenty-first ascent by balloon and sixth parachute jump. The gala was on Saturday, 9 June and Lily arrived with the captain the night before. She took a room at the White Lion Hotel at the top of Main Street.

That night she sat in the bar chatting and laughing with the locals. Travelling the country with a man who wasn't her husband and appearing in bloomers was controversial. Yet Lily easily dazzled everyone she met. She seemed so glamorous and modern when she rolled into town that the landlord's star struck daughters, Ellen and Ada Bowler, hung on her every word. According to the *Yorkshire Daily Observer* the star made a huge impression and 'during the weekend made many friends, including the daughters of the house who became very much attached to her.' The feeling was mutual with Lily delighting her fans by loving them right back, declaring 'she had never spent a pleasanter or happier week-end, her friends having treated her with true Yorkshire hospitality.'

Lily's stay in Haworth is likely to have included a visit to the first Brontë Museum, above the Yorkshire Penny Bank virtually next door to the White Lion. The nineteenth century sisters Charlotte, Emily and Anne had made the mill town a place of literary pilgrimage, thanks to novels such as *Jane Eyre*, *Wuthering Heights* and *The Tenant of Wildfell Hall*. The Brontës, long dead by Lily's visit, had loved balloons. They were children in 1828 when the celebrity aeronaut *du jour* was Charles Green. When he ascended from nearby Keighley and flew overhead to Colne, the gifted siblings had a perfect view from their home on the edge of the moor. The following year 13-year-old Charlotte Brontë was inspired to make aeronauts of the little king and queens in one of her earliest stories, *Tales of The Islanders* when they 'ordered a balloon' and 'steered our way through the air'. Years later Charlotte makes a passing reference to a balloon ascent in her novel *Villette*.

THE LOST HISTORY OF THE LADY AERONAUTS

In 1906 Haworth locals were less in thrall to the memory of the sisters than fans from further afield. Jolly, outgoing Leaping Lily was much more their cup of tea. Brontëmania was no match for balloonomania and the moorland made famous by Cathy and Heathcliff became the dramatic backdrop for Miss Lily Cove.

Bidmead's publicity machine combined with glorious sunshine drew 6,000 people for all the fun of the fair. Galas were eagerly anticipated among people used to working at least 60 hours a week in the local mills and on surrounding farms. They arrived in droves for a well-earned day out and a balloon to crown the excitement. Music, games, a Punch and Judy show, a conjuror and ventriloquist, acrobatics and sweet treats were the warm up for the lady aeronaut in her flying bloomers. Organizers could not relax about Lily reigniting enthusiasm for the gala until they had seen her pull off her performance that evening. Despite the razzmatazz, there were noticeable gaps in support for the event, which needed to make money for the nurses. The Friendly Societies had not turned out in any number, there was a lack of the usual cyclists in fancy dress and local businesses were lukewarm about attending. Haworth's big problem with street parades was its actual main street, famously steep, paved with setts and too much for some people. Despite this the procession included dignitaries, comic couples in fancy dress, and four Sunday school wagons with children decked out as fairytale characters or people of various nations. A fire engine also made its way through the city on the hill, as Haworth was sometimes known.

Like much of Haworth life, the gala was dominated by the wealthy Merrall family. Local grandees and major employers, they enjoyed the social clout that came with running one of Yorkshire's largest wool businesses. Many of the cups and trophies were named for the family and the nurses association was a pet cause among the Merrall ladies. For Lily, one line-up of local bigwigs looked much the same as another. But hers was a face one Merrall would never forget. Rich and eligible son Charlie made sure he was never far from the visiting celebrity and may even have been the one to book her in the first place. Rumours flew that the young gentleman was fair smitten with thoroughly modern Lily.

Children paraded in costumes such as Cinderella and Boadicea. Comic bands called Haworth Bingham Bangam and the Keighley Wiffum-Waffum-Wuffum struck up. With clear skies and good-humoured crowds the gala was off to a good start. But it was clear things were not going to plan with the headline act. Where people hoped to see a magnificent balloon straining to take off for the climax of the day's entertainment, they saw only increasingly frustrated attempts by Frederick to make the balloon rise. The bands played on but Lily was the main event and the 'leaping' now seemed in doubt. Lily's balloon relied on cheap coal gas from the local works and a pipe was laid to the show fields for the purpose. Frederick struggled to make the balloon rise as over a tense hour and a half one attempt after another ended in failure. He was puzzled and frustrated, blaming atmospherics and inferior gas. The balloon refused to leave the ground. Frederick fought to make the balloon behave as Lily and the disappointed crowd looked on. After the seventh attempt Charlie Merrall stepped in and called a halt.

This was exactly the sort of situation that could spark a balloon riot so Lily moved quickly to rescue the situation. She vowed to the crowd that she would try again in a couple of days. 'The circumstances preventing her ascent on Saturday were distinctly annoying to Miss Cove, who seemed to take a deep interest in her work and was quite looking forward to the trip to the clouds on that day,' according to the *Keighley Herald*. Just as Bidmead turned every crash, bang, wallop landing into a war story, Lily had to gloss over customer disappointment. So it was back to the White Lion, where she kept the locals happy with plenty of flattery – declaring plans to take holidays in Haworth – while he concentrated on logistics. They were both worried about the damaging impact on business if they didn't deliver. The failure on Saturday could easily spell disaster for Lily's reputation as a headline act on the circuit, so it was vital she kept both the crowds and the committees sweet. Grumbles in gala circles had to be dispelled. Specifically, she had to woo the Keighley Friendly Societies' Gala committee who were interested in booking her for the following week. Lily and Fred needed to keep the gigs coming in and the Keighley worthies were in danger of getting cold feet unless they saw Leaping Lily in action. They were waiting to see how the second attempt went before signing her up, with a meeting arranged for the day after. The booking hung on the Haworth jump going ahead as billed and Lily wasn't about to let one failed ascent blight her new life. Her exceptionally cheerful disposition triumphed again and news of the lady aeronaut's determination swelled spectator numbers to 7,000.

On Monday 11 June, Frederick spent the morning checking every inch of the equipment and made a discovery that explained why the balloon could not rise to the occasion on gala day. It had a tear in the fabric and must have been leaking. He repaired the damage to the balloon so that Lily could do the same for their reputation. It was a lovely summer evening when Charlie Merrall drew up outside the White Lion in his motorcar. Lily and Frederick stepped inside and were driven to the show field in style.

THE LOST HISTORY OF THE LADY AERONAUTS

The young aeronaut received a rousing reception. As the flight drew near 'she braced herself up wonderfully, and appeared to anticipate the ascent with eagerness,' according to a witness. Lily was determinedly on form, treating the appreciative crowd to her signature move, whipping off her skirt to reveal velvet-clad legs. The saucy strip was simply a way to have a practical outfit on her trapeze perch beneath the balloon and parachute ride to earth. Lily appeared in cheerful mood and chatted to those around her, telling one man about the kindness and hospitality she had enjoyed in Haworth. When her descent was done, she promised, she would rush back to the gala field to join in the festivities.

How much of this was a bravura performance to ensure the engagement went ahead is impossible to say. The failed attempts to raise the balloon on gala day must have rattled Lily and certainly she knew how many other lady aeronauts – most recently Adelaide Bassett and Edith Brookes – had died in ballooning accidents. Amid the carnival atmosphere and brave banter with the crowds, one shrewd eyewitness told a *Yorkshire Daily Observer* reporter that Lily seemed 'somewhat pale'. Maybe, he said, the failed first attempt had 'affected her spirits somewhat.' Whatever her true mood, Lily took a keen interest in equipment checks then sat on the trapeze. This time the balloon inflated perfectly and at 7.40pm began to float upwards, buoyed by a surge of cheers and whistles from those gathered on the ground. Balanced on the swing beneath her balloon, the parachute attached to its side, Lily appeared self-possessed and confident as she began to soar. Leaping Lily headed for the heavens to the sounds of an ecstatic crowd. Haworth Brass Band played with gusto and onlookers threw their hats into the air.

Lily drew more cheers as she fluttered her hankie, waving goodbye as the earth fell away. Captain Bidmead travelled below in a pony and trap, tracking her flight. Behind him was Charlie Merrall and it is doubtful Frederick had any say in the matter. As proud owner of the first motorcar in Haworth, Charlie seemed determined to impress Lily by driving along below the balloon as it soared across wild open moorland, just like the society gents of the Aero Club in London. The drill was to wait until 700 feet then jump from the trapeze, her weight snapping the cord that attached the parachute to the balloon, and drift to earth in the performance she had perfected.

Suddenly, something went catastrophically wrong. She began plunging towards Ponden reservoir, 30 acres of water in a valley near Stanbury. Lily was going too fast for the parachute to open in time. The *Yorkshire Daily Observer* reports:

'Those who had seen several parachute descents say that the lady attempted to come down before a height had been attained sufficient to allow time for the machine to open properly. However this may be, instead of expanding fully and supporting Miss Cove, in the ordinary way, it does not appear to have more than slightly opened at most, and parachute and parachutist came down through the air like a dead weight.'

To the utter disbelief of those on the ground she came free of the parachute altogether and a nightmare unfolded in the sky. Spectator Robert Rushworth saw her through his field glasses and could only watch in horror as she plunged headfirst toward the ground, cartwheeling helplessly in the air and crashing into a field near the reservoir beneath Ponden Hall. The first on the scene was Cowling Heaton who ran a café at nearby Scar Top. He raced to the stricken Lily and found her still breathing, her eyes flung open but seemingly blind with shock. He took her into his arms and said, 'My good woman, if you can speak, do.'

A frantic Frederick was right behind, running to Lily's side. Behind him was Charlie. It was too late. Her legs and skull were smashed, blood running from her mouth, nose and eyes. The men could only sink to their knees as moments later Lily died where she fell, never speaking a word, never able to explain what had gone so fatally wrong. A doctor arrived and with one glance could see she was dead. Sick at heart they lifted her broken body onto a stretcher, carrying Lily to a covered cart in Hob Lane for the mournful trek back to Haworth.

Two miles away at the gala field there was unease in the air, the merrymaking muted. There was a feeling that things were not right though no-one in Haworth had seen the accident. The band was still poised to strike up *See the Conquering Hero Comes*. The holiday crowds gathered on the hillsides near Ponden to see Lily jump were not so lucky. They witnessed Lily's horrific plunge and joined the rush towards where she lay. Back at the gala field a relieved cheer went up when Charlie's car finally appeared, spectators assuming he had squired Lily back to town. Instead the ashen-faced young gentleman stepped out of the car and told them she was dead. People stared in total shock as the cart carrying her corpse moved through the village and the grim reality rippled through the crowd. The proof of the tragedy was a poignant glimpse of blood-streaked blonde hair trailing from beneath the hasty shroud. Some onlookers sobbed, others simply watched in appalled silence as she was taken back to the White Lion, carried inside and the coffin maker called. The landlady, mother of Ellen and Ada, told a reporter: 'We'd made arrangements to spend such a jolly evening, but they brought her back dead.'

A stark telegram was sent to Thomas Cove in London. His daughter would never leave Yorkshire.

The *Keighley News* told the sad story:

> 'The happy, enthusiastic crowd of an hour before was changed into a melancholy, despairing assembly. The news was staggering. Many could scarcely credit that the blithe, vivacious, fearless young lady who a very short time before had ascended, full of hope for a successful performance, now lay lifeless. There was many an aching heart in that throng, and many a tear rose unbidden to the eye as the vehicle conveying the body passed the vicinity of the field from which the ill-fated ascent had been made.'

From 8.30pm until midnight, knots of people stood in the streets discussing the awful tragedy and 'a deep gloom weighed on the spirits of all. It was an experience Haworth never wishes to know again.'

As word spread journalists flooded in, closely followed by day-trippers who wanted to see the exact spot where Lily fell to her death. 'Needless to say the tragedy entirely changed the peaceful lethargy of the home of the Brontës,' notes the *Keighley Herald*. 'The people gathered at the street corners on Tuesday gazed with morbid interest on the unusual sight of a large band of inquisitive pressmen seeking details of the previous night's fatality.' Haworth was feverish with speculation about how 'the poor lass' had met her end. Was someone to blame for her death? Or did Lily jump to her doom on purpose? All eyes were on Frederick and though visibly upset, he spoke to newsmen immediately in a bid to quash the gossip.

'Captain Bidmead emphatically declared that the affair was a pure accident,' reports the *Keighley News*. 'The girl was in the highest spirits, and on the best terms with all her friends. She had never had any mishap before. She had been one of the most reliable girls that one could desire.'

Her last descent had been a week earlier in Cambridge, according to Bidmead, where 'she was always cool,' and 'did not know the meaning of fear.' Except, that is, when it came to water. Lily was terrified of landing in water. Frederick believed she saw herself drifting towards the reservoir beneath Ponden Hall and panicked. 'He attributed Miss Cove's terrible fate to her horror of water,' the paper explains. 'He had frequently urged Miss Cove to take swimming lessons, but no-one had been able to persuade her to go to the swimming baths.' Though under strict orders never to unfasten the parachute it was easy enough for Lily to do. She probably thought she could hold on but lost her grip and plummeted around 60 feet to the ground. Frederick relived the awful moment when he discovered her fate:

> 'When we came up to the spot where she had fallen, two or three people who had been watching the ascent from the surrounding hills were on the spot, and told me she was dying. It was a terrible shock to me for I never had a better or more promising assistant.'

The parachute the captain made specially for his talented protégée lay uselessly on the moorland heather, almost 20 yards away. If she had followed his instructions and kept her head all would have been well, he was quick to point out. 'Miss Cove really went further than she should have done,' reports the paper. 'He told her to drop just over by the mill. If she had done so he would have been with her in a couple of minutes.'

While Lily's friends in Yorkshire and London reeled from the shock of her death, newspapers around the world reported the event with varying degrees of sympathy. Under the headline 'Lady Parachutist Killed at Haworth,' the *Yorkshire Daily Observer* relayed the disaster of 'Miss Cove, who had undertaken to make a parachute descent, falling like a log to the earth from a considerable height, in the full gaze of a large number of horrified spectators, and being instantly killed.' Meanwhile the *Keighley News* wagged a stern finger about the 'certain class' of people who were thrilled by the element of danger in ballooning events. Under the vivid headline 'Young Woman Dashed to Death' the editorial thundered:

> 'Public interest in this class of performance has not shown any diminution and so ingrained among a certain class is the love of morbid excitement, the performance attended by risk of injury and even death, that were another parachute descent announced in the district today a great many would be found only too willing to pay to witness it.'

THE LOST HISTORY OF THE LADY AERONAUTS

The editor was not the first or the last to express fury about skydiving women and the appreciative audience they attracted. On the day of Lily's funeral, politicians leapt to their feet in all-male Westminster to demand a ban on women performing dangerous stunts. In the House of Commons debate of 14 June 1906, Sir Arthur Fell said:

> 'I beg to ask the Secretary of State for the Home Department whether his attention has been called to the death of Miss Cove when descending from a balloon in a parachute on June 11th and whether he proposes to take any steps to prohibit such exhibitions in the future.'

Home Secretary Herbert Gladstone replied:

> 'My attention has been called to this shocking case. I have prepared and hope to introduce shortly a Bill extending the Dangerous Performances Acts to all women whatever their age may be.'

Across the Atlantic, though, the American press saw things differently. The *New York Times* took up the cause of freedom for female performers who chose the same life as Lily. On 1 July 1906, the leader column was devoted to an impassioned plea to the British not to make a hasty law that might spell the end of every kind of exciting show. Headlined 'Dangerous "turns" by women may be stopped in England' it highlights Gladstone's threat to outlaw women (no-one objected to men) doing dangerous stunts such as jumping from balloons. The solution was to simply bracket women with children in deciding what was best for them. 'Now the tragic death of Miss Cove, by the failure of her parachute, has brought the matter forward in the most urgent manner...' but unlike its British counterparts, the paper made a powerful argument for resisting such a law. It would, warned the Americans, spell the end of every kind of stirring sideshow, gala and entertainment performed by daring women and enjoyed by all.

Back in Britain female performers were described in one report as having 'nerves of iron and muscles of steel' as they mobilized to save their jobs. A series of protests across the country, including one in London's Hyde Park, persuaded the government to drop the Bill. Meanwhile, the *Keighley Herald* was not deflected in its dogged duty to report comprehensively on all the events of the previous Saturday and Monday – Gala worthies, competitions and festivities first; the fate of Lily Cove second. Before the internationally-reported story of her sensational death was relayed, there were such matters as the children's costume parade, the 'best "get-up" in fancy dress' prize and the name of every person on the many organizing committees. True to the mission of a good local paper at a big local event, the headlines ran in descending order of local importance. 'Haworth Gala', declared the *Keighley Herald* when reporting the week's events. Then came 'Brilliant weather and a large attendance' and only then, 'Parachute fatality: lady aeronaut's terrible death'.

The inquest into Lily's death was packed, with every detail reported in the *Keighley Herald*, *Keighley News* and *Yorkshire Daily Observer*. Held less than 24 hours after the tragedy, rumours were rife about possible foul play, with gossip linking Lily's death to an imagined love rivalry between manager Frederick and playboy Charlie. Neither had the whisper that Lily deliberately jumped to her death gone away. However, the police report stated that 'no blame or suspicion appeared to attach to anybody.' District coroner Edgar Wood presided over the inquiry at the Haworth District Council Offices. Jonas Bradley of Stanbury, who had watched Lily's flight from Haworth Moor, was appointed as foreman of the jury.

The spotlight trained once more on Captain Frederick Bidmead, the first witness called to help solve the mystery. Stepping forward for his grilling, he began by paying tribute to Lily as an experienced artist who had made 20 successful ascents and descents over the last two years. On the previous day everything in connection with the performance was satisfactory and under his personal supervision. When the balloon began to rise, 'Miss Cove was not the least nervous and seemed in a cheerful mood.'

The parachute paraphernalia was brought out and Bidmead talked the jury through how it worked:

> 'The device is quite simple: First of all the parachute is fastened to the balloon by the breaking cord. On the hoop at the bottom of the parachute two cords with the hooks referred to are attached to the shoulder hooks on the strappings of the aeronaut so that even if the person leaves hold or faints he or she is supported by the hooks. The parachute, of course, is severed from the balloon by the cord snapping with the weight of the aeronaut's body.'

The balloon 'rose steadily and sailed away very nicely' on the fateful day and Lily floated along for about nine minutes before making her parachute jump.

So, what had gone so wrong? Frederick had not seen Lily leave the balloon because he lost sight of her for about a minute as she disappeared over the skyline, but knew she had jumped when the balloon shot up. The next time he laid eyes on her she was unconscious on the ground, unhooked from the parachute that lay uselessly some distance away. It was impossible for the parachute to have become unfastened by itself and a Superintendent Tebbutt voiced the only two options. Either it was interfered with or Lily undid it herself, but why?

'She must have unfastened them on account of being afraid of dropping into the reservoir,' the captain said, presenting again his preferred solution to the puzzle. Lily could not swim, Frederick told the court as he had told the press, and had 'a perfect horror of dropping on water.' Certainly, Lily knew that drowning was a very real danger in her line of work. A decade earlier Louisa Maud Evans was dragged under by her parachute. Seeing a large reservoir loom into view may have filled Lily with panic that she faced the same fate.

The inquest jurors were keenly aware of all the speculation about Lily's death and determined to hold every possible explanation up to the light. Village gossip suggested Lily actually wanted to create a sensation by entering the water, according to one juror. It was put to Bidmead that 'a report had been current in Haworth during the day that she could [swim], and that she expressed a desire to drop into the dam.' The aeronaut repeated that Lily could not swim, though he had wanted her to learn. Or could she have loosened the rings out of sheer bravado in order to come down hanging on by her hands? Eventually the coroner stepped in to back up Bidmead's theory. 'Personally I think she did so in order to avoid the water,' he said. If Lily had simply kept her seat under the balloon she would have come down steadily, a tactic Frederick had advised if she ever felt in danger. Instead she became anxious, misjudged her height and tried to unhook herself from the parachute in case she hit the water.

A traumatised Cowling Heaton then took the stand and described how the balloon 'exploded' and a minute later he watched Lily falling head over heels and landing headfirst. Overcome at the memory, it took a while to draw out his story. *The Keighley Herald* notes, 'The sad circumstances of the affair had no doubt considerably affected the witness and he continued his evidence under deep emotion.' Little wonder. He started the evening watching a summer entertainment and ended it by cradling a young woman as she lay dying. He told the hushed room that Lily seemed to let out two sobs and he lifted her onto his knee, with her head resting on his shoulder. She did not speak and all he could do was send a boy running for water as her life was ending. From what he saw, she would have been safe if she had stayed with her parachute but accused her of trying to show off. 'It seemed to me that she had been trying to be clever,' he said.

The next witness, Robert Rushworth, watched the whole thing through field glasses from half a mile away. He saw Lily shrugging her shoulders and was convinced she detached herself from the parachute before jumping. Sergeant David Pearson testified that he was present at the ascent and had seen the parachute rings firmly attached to Lily's shoulder hooks. Dr Robert Thompson then described her fatal injuries as fractures to both legs and probably her skull. Her neck was bruised and half her head was covered in blood. Having exhausted every theory the inquest recorded a verdict of accidental death and, like so many juries before and after, called on the Home Secretary to ban such performances. Foreman and witness Jonas Bradley declared them 'lowering to the public taste'. Lily had clearly died as a result of falling from a parachute but the chain of events during her final minutes would remain a mystery.

The shocking week in the city on the hill concluded on the afternoon of Thursday, 14 June 1906. Just three days after she happily fluttered her handkerchief from her seat in the sky, adoring crowds once again converged for Lily's funeral. While newspapers relayed every detail of the dreadful death across the world and the great and the good entered the brief parliamentary furore over outlawing dangerous stunts by female balloonists, Haworth came together to bury its adopted darling. Frederick brought Lily's dad up from London and bought him a new black suit for the funeral. It felt like his duty, whether or not he knew Thomas's history.

Lily, at least, did not have to suffer seeing her father. Before the coffin lid was nailed shut women gathered to look down on her pale young face one last time. The Reverend Thomas Story conducted a short service at the White Lion, remarking that 'strange and unexplainable things happen'. Haworth Gala Committee stalwarts carried the coffin of pitch pine in relays through the village and out to the cemetery on the edge of the moor. Not since the funeral of the Reverend Patrick Brontë 45 years earlier had such a huge crowd gathered to mourn along the moor town roads. Virtually the whole population turned out to accompany Lily on her final journey, all curtains drawn and shutters closed out of respect. Hundreds more came from neighbouring villages. Men stopped working in the stone quarry, removing their caps and falling silent as the cortege and crowd passed slowly by. The young Cockney balloonist was lowered into the Yorkshire earth, within sight of the Ponden field where her life ended, her funeral and headstone funded by a village whip round. Charlie sent a wreath of pink roses.

THE LOST HISTORY OF THE LADY AERONAUTS

Lily Cove was dead before her twenty-first birthday but the *Keighley Herald* summed up the lasting impact she made on her final audience:

> 'All of Haworth seemed to have bestirred itself in order to pay a final tribute of sympathy to the relatives of one, who less than a week ago, had come into their midst a happy, enthusiastic and plucky young aeronaut.'

As with every female aeronaut since 1784, pluck could only get you so far. Lily was brave, but went to an early grave. And that, for everyone concerned in this mystery above the moors, was that for the next century. Captain Bidmead deemed blameless, Lily accused of mindless panic and failing to follow orders, her death officially an accident. When I took a closer look at Fred's version of events, however, something did not add up. Several things, in fact.

The manager's repeated assertion that Lily was a very experienced parachutist, for instance. *The Times and Express* quotes him saying 'as recently as Whit-Monday she made a very successful parachute descent at Carmarthen.' However, the Welsh *Evening Express* for 5 June 1906 makes no mention of Lily – or any other aeronaut, male or female – when describing the Whitsuntide ascent and descent by Captain Bidmead. Neither does the Welsh press refer to Lily ever having performed there when reporting the tragedy. Bidmead also said Lily's most recent ascent was the week before, on 4 June in Cambridge. Yet the only record of Bidmead being there was in January of that year, when he was sued by a gala committee for a failed balloon ascent the previous August. Bidmead shirked responsibility, blaming another 'unforeseen accident'. So it is fair to ponder whether Bidmead's claims for Lily's credentials were true.

Also, Bidmead's iron insistence that his safety checks were all 'first class' was accepted by press, police and jurors who were hardly familiar with skydiving equipment. Time and again in interviews and in court, Bidmead insisted it was impossible for Lily's parachute not to open, dropping his handkerchief by way of illustration. Yet elsewhere he relates his own sky scrapes caused by parachutes failing to open. And if Bidmead had worked with Lily for two years, why did he take out a 'Wanted' ad in the theatrical newspaper *The Era* seven weeks before the Haworth gig, saying 'Captain Bidmead has a few vacant dates ... Lady parachutist write immediately.'

Bidmead's airborne disasters did not begin or end in Haworth. Less than two months after Lily's funeral, he was in the papers again for another flop.

THE LILY COVE MYSTERY

Back in Carmarthen, he was unable to make an August ascent because of 'a mishap to the balloon'. Mishaps, accidents, court cases and death follow Captain Bidmead around. He even had unsettling links to another female fatality, Louisa Maud Evans, the girl who perished in Cardiff a decade earlier under the dubious care of Auguste Gaudron. Bidmead was working with the Gaudrons in that year of 1896 as another inquest into another parachutist discussed how such a thing could happen. A cynic might note that from the moment poor Lily hit the ground, the showman was free to portray the whole, horrible thing as an accidental suicide or a failure to follow his instructions.

In short, Lily's own fault.

We will never know if Bidmead had blood on his hands. There are only questions that won't go away. What had Lily told her new friends over that party weekend in the pub? What suspicions were shared on street corners the night of the accident? If Captain Frederick Bidmead was not telling the whole truth, it throws a chilling new light on his words to a reporter in the aftermath of the tragedy. 'I can't get it out of my mind,' Frederick confessed. 'Last night I saw it in a dream. It haunts me.'

Chapter 11

Balloonomania Sunset

The decade before the First World War was the last hurrah for the lady aeronauts before aeroplanes changed the sky forever. The female pilots and skydivers of lighter-than-air flight displayed an impressive combination of gumption, gut instinct and presence of mind. Resourceful women employed balloons as tools of personal and economic emancipation and now they were recruited to the fight for political freedom, too. In the final days of balloonomania, charismatic performers and airborne activists proved that you really could not keep a good woman down.

The most famous of all the Edwardian lady parachutists was Dolly Shepherd, who lived to blow out 96 candles compared to Lily Cove's 20. Like Letitia Sage, Margaret Graham and Gertrude Bacon, Dolly penned a memoir and *When the 'Chute Went Up* offers a unique insight into the final days of balloonomania.

In 1903 Alexandra Palace in North London was *the* place to go for entertainment. There were carousels, boating lakes, horse races, carnivals and of course, balloon rides. Dolly, from Southgate, was 16 and desperate to see John Sousa, the American famous for his marching music. The concert was a sell-out (not that she could have afforded a ticket) and she hatched a plan to watch for free. She turned up on the day and asked for a job as a waitress. Delighted that her plan worked, her hands sore from clapping, she turned back to her new job and was stunned to see Sousa himself take a seat at one of her tables. He was joined by a dapper Frenchman with piercing eyes, a waxed moustache and a balloon on his navy blue cap. It was Auguste Gaudron, the aeronaut. Then another American with a flowing beard, a larger waxed moustache, a cowboy hat and boots with spurs sat down too. It was Samuel Cody, the Wild West showman and pioneering aviator. Gaudron and Cody were at the centre of the aeronautical world and for Dolly, it was a fateful moment. She craved a more exciting life than waitressing and another woman found herself in the right place at the right time.

'Ally Pally' was a hub for early aviation experiments and Auguste and Samuel became regulars at Dolly's table, where she was drawn into conversations about daredevil life. The job that was only a canny way to see a concert became the door to an exciting world, one where she was a perfect fit. When the north London teenager volunteered as a stand-in for the American's sharp-shooting act (he fired an egg from her head while blindfolded) the Frenchman with the piercing eyes spied evidence of that all-important pluck. Dolly with the wasp waist and iron resolve was definitely lady aeronaut material, though it was another year before he offered her an ascent. The captain gave Dolly thirty minutes of parachute training, mainly in how to fall backwards on landing, and she was ready to don her knickerbocker suit and board the basket. Auguste took her up to 2000ft, pointed out a field to aim for and shouted 'Go!'

> 'My heart rose into my mouth as I plummeted for what seemed far too long, dropping like a stone. I could hear the rapid flap-flap-flap of the silk streaming after me as the canopy broke from the balloon netting and sucked at the rush of air, and then at last there was a big whoooooosh...'

The parachute opened and Dolly describes in her memoirs that first taste of drifting alone through the clouds. 'Suspended there in the clear, warm air, high above the land of mere mortals, I experienced a sense of elation such as I had never known.'

Dolly was a natural and gladly pocketed her first fee of £2 10s but did not know the whole story behind her sudden big break. Thrilled with her new job, the 17-year-old was unaware that she was filling the 'chute of Maud Brooks, who died of her injuries after an accident in Dublin. By the time Dolly did know, she understood why Maud was never discussed. Early parachutists were in permanent danger and could not afford to think about it too much. Sudden death was a very real possibility, as Louisa Evans, Edith Brookes, Edith Cook, Adelaide Bassett, Lily Cove and others proved with tragic regularity. Everyone in the ballooning world knew the ones who never made it home. Gaudron's doomed skydivers had made headlines since the death of little Mademoiselle Albertina in 1896 but inside the team they were tactfully ignored.

For all his gentlemanly ways, Auguste had a chilling way of dealing with the deaths of his aeronauts. He simply did not discuss them. 'From time to time a member of our team might "disappear",' says Dolly:

> 'Nothing would be said. He or she would just not be seen at any more shows, and if questioned, Captain Gaudron would

merely say that the aeronaut in question had "left the team". They had left, sure enough!'

She had to put the aeronauts killed on the job from her mind:

> 'We learnt not to question these departures, for death was a subject on which we did not dwell. We might read of such an event in a newspaper, but if we did, our reaction was that of most people who flirt with danger: it might happen to *them* but never to *me*.'

She knew it was danger that shifted tickets and frankly admitted it gave her a kick, too. Dolly moved on to ascending with paying passengers and watching their eyes widen as she finished her little guided tour of the sights below before bidding them cheerio and jumping from the basket. Where other women realized too late that they had made a terrible mistake, Dolly thrived on the pure rush of adrenalin:

> 'What lingered in my mind was the dream-like ascension into the skies; the exquisite excitement of the long drop from the basket; the gentle ride down under the smiling canopy; the sense of achievement as I scrambled to my feet after the landing. These were the delights that captured me.'

Her act evolved into a daring solo. The basket was dispensed with and she would run into the sky holding on to a trapeze beneath the balloon as it rose, then check the little altimeter she wore on her wrist before releasing her parachute and floating back down. This had the added commercial advantage of only needing a small and cheap-to-fill balloon. In 1906, the year Lily Cove died, Dolly had an awful insight into the final moments of her unfortunate contemporary. For several minutes during a jump in the Midlands, Dolly was convinced she would die. The 'chute failed to open until the last moment and she landed badly winded but uninjured. The episode taught her to double-check the ropes were untwisted, but her nerve remained intact.

What really set Dolly Shepherd apart from poor Lily (and Louisa Evans and Edith Brookes) was her ability not to panic. She had the mindset of a commando, courage coupled with total focus. When things went wrong, refusing to panic was what kept you alive. Singing helped, too. The next time she was 4000ft over Coalville she picked out her landing spot and gave the ripping cord the usual tug to release the parachute. As in a nightmare, nothing happened. She tried over and again and felt the panic rise before consciously calming herself by talking out loud. 'Now what do I do?' she asked her balloon. There was nothing for it but to simply hang on until it descended itself. It was then she saw that the flap had blown across the neck of the balloon and the gas was trapped:

> 'My heart dropped, and for a few moments I slumped there, my mind a blank. But this wouldn't do. I *couldn't* give up.

I *had* to hang on. When I regained control of myself, I began to think constructively. With the sling to take most of the weight of my body, I resolved that I could stay there just as long as it would take for the balloon to tire of this silly game and return us both to earth.'

That was when she started to sing. It was a trick her policeman father had taught her for times of trouble. 'Pale hands I've loved, beside the Shalimar...' she crooned to the clouds, from the parlour hit *The Kashmiri Song*. Then, 'Goodbye, Dolly, I must leave you...' wishing the balloon would take the hint, then her father's favourite hymn, 'There is a happy land, far, far away...' She went through every song she knew, fighting to hold on as her arms grew painful, cold and tired, hating her balloon, 'some grotesque monster now, relentlessly carrying me higher and higher, like some mad abductor hauling me off to a distant and secret lair.'

She had one thought, to keep her arms from going numb. If she let go she would fall 12000ft. She removed one hand at a time to blow on them. One by one, she bit the end of each finger. Growing delirious and weak she gave in to wondering whether she would feel the 'crump' of hitting the earth but then she was descending, landing semi-conscious on the grass, a horse licking her cheek. She staggered to a nearby cottage and discovered she was in Whissendine. After a reviving drink, the father gave her a lift on his bike to the railway station.

Captain Gaudron did not pay full-time wages. Alma Beaumont quit over money in 1896 and a decade later Dolly needed a day job between bookings; that meant the Ostrich Feather Emporium in Holborn, owned by her aunt. The stoles, hats, dresses and feather boas made by Dolly and her friends were popular with elegant ladies of the era, from the Aero Club to 'Ally Pally'. She worked from 8.30am to 8pm with 45 minutes for lunch and kept the women she worked with entertained with tales of derring-do and little treats from her parachute earnings. They hung on her stories but one in particular was agog. Louie May wanted to be an aeronaut too – as long as her fiancé never found out. Gaudron agreed, gave her the usual half hour training and Louie and Dolly rose together from Ashby de la Zouch in Leicestershire for a double drop on 9 June 1908. 'Together we ran forward beneath the rising balloon, to be lifted smoothly into the air alongside each other,' says Dolly. Higher and higher they went, Dolly waving a silky union jack and never for a moment realizing she was embarking on the most dangerous ascent of her life.

Louie was loving it until the time came to tug the cord and the release mechanism failed. They were at 8000ft when Dolly swallowed her own panic as she realized that once again they would have to hang on for dear life until the balloon came down. Not once did she consider saving herself and abandoning her friend. Instead she gave a little pep talk. Hang on, this had happened before, don't look down, look up, they would be fine, but *hang on*. She watched Louie's lips turning blue, terror overtaking her and knew Louie could not hang on. Once again Dolly's extraordinary courage and quick thinking came into play. It was all she had to save Louie from an appalling death. She paid her companion the highest accolade. 'You are very plucky,' Dolly called out and told Louie the plan. It was to execute the most audacious mid-air rescue of all time. 'Don't worry, I won't leave you, I've made up my mind,' Dolly shouted. 'You're coming down on my parachute.'

She managed to haul her friend over using the connecting rope, then persuade her to move from one parachute to the other and wrap herself around Dolly. The heart-stoppingly dangerous transfer happened 11,000ft above ground, with Dolly feverishly praying her arms could take both their weights and that the parachute would open. There was only one way to find out. They began to fall, too fast with so much weight on one parachute and even then Dolly was reassuring her friend that they would be all right. When they hit the ground, Louie was all right. It was Dolly who appeared to have broken her back.

Nursed by the farmers who found her, Dolly was fed brandy in milk for three days to keep her sedated as Gaudron and the doctors came and went. Only time would tell whether she would 'leave the team' like her predecessor, Maud. As she hovered between life and death, her heroism made headlines and the press kept a vigil. Eventually she was out of danger and her back, like parachute ropes, had to be untwisted. With only a knotted hankie to bite on and a stiff brandy for anaesthetic, she was pulled back into shape. Dolly was paralysed from the waist down and a specialist from London said she would never walk again. He recommended a hospital for incurables. The local doctor did not agree. In a scene reminiscent of an early Frankenstein film, the farmer assisted the family physician Dr Allen in an experimental treatment where primitive electric plates were placed on her damaged back. Dolly waited. The farmer sweated. Everyone watched in silence. Then Dolly felt a tingling. The feeling was returning to her back and legs. By the end of a week she was on her way to recovery. Everyone was overjoyed, except the London doctor who turned on his heel and flounced off.

While Dolly recuperated Auguste Gaudron had a problem. He was a practical man and having his star parachutist out of action left him short staffed. It was only decades later that Dolly discovered the secret arrangement he made with her mother while she was learning to walk again. The Madame Papillon who appeared over London in 1908 was Dolly's mother. She helped hold the fort while her famous daughter recovered, but made the captain promise never to tell.

Despite everything, Dolly had not finished with balloons. She had to go up again to prove that she could. A mere eight weeks after crashing to earth under Louie (who had been whisked away from the feather shop by her furious fiancé), she staged a comeback in Ashby. They were so happy to see her back that a brass band escorted her from the station. This time Dolly was scared but after a perfect descent, 'I rose to my feet, happy to be a parachutist again.' One evening in 1912 her career as the last of the lady aeronauts ended where it had begun, at 'Ally Pally'. Aged 25 and famous across the land, Dolly hung in the silent sky feeling at peace with the world. 'The silence of the sky was suddenly broken,' she says. 'It was a voice. I did not imagine it. It spoke once, quite clearly, then no more. "Don't come up again, or you'll be killed," it said.' Whether she heard the voice of God or her subconscious, she did not argue and for the very last time, pulled the rip cord and floated gently back to earth.

When Dolly had saved Louie and almost killed herself, the usual arguments appeared in the local press. Certain men would never approve of stuntwomen and wanted them stripped of the right to work. The Reverend Edmund Pigott considered Dolly's displays pandered to base instincts and should be forbidden. He was joined by Caleb Hackney who opined, 'Can not public opinion, perhaps supported by some exalted personage, put an end to parachute descents by females?' Two years earlier the *New York Times* argued at length on posthumous behalf of Leaping Lily, but Dolly put it in a nutshell for leaping ladies everywhere. 'What a dull world it would be if it were full of Reverend Pigotts and Caleb Hackneys!'

THE LOST HISTORY OF THE LADY AERONAUTS

Dolly once remarked that she seemed to have led a charmed life. It would be more accurate to describe it as a courageous one. In her nineties, she enjoyed a flight with the Red Devils and remained fascinated by developments in parachutes. No-one ever succeeded in banning women from skydiving and Dolly never forgot her glory days. 'I could see a young girl making her determined way up the hill to the Alexandra Palace in the spring of 1903, heading for adventures and pleasures untold,' she writes at the close of her astonishing life story.

The golden age of women and balloon flight began with Madame Thible singing her heart out over Lyon in 1784 and ended with Lily and Dolly chatting up the crowds before heading for the clouds in the 1900s. Little wonder that feisty Edwardian women used the sky to fight for political freedom, too. 'Suffragettes in Mid-Air' ran a February 1909 headline in the *Essex County Chronicle*, reporting on a daring act of aerial propaganda by one Muriel Matters in a dirigible balloon:

> 'During its progress the balloon reached a height of about 3,500ft, and passed the Houses of Parliament when they were so high that they could just distinguish the buildings. Miss Matters threw out 56lb. of hand-bills, which dropped "as the gentle rain from heaven, upon the place beneath."'

Like Letitia Sage at the start of our story, Muriel was an actress. She made her name with the feminist flight over the opening of Parliament. Born in south Australia, where women won the vote in 1894, she moved to London in 1905 to fight for the Women's Freedom League. Muriel knew that no-one could ignore a balloon. Not those of the Aero Club aristos, not those of the parachuting showgirls and certainly not one emblazoned with 'VOTES FOR WOMEN' and pointed at Parliament. According to the *Daily Express*:

> 'The suffragists, not content with their infantry assaults, cavalry parades, motor and char-a-banc demonstrations, and steamboat trips, took to the air yesterday. At least, Miss Muriel Matters, one of their youngest but more determined warriors did. She sailed aloft from Hendon in the diminutive basket of a cigar-shaped dirigible balloon for the very latest thing in suffragist dashes to Westminster.'

Muriel was a true liberated aeronaut. She wore an overcoat to protect against the rotten eggs and fish lobbed when she spoke at rallies and earned her suffragette spurs in October 1908 by chaining herself to the grille of the Ladies Gallery in the House of Commons. The metal grille was a loathed symbol of female exclusion and as Muriel held forth on the female vote to the startled members below, fellow protester Violet 'Tilly' Tillard lowered campaign literature on a piece of string. That may have been the moment the dirigible idea dawned. Why stick with string from a balcony? Why not take to the skies and scatter pamphlets all over London? Muriel was aided and abetted by Henry Spencer, one of the balloon-making brothers who were friends with many of the lady aeronauts, and an enthusiastic supporter of female equality. Muriel set off from Hendon with Henry in his airship, which bore those three controversial words, votes for women, across the gas bag. Muriel told the BBC in 1939:

> 'We loaded up about a hundredweight of leaflets, then I climbed into the basket. Mr Spencer joined me and we rose into the air, travelling towards Cricklewood. We ascended to over three thousand feet. It was very cold but I got some exercise throwing the leaflets overboard. Mr Spencer occasionally clambered out along the framework to make some adjustment. He was rather like a spider walking across its web, for the rigging was quite open with nothing between him and the earth and suddenly I realized that if he fell off I hadn't the first idea how to manoeuvre the airship. Not that I bothered much about that. I was far too busy making a trail of leaflets across London.'

As ever, the balloon went exactly where it wanted, which was away from Westminster and into the branches of a tree in Surrey. Muriel did not mind. She was unscathed and content with the publicity for the movement. She later went on to work with Sylvia Pankhurst in socialist education projects around Bow, Lily Cove's old East End neighbourhood. Just like Lily, Dolly and all their sky-sailing sisters, Muriel upheld the true tradition of the balloonistas who used flight to fight for their freedom:

> 'Daring? Well yes I suppose it was daring as one looks back from the point of view of age and, perhaps, wisdom. But at the time I didn't stop to think what a risky venture it was. I was young and the experiences of the suffragettes soon taught one to be tough.'

In the century and a quarter before powered aircraft, lady aeronauts were up, up and away on the wild frontier of balloon flight. It was always a tough life but even when the risks were appalling, the rewards were glorious.

Bibliography

BACON, Gertrude, *Memories of Land and Sky*, Methuen & Co. Ltd, 1928.
BAKER, John A. and Pritchard, Norman, *Balloons and Ballooning*, Shire Publications, 1986.
BARKER, Juliet, *The Brontës*, Abacus, 2010.
BASSETT, Preston R., *Aerial Adventures of Carlotta, The Lady Aeronaut or Sky-Larking in Cloudland, being hap-hazard accounts of the Perils and Pleasures of Aerial Navigation*, American Heritage, August 1966.
BRONTË, Charlotte, *Tales of the Islanders*, The Berg Collection, New York Public Library, 1829.
CONLIN, Jonathan (editor), *The Pleasure Garden, from Vauxhall to Coney Island*, University of Pennsylvania Press, 2012.
CORN, Joseph J. (editor), *Into the Blue: American Writing on Aviation and Spaceflight*, The Library of America, 2011.
CROUCH, Tom D., *The Eagle Aloft: Two Centuries of the Balloon in America*, Smithsonian Institution Press, 1983.
DARNALL, Diane Thomas, *The Challengers: a Century of Ballooning*, Hunter Publishing Company, 1989.
GARDINER, Leslie, *Lunardi,* Airlife Publishing, 1984.
GORDON, Charlotte, *Romantic Outlaws: the Extraordinary Lives of Mary Wollstonecraft & Mary Shelley*, Windmill Books, 2016.
HARRIS, Sharon M, *Dr. Mary Walker: An American Radical*, 1832-1919, Rutgers University Press, 2009.
HEWITT, Peggy, *Brontë Country: Lives and Landscapes*, Sutton Publishing, 2004.
HIGHFILL, Philip H., BURNIM, KALMAN A., LANGHANS, Edward A., *A Biographical Dictionary of Actors, Actresses, Musicians, Dancers, Managers & Other Stage Personnel in London, 1660-1800*, Southern Illinois University Press, 1984.
HODGSON, J.E., *The History of Aeronautics in Great Britain*, Oxford University Press, 1924.

BIBLIOGRAPHY

HOLMES, Richard, *Falling Upwards: How We Took To the Air*, William Collins, 2014.

JACKSON, Donald Dale, *The Aeronauts*, Time-Life Books, 1981.

LYNN, Michael R., *The Sublime Invention*, Pickering & Chatto, 2014.

MARLOW, Joyce, *Suffragettes: The Fight for Votes for Women,* Virago, 2000.

MOOLMAN, Valerie, *Women Aloft*, Time-Life Books, 1981.

PEACEY, Nick, *The Inflations and Deflations of the Spencer Family: Balloons, Bikes and Electric Camels,* Goggled Dog Publications, 2013.

PENNY, John, *Up, Up and Away!: an Account of Ballooning In and Around Bristol and Bath 1784 to 1999*, Bristol Branch of the Historical Association, 1999.

RIDDLE, Brian, *Turner and Aerostation*, Turner Society News 116, Autumn 2011.

SHEPHERD, Dolly, *When the 'Chute Went Up... : the Adventures of an Edwardian Lady Parachutist*, Robert Hale, 1984.

VERNE, Jules, *A Winter Amid the Ice, and Other Thrilling Stories*, The World Publishing House, New York, 1877.

WALPOLE, Horace, *Horace Walpole's Correspondence*, The Lewis Walpole Library, Yale, USA.

WILEY, Frank W., *Montana and the Sky*, Montana Aeronautics Commission, 1966.

Archives

The Cuthbert-Hodgson Collection and the Major B.F.S. Baden-Powell Collection of Aeronautical Cuttings, the National Aerospace Library, Farnborough.

Chawton House Collection of Works by Early Women Writers.

The British Balloon Museum and Library.

Index

Artillery Ground, London 23, 30-2

Bacon, Gertrude 1, 10, 115-7, 119, 120, 124, 125, 170
Bacon, Reverend John M. 115, 120, 125, 170
Balloons –
   Áerostat *Réveillon* 3, 12
   British Balloon 17, 18, 21
   La Gustave 14-6
   Le Flesselles 14
   Royal George 37, 65, 74
   Skylark 145, 146
   Valkyrie 133
   Vesperus 104
Bassett, Adelaide 150, 160, 171
Beaumont, Alma 147-50, 173
Bidmead, Captain Frederick 155, 156, 160, 162, 165, 169
Biggin, George 32, 34, 37, 38, 40-3, 45-7, 50-2
Blanchard, Jean-Pierre 17, 21, 56, 142
Blanchard, Sophie 8, 10, 21, 56, 64, 127, 142, 144
Bonaparte, Napoleon 56, 57, 60
Bradley, Lucretia 104
Broadwick, Tiny 109, 114
Brookes, Edith 151, 160, 171, 172
Brookes, Maude 151

Brunswick, Charles, Duke of 80, 82-6, 92, 93, 95
Butler, Vera 10, 130

Cavallo, Tiberius 3, 4
Charles, Jacques 2, 4, 65, 66
Cove, Lily 10, 153, 154, 158, 165, 168, 170-2, 177
Covent Garden Theatre, London 7, 21, 31
Crystal Palace, London 91, 92, 117, 118, 130, 139, 141
Currie, Capt. R.W. 81, 84, 88, 94

d'Arlandes, François Laurent 4, 5
Dare, Leona 107, 108
de Lagarde, Miss 4, 12, 13
de Moret, Chevalier 7, 8, 36

Evans, Louisa Maud 146, 166, 169, 171, 172
Errington, Harriot 52, 53

Fleurant, Mr. 14-6
Fley, John 89, 90, 96

Garnerin, André-Jacques 61, 142
Garnerin, Elise 62, 142, 144
Garnerin, Jeanne-Geneviève 142, 143

INDEX

Gaudron, Captain Auguste 145-7, 155, 169, 170, 171, 175
Graham, George 65, 71, 72, 74, 78, 99
Graham, Margaret 10, 74, 75, 77, 78, 90, 99, 137, 170
Granville, Charlotte 139, 140
Green, Charles 74, 89, 143, 157
Grice, Miss 18, 19, 23, 27, 36

Harbord, May Assheton 11, 132
Harris, Thomas 65, 72, 78

Jeffries, John 17, 57
Johnson, Madame 101-4, 114

Lister, Anne 88
Louis XVI, King of France 2, 3, 5
Lunardi, Vincent (Vincenzo) 6, 17, 30
Lyon 4, 13-5, 176

Marie Antoinette, Queen of France 1, 3, 5
Matters, Muriel 176
Merrall, Charlie 159, 160
Merton, Marie 145
Montalembert, Countess 4, 12, 13
Montalembert, Marchioness 4, 12, 13
Montalembert, Marquis 12, 13
Montgolfier, Jacques-Étienne 1, 3
Montgolfier, Joseph-Michel 1, 12, 14, 16, 61
Myers, Carl 110
Myers, Mary 10, 110

Pilatre de Rozier, Jean-Francois 4, 5, 24, 25, 35, 41

Podenas, Charlotte, Countess 4, 12, 13
Pollock, Charles 133

Ranelagh Gardens, London 43, 138, 141
Rossiter, Mr. 66, 70, 74
Royal Aero Club 11, 130-3, 139-41, 145, 160, 173, 176

Sage, Letitia 9, 29, 31, 32, 36, 38, 50, 127, 135, 170, 176
Shepherd, Dolly 10, 153, 170, 172
Simonet Leonora 21, 24-8, 51
Simonet, Louis 21, 22
Simonet, Rosine 21, 22, 24-8, 51
Spencer, Marina 145
Spencer, Percival 118
Spencer, Stanley 117, 119, 123, 130
Stocks, Jane 65, 77-9, 84

Teano, Vittoria Colonna, Princess of 11, 134-6, 139, 141
Thible, Elisabeth 4, 14-7, 27
Tytler, James 6, 30

Van Tassel, Jeanette 108-9
Vauxhall Gardens, London 90, 96
Vernon, Rear Admiral Sir Edward 17, 18, 22
Versailles 1, 3, 5, 12, 30, 125

Wilson, Harriette 10
Wise, John 104, 106

Zambeccari, Count Francesco 17-9, 22, 23, 36